Ke beaches

Lizzie Williams

Credits

Footprint credits
Editor: Alan Murphy
Production and Layout: Angus Dawson,
Elysia Alim, Danielle Bricker
Map editor: Kevin Feeney

Managing Director: Andy Riddle
Commercial Director: Patrick Dawson
Publisher: Alan Murphy
Publishing Managers: Felicity Laughton,
Nicola Gibbs
Digital Editors: Jo Williams, Tom Mellors
Marketing and PR: Liz Harper
Sales: Diane McEntee
Advertising: Renu Sibal
Finance and Administration: Elizabeth
Taylor

Photography credits
Front cover: Artur Tiutenko/Shutterstock
Back cover: Steffan Foerster/Shutterstock

Printed in Great Britain by CPI Antony Rowe,
Chippenham, Wiltshire

MIX
Paper from
responsible sources
FSC
www.fsc.org FSC® C013604

Every effort has been made to ensure that
the facts in this guidebook are accurate.
However, travellers should still obtain
advice from consulates, airlines, etc about
travel and visa requirements before travelling.
The authors and publishers cannot accept
responsibility for any loss, injury or
inconvenience however caused.

Publishing information
Footprint *Focus Kenya's beaches*
1st edition
© Footprint Handbooks Ltd
September 2011

ISBN: 978 1 908206 29 9
CIP DATA: A catalogue record for this book
is available from the British Library

® Footprint Handbooks and the Footprint
mark are a registered trademark of Footprint
Handbooks Ltd

Published by Footprint
6 Riverside Court
Lower Bristol Road
Bath BA2 3DZ, UK
T +44 (0)1225 469141
F +44 (0)1225 469461
www.footprintbooks.com

Distributed in the USA by Globe Pequot Press,
Guilford, Connecticut

The content of Footprint *Focus Kenya's
beaches* has been taken directly from
Footprint's *Kenya Handbook* which was
written and researched by Lizzie Williams
and Michael Hodd.

Contents

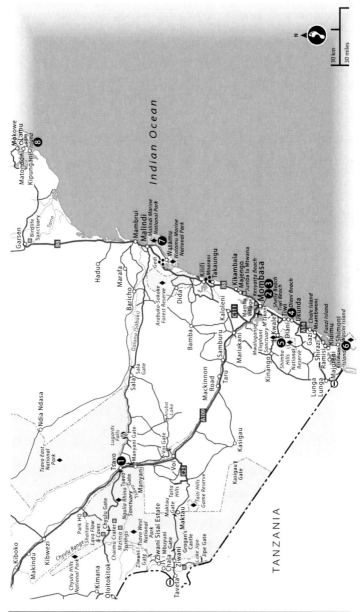

Southern Kenya is one of the most visited regions of the country. The major game parks in the region are a big draw: Tsavo West and Tsavo East, on either side of the Nairobi–Mombasa road, make up the largest park in the country. Another reason for their popularity is their closeness to the coast; visitors to this region can go on safari and also spend some time on the beach.

Kenya's southern coast has a separate cultural history from the rest of the country. Mombasa, Kenya's second city, has a history dating back several hundreds of years, when the Persians, Arabs, Indians and Chinese visited the East African coast to trade in slaves, skins, ivory and spices. The beaches here are of fine white sand and there are plenty of activities on offer including diving, snorkelling and windsurfing. There are marine national parks aplenty off the coast protecting the important marine life which can be experienced by dhow, glass-bottomed boat, or in a closer encounter, through a mask. Here the colourful coral reefs teem with fish, dolphins and turtles, and the aqua blue Indian Ocean provides near perfect visibility.

In the extreme north are the intriguing islands of Lamu, which make for a fascinating excursion into the old Swahili way of life. The old town of Lamu, known locally as Mkomani, was declared a UNESCO World Heritage Site in 2001 for its cultural importance and for being the oldest, best-preserved and still-functioning Swahili settlement on the East African coast. The islands have some wonderful deserted beaches, very atmospheric places to stay and seafood to die for. Lamu really is a paradise; it is so serene and beautiful that you are likely to want to stay forever.

Planning your trip

Getting there

Air

Kenya is the cheapest country in East Africa to get to by air and consequently is a good place to start off a tour of the region. There are several airlines that fly into Kenya from various cities in the world and airfares are very competitively priced. The main point of arrival is Nairobi's **Jomo Kenyatta International Airport**, though there are also a substantial number of scheduled and charter flights from Europe to **Moi International Airport** in Mombasa. Airport information can be found at www.kenyaairports.co.ke, or see details of arriving at the airports in the Nairobi or Mombasa chapters. Nairobi is a nine-hour flight from London and Mombasa is about 11 hours. Because of the proximity of the Northern Circuit national parks in Tanzania, which are accessed from Europe, many visitors going on safari to Northern Tanzania also fly into Nairobi as it is closer than Tanzania's capital Dar es Salaam.

The cheapest plane tickets are in the 'off season', from February to June and again from October to early December. If you do have to go during peak times, book as far in advance as you can, particularly if you aim to get there in mid-December when flights get full very quickly. If you are short of time, a package holiday could well be a useful option, particularly if you go out of the peak season when you can get excellent deals. Beach holidays are far cheaper than safaris. It is a good idea to find out as much as you can about the hotel in the package deal before going, although you can always stay elsewhere if necessary. It is sometimes the case that a package trip to the coast will be cheaper than a flight alone. Once on the coast there is then the option to book a short overnight safari to one of the parks.

Getting around

Kenya has an efficient transport network linking its towns and cities. There are regular flights between Nairobi and the coast and Kisumu, and further afield to Tanzania and Zanzibar. There is an overnight train service between Nairobi and Mombasa that is a fairly enjoyable, if not slow experience, and in recent years there have been great improvements of standards of the bus and *matatu* (minibus) services. It is quite feasible for a visitor to move around by public transport, which is cheap and efficient, but be aware of petty theft not only on the vehicles but in the bus stands and stations.

Air

Kenya Airports Authority ① *www.kenyaairports.co.ke*, established by the government in 1991, oversees the management and administration of the airports which include passenger services and freight services for horticultural and agricultural goods, for example the flowers and vegetables flown out of Eldoret International Airport daily headed for European supermarkets. Today internal travel in Kenya is regular and efficient and the introduction of 'no-frills' airlines have introduced competition and flights are very affordable. The following airlines offer daily scheduled flights. Specific schedules are detailed under each relevant chapter.

Don't miss...

1 Tsavo National Park, page 32.
2 Fort Jesus, page 46.
3 Eating dinner on the romantic white-sailed dhow Tamarind, page 53.
4 Kitesurfing along Diani Beach, page 62.

5 Shimba Hills National Reserve for views of Mount Kilimanjaro, page 66.
6 Wasini Island, page 68.
7 Watamu or Malindi marine national parks, pages 88 and 95.
8 Lamu Old Town, page 116.

Numbers relate to map on page 4.

All tickets can also be bought directly from desks at the airports. **Kenya Airways** ① *5th floor, Barclays Plaza, Loita St, city centre, T020-327 4747, airport T020-642 2000, general enquiries T0208-283 1818, www.kenya-airways.com*, has daily flights from Jomo Kenyatta International Airport to Kisumu, Malindi, Lamu and Mombasa, plus regional destinations.

Fly 540 ① *ABC Place, Westlands, T020-445 3252, airport T020-827 521, www.fly540.com*, has flights from Jomo Kenyatta International Airport to Eldoret, Kisumu, Lamu, Malindi, Masai Mara and Mombasa. It now also operates daily flights between Nairobi and Entebbe in Uganda.

Air Kenya ① *based at Wilson Airport, T020-605 745, www.airkenya.com*, has flights between Nairobi and Amboseli, Kilimanjaro, Lamu, Lewa Downs, Malindi, Masai Mara, Meru, Mombasa, Nanyuki and Samburu. It also code shares with **Regional Air** in Tanzania and offer flights from Nairobi to Kilimanjaro, Dar es Salaam and Zanzibar.

Safarilink ① *based at Wilson Airport, T020-600 777, www.safarilink-kenya.com*, has flights between Nairobi and Amboseli, Kiwayu, Lamu, Lewa Downs, Masai Mara, Nanyuki, Samburu and Tsavo. It code shares with **Air Excel** in Tanzania so have flights from Nairobi to Kilimanjaro.

In addition to scheduled flights there are many air charter services based at Wilson Airport, Nairobi, which can arrange private flights in small six- to eight-seater planes to over 150 airstrips spread all over the country. As well as ferrying tourists around, some of these companies have been involved in distributing food and medical aid in the Northern Kenya and southern Sudan and Somalia regions in recent years, as well as providing air access to the refugee camps for aid workers. These include **ALS** ① *Wilson Airport, T020-603 706, www.als.co.ke*; **Aero Kenya** ① *Wilson Airport, T020-601001, www.aerokenya.com*; **Capital Airlines** ① *Wilson Airport, T020-603 357, www.capitalairlines.biz*; and **Z-Boskovic Air Charters** ① *Wilson Airport, T020-602 026, www.boskovicaircharters.com*.

Rail

Nairobi Railway Station ① *T020-221 211*, is to the south of Haile Selassie Avenue, at the very end of Moi Avenue. Despite Kenya's long association with what was the Uganda Railway, which effectively founded the colony, in recent years due to chronic under-investment the railway is close to collapse with dilapidated rolling stock, and frequent derailments and breakdowns. Added to this, part of the railway in the north of the country was ripped up during the post-2007 election violence so the service from Nairobi to Kisumu is no longer operational. For now, there's only the overnight train between Nairobi and Mombasa. This used to be an historic and authentic rail experience and an excellent way of getting to the coast, but these days and thanks to breakdowns of other freight trains using the same track, which subsequently block the line, this journey can be painfully slow.

Road

The present road transport network comprises a variety of roads ranging from forest and farm tracks to multi-lane urban and suburban highways. The system is divided into classified and unclassified roads, with a total network of 151,000 km. Out of the classified network of 62,667 km, 7943 km are tarred (compared with 1811 km at Independence), 26,180 km are gravel and the rest are dirt.

Bus and matatu

The most popular form of public transport in Kenya is the *matatu*, which has become a national icon and a large part of Kenyan modern culture. A *matatu* is a minibus, usually a Nissan, with a three-tonne capacity, hence the name *matatu* – *tatu* means 'three' in Kiswahili. Safety records for public transport have been pretty awful in the past with many road accidents involving overcrowded buses and *matatus* and some large derailments on the railways. However, since the government instigated new regulations in 2003, public transport in Kenya has undergone quite a transformation. While the vehicles introduced at the time are starting to show their age, overall they have contributed to positively getting the accident rate down. All buses, *matatus*, taxis and any vehicle carrying paying passengers must be licensed and have a yellow stripe around them, and *matatus*, which were once famously painted in lots of bright colours and murals, are now mostly uniformly white. Buses are still different colours, although each company has smartened up their image and many of the buses from the same fleet are in the same colour. **Metro** red buses have been introduced to Mombasa, and green **City Hoppers** in Nairobi, which are gradually taking over the old fleet of city buses. All public buses and *matatus* now have to be speed governed at 80 kph. Every vehicle has been fitted with seat belts and it is now law for every passenger in any vehicle to buckle up. Police issue on-the-spot fines to passengers who haven't got seat belts on. The number of passengers has been governed to stop the overcrowding. In *matatus* this has been restricted to 15 passengers, all with their own seat, with a seat belt. The police also frequently stop the vehicles and count how many people are on board. The same goes for larger buses where standing is no longer permitted and everyone gets their own seat. These regulations have improved safety and comfort, meaning that it is now reasonable for independent travellers to move around Kenya on buses and *matatus*. There are lots of private bus companies operating in Kenya, and the system is very good on the whole, being reliable, running on time and offering cheap fares. In addition, the accident rate on the roads has fallen dramatically in recent years. The larger buses cover the long-distance routes and you will be able to reserve a seat a day in advance, whilst the *matatus* do the shorter distances and link the major towns and usually go when full. If you have problems locating the bus station, alternatively called bus stand or bus stage in Kenya, or finding the right bus in the bus station, just ask around and someone will direct you. In Nairobi and Mombasa city buses operate on set routes with formal bus stops, while *matatus* follow the same routes and can be flagged down anywhere.

Packing for Kenya

Before you leave home, send yourself an email to a web-based account with details of traveller's cheques, passport, driving licence, credit cards and travel insurance numbers. Be sure that someone at home also has access to this information. A good rule of thumb is to take half the clothes you think you'll need and double the money. Laundry services are generally cheap and speedy in Kenya and you shouldn't need to bring too many clothes. A backpack or travelpack (a hybrid backpack/suitcase) rather than a rigid suitcase covers most eventualities and survives the rigours of a variety of modes of travel. A lock for your luggage is strongly advised – there are cases of pilfering by airport baggage handlers the world over.

Light cotton clothing is best, with a fleece or woollen clothing for evenings. Also pack something to change into at dusk – long sleeves and trousers (particularly light coloured) help ward off mosquitoes, which are at their most active in the evening. During the day you will need a hat, sunglasses and high-factor sun cream for protection against the sun. Modest dress is advisable for women, particularly on the coast, where men too should avoid revealing shoulders. Kenya is a great place to buy sarongs – known in East Africa as *kikois*, which in Africa are worn by both men and women and are ideal to cover up when, say, leaving the beach. Footwear should be airy because of the heat: sandals or canvas trainers are ideal. Trekkers will need comfortable walking boots, and ones that have been worn in if you are climbing Mount Kenya. Those going on camping safaris will need a sleeping bag, towel and torch, and budget travellers may want to consider bringing a sleeping sheet in case the sheets don't look too clean in a budget hotel.

Car

Driving conditions The key roads are in good condition; away from the main highways the majority of roads are hazardous. The minor roads of unmade gravel with potholes can be rough going and they deteriorate further in the rainy season. Road conditions in the reserves and national parks of Kenya are extremely rough. During the rainy season, many roads are passable only with 4WD vehicles. Even some of the tarred roads are in poor shape: cracked, crumbling and littered with small and not-so-small potholes. There is little road maintenance and when re-tarring of the roads does occur, the new tar that is laid is so thin it deteriorates within months. On hills, heavy vehicles with hot tyres curve the tar into steep ridges, making the roads very bumpy. Added to this are Kenya's speed bumps (hardly necessary when the potholes do a fine job of slowing traffic down), which are in place every few metres wherever there is any kind of settlement and are prolific all over the towns. It is still possible to drive on Kenya's main roads in a normal saloon car, although the going is slow and you will have to take extra care to avoid the deeper potholes. A 4WD is recommended as the high clearance is better for the potholes, and is essential if you are going off the tarred roads or into the game parks. If you break down, it is common practice in Kenya to place a bundle of leaves 50 m or so in front of and behind the vehicle to warn oncoming motorists. Note when parking in the towns, you pay a small fee to a parking official who will give you a ticket to display in the window.

Car hire Renting a car has certain advantages over public transport, particularly if you intend visiting any of the national parks or remoter regions of the country, or there are at least four of you to share the costs. You should be able to rent either at a fixed price per day or by mileage. If you are organizing your own safari by hire car, it requires careful planning, and you need to be confident about driving on the poor roads. A 4WD is essential. Minimum engine size should be 1300cc, as anything smaller cannot cope with the rough roads in the game parks. Make sure that the car is not more than two years old. Driving is on the left side of the road.

To hire a car you generally need to be over 23, have a full driving licence (it does not have to be an international licence, your home country one will do – with English translation if necessary), and to leave a large deposit (or sign a blank credit card voucher). Always take out the collision damage waiver premium as even the smallest accident can be very expensive. Costs vary between the different car hire companies and are from around US$40-80 per day for a normal saloon car, rising to US$120-180 for a 4WD. Deals can be made for more than seven days' car hire. It is important to shop around to get the best-value rates. Things to consider include whether you take out a limited mileage package or unlimited mileage depending on how you many kilometres you think you will drive. For example, a company may offer a package for US$60 per day, with 200 km free per day, and any mileage after that at US$0.25 per km. If you think you are going to be driving for more than 200 km a day then a more expensive unlimited mileage package may be better. Also check the insurance policies. Some of the companies that offer the cheapest rates have no insurance policies at all where in the event of an accident, the hirer is responsible for costs, or, a costly option if the car gets stolen, reimbursement of the value of the vehicle. Alternatively it is best to take out an additional insurance of about US$10-25 per day on top of the car hire rates to cover these eventualities, although you'll still be liable of an excess of around US$500-1000. Finally, 16% VAT is added to all costs. It is essential to shop around and ask the companies about what is and what is not included in the rates. For car hire companies in Nairobi. If you think you may not be that confident in driving in Kenya but still want the flexibility of your own vehicle, most companies can organize drivers for additional expense. However, for a group of four people, this option is going to be no cheaper than booking on an organized budget camping safari.

Taxi

Hotels and town centres are well served by taxis, some good and some very run-down but serviceable. Hotel staff, even at the smallest locations, will rustle up a taxi even when there is not one waiting outside. If you visit an out-of-town location, it is wise to ask the taxi to wait – it will normally be happy to do so for the benefit of the return fare. Up to 1 km should cost US$1. Very few of the cabs have meters, and you should establish the fare (*bei gani?* – how much?) before you set off. Prices are generally fair as drivers simply won't take you if you offer a fare that's too low. A common practice is a driver will set off and then go and get petrol using part of your fare to pay for it, so often the first part of a journey is spent sitting in a petrol station. Also be aware that seemingly taxi drivers never have change, so try and accumulate some small notes for taxi rides.

Tuk-tuks

A *tuk-tuk* is a motorized three-wheeled buggy; cheap and convenient, they are starting to feature in many Kenyan towns and cities. The driver sits in the front whilst two to three passengers can sit comfortably on the back seat. They are still quite a novelty and as yet there are few around, but the idea is catching on quickly and in the future they should offer a service that is at least half the price of regular taxis. They do not however, go very fast so for longer journeys stick to taxis.

Boda boda A *boda boda* is a bicycle taxi with one padded seat on the back, and so named as they were first popular in the border towns to transport people across no man's land between the border posts of East Africa and the cyclist would shout out '*boda boda*' offering his services. They are very popular along the coast and in the smaller towns, although not in Nairobi and Mombasa, and cost next to nothing. The driver/cyclist does an excellent job of cycling and keeping the bike balanced with you on the back of it, although you are still advised to hang on to the seat. A word of warning to the ladies, however, if you are wearing a skirt you will have to sit side saddle, which makes the bike far more wobbly.

Trucks
Overland truck safaris are a popular way of exploring Kenya by road. They demand a little more fortitude and adventurous spirit from the traveller, but the compensation is usually the camaraderie and life-long friendships that result from what is invariably a real adventure, going to places the more luxurious travellers will never visit. The standard overland route most commercial trucks take through East Africa (in either direction) is from Nairobi: a two-week circuit into Uganda to see the mountain gorillas via some of the Kenya national parks, then crossing into Tanzania to Arusha for the Ngorongoro Crater and Serengeti, before heading south to Dar es Salaam, for Zanzibar. If you have more time, you can complete the full circuit that goes from Tanzania through Malawi and Zambia to Livingstone to see the Victoria Falls, and then another three weeks from there to Cape Town in South Africa via Botswana and Namibia. There are several overland companies and there are departures almost weekly from Nairobi, Livingstone and Cape Town throughout the year.

Overland truck safari operators
In the UK Dragoman, T01728-861 133, www.dragoman.co.uk. Exodus Travels, T020-8675 5550, www.exodus.co.uk. Explore, T0845-0131 537, www.explore.co.uk. Kumuka Expeditions,T0778-6201 144, www.kumuka.com. Oasis Overland, T01963-363 400, www.oasisoverland.co.uk.

In South Africa Africa Travel Co, T021-385 1530, www.africatravelco.com. Wildlife Adventures, T021-385 1530, www.wildlifeadventures.co.za.

Sleeping

There is a wide range of accommodation on offer. At the top end are game lodges and tented camps that charge US$300-1000 per couple per day; mid-range safari lodges and beach resorts with self-contained double rooms with air conditioning charge around US$150-250 per room; standard and faded small town hotels used by local business people cost around US$50-100 per room; and basic board and lodgings used by local travellers are under US$10 a day. At the top end, Kenya now boasts some accommodation

Sleeping and eating price codes

$$$$ over US$300   **$$$** US$100-300   **$$** US$50-100
$ under US$50
Prices are for a double room in high season, including taxes.

Eating price codes
$$$ over US$30   **$$** US$15-30   **$** under US$15
Prices refer to the average cost of a two-course meal for one person, not including drinks or service charge.

options that rival the luxurious camps in southern Africa – intimate safari camps with an amazing standard of comfort and service in stunning settings. The beach resorts too have improved considerably in recent years, and there are some luxurious and romantic beach lodges and hotels in commanding positions. At the budget end there's a fairly wide choice of cheap accommodation. A room often comprises a simple bed, shared toilet and washing facilities, and may have an irregular water supply; it is always a good idea to look at a room first, to ensure it's clean and everything works. It is also imperative to ensure that your luggage will be locked away securely for protection against petty theft especially in shared accommodation. For more expensive hotels, airlines, game park entrance and camping fees, a system operates whereby tourists are charged approximately double the rate locals are charged – resident and non-resident rates – although these can be paid in foreign currency as well as Kenyan Shillings. The word hotel (or in Kiswahili, *hoteli*) means food and drink, rather than lodging. It is better to use the word guesthouse (in Kiswahili, *guesti*).

Generally accommodation booked through a European agent will be more expensive than if you contact the hotel or lodge directly. Kenya's hoteliers are embracing the age of the internet, and an ever-increasing number can take a reservation by email or through their websites. Low season in East Africa is generally around the long rainy season from the beginning of April to the end of June, when most room rates drop considerably. Some establishments even close during this period.

Hotels

There are roughly 75,000 hotel beds in over 2000 licensed hotels within the country. A large majority of these are found in the coastal region, thanks to the rapid development of tourism infrastructure and beach resorts in the late 1970s and early 1980s. Some of the beach hotels are resorts with a range of watersports and activities where guests stay for their entire holiday, and while they will appeal to those who enjoy the all-inclusive package holiday experience; they may not appeal to more independent travellers. However, also on the coast are some small, simple beach cottage type of accommodation, which are mostly in good locations and are excellent value. A few international hotel chains, such as **Hilton International** and **Intercontinental Hotels** among others, have hotels in Nairobi. Most local town and city hotels tend to be bland with poor service, although there are a number of characterful hotels that have been around since the colonial days, such as Nairobi's **The Norfolk** or the **Country Club** in

Naivasha. Prices of hotels are not always a good indication of their quality, and it is sensible to check what you will get before committing yourself, though prices are often negotiable, even in large hotels. On the coast and in the game parks, you can expect to pay more in the high season, particularly mid-December to mid-February. Low season in Kenya is generally 1 April-30 June (excluding Easter weekend). The town and city hotels tend to keep their rates the same year round.

Self-catering and homestays
Renting a private property is a good way to gain a new perspective on Kenya and relax on your own. The real advantage of a Kenyan homestay is the opportunity to spend time with Kenyans and their families, and to share the benefit of their many years of local experience. These are often surprisingly good value if you intend to stay for a while. They vary from rustic cottages in the bush or historic Swahili mansions on the coast, to serviced city apartments. Many of the homes used as homestays are in the highland areas of Kenya, legacies of the pre-Independence settlers, and the coastal belt; very few are near the game parks. Homestays tend to be more expensive than hotels and are often built into the more expensive, individually tailored itineraries. Such properties can either be booked privately or through a travel agent or safari operator. There is also an increasing number of self-catering apartments for rental especially at the coast. Often assistance with cleaning and cooking is available. Whilst some of these facilities are custom built, many are holiday homes leased out when not in use by the owners. These range from quite simple and basic beach cottages to sophisticated villas. For more information contact **Kenya Holiday Villas** ⓘ *www.kenyaholidayvillas.com*, or **Kenya Safari Homes** ⓘ *www.kenyasafarihomes.com*. Each website has a full description, including photos of each property.

Hostels
There are only a handful of hostels around the country, affiliated with the Youth Hostelling Association, YMCA and YWCA, and most are clean and safe and very cheap. Nevertheless they tend to be very spartan and generally cater for long-term residents such as students or church groups.

Camping
There are many campsites all over Kenya. They are usually very cheap with basic amenities and some are very good. Camping is essential if you are on a tight budget but want to explore the national parks. You should always have your own tent and basic equipment as these cannot always be hired at the sites. You should also carry adequate supplies of fresh water, food, fuel and emergency supplies. Do not rely on local water supplies or rivers and streams for potable water. Any water taken from a stream should be filtered or boiled for several minutes before drinking. If you are trekking and planning to wild camp outside of official or designated campsites, seek local advice in advance. The land on which you are planning to camp may be privately owned or be traditional lands under the control of a nearby village. In some instances, advance permission and/or payment is required. If camping near a village, as you may be asked to do, remember to be culturally sensitive.

Safari options

All safari companies offer basically the same safari but at different prices, which is reflective of what accommodation is booked. For example, you could choose a two-day safari of the Masai Mara and the options would be camping (the companies provide the equipment) or a lodge safari, making it considerably more expensive. For those that want to spend more, there is the option of adding flights between destinations or staying at one of the luxury private tented camps in the private concession areas on the edges of the parks. Everyone is likely to have the same sort of game-viewing experiences, but the level of comfort you want on safari depends on where you stay and how much you spend.

Hotels and lodges These vary and may be either typical hotels with rooms and facilities in one building or individual *bandas* or *rondavels* (small huts) with a central dining area. Standards vary from the rustic to the modern, from the simply appointed to the last word in luxury. Efforts are usually made to design lodges that blend into their environment, with an emphasis on natural local building materials and use of traditional art and decoration. Most lodges serve meals and have lounges and bars, often with excellent views or overlooking waterholes or salt licks that attract game. Many have resident naturalists, as well as guides for organized walks or game drives.

Tented camps A luxury tented camp is really the best of both worlds. They are usually built with a central dining area. Each tent will have a thatched roof to keep it cool inside, proper beds and a veranda and they will often have a small bathroom at the back with solar-heated hot water. But at the same time you will have the feeling of being in the heart of Africa and at night you will hear animals surprisingly close by. Tented camps can be found in many of Kenya's national parks and game reserves, as well as on private game ranches and sanctuaries.

Campsites There are campsites in most national parks. They are extensively used by camping safari companies. Vehicles, guides, tents and equipment, as well as food and a cook, are all provided. They are often most attractively sited, perhaps in the elbow of a river course but always with plenty of shade. Birds are plentiful and several hours can be whiled away birdwatching. Some campsites have attached to them a few *bandas* or huts run by the park where you may be able to shower. Toilet facilities can be primitive – the 'long drop', a basic hole in a concrete slab, being very common. Most camps are guarded but despite this you should be careful to ensure that valuables are not left unattended. If you are camping on your own, you will almost always need to be totally self-sufficient with all your own equipment. The campsites usually provide running water and firewood. Camping should always have minimal impact on the environment. All rubbish and waste matter should be buried, burnt, or taken away with you. Do not leave food scraps or containers where they may attract and harm animals. Campers should also take care of wildlife. Do not leave fruit or other food inside tents, it can attract monkeys, baboons, and even in some areas elephants, resulting in destruction.

Eating and drinking

Food

Kenyans are largely big meat eaters and a standard meal is *nyama choma* – roasted beef or goat meat, usually served with a spicy relish, although some like it with a mixture of raw peppers, onions and tomato known as *kachumbari*. This is usually prepared on simple charcoal grills outside in beer gardens. The main staple or starch in Kenya is *ugali*, a mealie meal porridge eaten all over Africa. In Kikuyu areas you will find *irio*: potatoes, peas and corn mashed together. A popular Luo dish is fried *tilapia* (fish) with a spicy tomato sauce and *ugali. Githeri* is a bean stew. Cuisine on mainland Kenya is not one of the country's main attractions. There is a legacy of uninspired British catering (soups, steaks, grilled chicken, chips, boiled vegetables, puddings, instant coffee). Small town hotels and restaurants tend to serve a limited amount of bland processed food, omelette or chicken and chips, and perhaps a meat stew but not much else. Asian food is extremely good in Kenya and cheap, and an important option for vegetarians travelling in the country. Many Indian restaurants have a lunchtime buffet where you can eat as much as you want for less than US$10 a head. Other cuisines include Italian, French, Chinese, Japanese and even Thai, though these can only be found in the upmarket Nairobi restaurants and coastal resorts. Also on the coast, the Swahili style of cooking features aromatic curries using coconut milk, fragrant steamed rice, grilled fish and calamari, and delicious bisques made from lobster and crab. Some of the larger beach resorts and safari lodges offer breakfast, lunch and dinner buffets for their all-inclusive guests, some of which can be excellent while others can be of a poor standard and there's no real way of knowing what you'll get. The most important thing is to avoid food sitting around for a long time on a buffet table, so ensure it has been freshly prepared and served. Restaurant prices are low; it is quite possible to get a plate of hot food in a basic restaurant for US$3 and even the most expensive places will often not be more than US$30 per person. The quality, standard and variety of food depends on where you are and what you intend to pay. Various Western-style fast foods are becoming ever more popular such as chips, hamburgers, sausages and fried chicken. Finally, the service in Kenyan restaurants can be somewhat slower than you are used to and it can take hours for something to materialize out of a kitchen. Rather than complain just enjoy the laid-back pace and order another beer.

A variety of items can be purchased from **street vendors** who prepare and cook over charcoal, which adds considerably to the flavour, at temporary roadside shelters (kiosks). Street cuisine is pretty safe despite hygiene methods being fairly basic. Most of the items are cooked or peeled, which deals with the health hazard. Savoury items include chips, omelettes, barbecued beef on skewers (*mishkaki*), roast maize (corn), samosas, kebabs, hard-boiled eggs and roast cassava (looks like white, peeled turnips) with red chilli-pepper garnish. Roadside stalls selling *mandazi* (a kind of sweet or savoury doughnut), roasted maize, grilled, skewered meat, or samosas are popular and very cheap. Fruits include oranges (peeled and halved), grapes, pineapples, bananas, mangoes (slices scored and turned inside-out), paw-paw (papaya) and watermelon. These items are very cheap and are all worth trying, and when travelling, are indispensable.

Most food produce is purchased in open-air markets. In the larger towns and cities these are held daily and, as well as selling fresh fruit and vegetables, sell eggs, bread and meat. In the smaller villages, a market will be held on one day of the week when the farmers come to sell their wares. Markets are very colourful places to visit and just about any fruit or vegetable is available. Other locally produced food items are sold in supermarkets, often run by Asian traders, whilst imported products are sold in the few upmarket supermarkets in the larger cities such as Nakumatt.

Drink
Sodas (soft drinks) are available everywhere and are very cheap, the bottles are refundable. Apart from the usual Cokes and Fantas look out for Krest bitter lemon and ginger ale, and the rather delicious Stoney's Ginger Beer. The other common drink throughout the country is *chai*, milky sweet tea, which is surprisingly refreshing. When available, fresh fruit juices are very good as they are freshly squeezed. Bottled water is fairly expensive, but is available in all but the smallest villages. Tap water is reputedly safe in many parts of the country, but is only really recommended if you have a fairly hardy traveller's stomach. If you don't have a strong stomach, do not use tap water to brush your teeth and avoid ice and washed salads and fruit if possible. Also see the health section for more information about food and water hygiene.

Kenyan beer is very good: *Tusker*, *White Cap* and *Pilsner* are the main brands sold in half-litre bottles. Fruit wines are also popular; they come in a variety of different flavours but tend to be sweet. Papaya wine is widely available, but is a little harsh.

Spirits tend to be extremely expensive and imported brands can be found in the supermarkets and in bars. Local alternatives that are sold in both bottles and sachets of one tot include *Kenya Cane*, a type of rum, and the sweet *Kenya Gold* coffee liqueur.

Traditional Kenyan drinks include *chang'aa*, a fierce spirit made from maize and sugar and then distilled. Sentences for distilling and possessing *chang'aa* are severe and it is sometimes contaminated. It has been known to kill so think twice before tasting any. Far more pleasant and more common are *pombe* (beer), brewed from sugar and millet or banana depending on the region. It is quite legal, tastes a bit like flat cider and is far more potent than it appears at first. **Palm wine** is drunk at the coast.

Festivals and events

All along the coast and in the northeast the **Islamic calendar** is followed and festivals are celebrated. These include the beginning and end of **Ramadan** (variable); **Islamic New Year** (Jun) and **Prophet's birthday** (Aug). On Lamu the Islamic **Maulidi Festival** is held each year (see box, page 123).

January
New Year's Day Dhow Race, Shela Beach on Lamu, is an important event on the island. Only 8 captains are invited to race, so winning the race is a great honour. *Dhows* are brightly decorated and festivities last well into the night. See box, page 126.

June
1 Jun Rhino Charge. This is an off-road 4WD motor rally and fund-raising event to raise money for the fencing of the Aberdares National Park, which is almost complete, and provide solar power to electrify it. The winner is the car that visits all of the 10 control points along the course and has the lowest mileage within the allocated 10 hrs of driving time. Contact **Rhino Ark**, T020-213 6010, www.rhinoark.org.

Safaricom Marathon, at Lewa Wildlife Conservancy. A fundraising event to support the conservancy on the Laikipila Plateau amongst other good community causes. Both the half and full marathons attract runners from all over the world, including many world-class Kenyan long-distance runners. They are hard runs at altitude and the course is held within the game conservancy. Helicopters are used to keep an eye out for elephant and predators along the course. It is a unique experience! You can take part or watch. Contact **Lewa Wildlife Conservancy**, T064-31405, www.lewa.org.

August
1st weekend in Aug Maralal International Camel Derby, operating since 1990, and from 1998 the event has been coupled with the **Kenya Amateur Cycling Association Race**. Visit www.yaresafaris.com.

October
Nairobi Air Show, held at Wilson Airport on Kenyan Aviation Career Day, features fly-bys by military and historical aircraft and helicopters, formation flying and parachuting displays. There's also plenty of on-the-ground entertainment and food and drink tents and it's a good family day out. See www.nairobiairshow.com.

December
Early Dec **Craft Fair**, Ngong Racecourse, Nairobi, is a large craft fair with many home-made items from all over Kenya: curios, soaps, jams, furniture, toys, embroidery and quilted items.

East African Safari Classic, has been going since 1953 and was first car rally run to celebrate the queen's coronation. It runs for 3 days over a course of about 3000 km. It goes all over the country on some of the worst roads and often in appalling weather. Watching is exciting especially from a good vantage point in the Rift Valley where the cars go charging up and down the escarpments. **Note** For the first time since 1972, the 2009 event will be run in Tanzania. Contact **East African Safari Classic**, Nairobi, T020-445 0030, www.eastafricansafarirally.com.

Parks and safaris

National parks and reserves
Kenya's wildlife is one of its greatest assets and many of the parks and reserves offer a glimpse of a totally unspoilt, peaceful world. Marine life is also excellent and is preserved in the marine national parks off Malindi, Watamu and Kisite. Along with the wildlife, some of the parks have been gazetted to preserve the vegetation and unique locations such as Mount Kenya or the Kakamega Forest. Some of the parks and reserves are world famous, such as the **Masai Mara** and **Amboseli**, and have excellent facilities and receive many visitors. Many others rarely see tourists and make little or no provision in the way of amenities for them.

It is essential to tour the parks by vehicle and walking is prohibited in most of the parks. The exceptions to this are Hell's Gate, parts of Nakuru and Saiwa Swamp National Park near Kitale, and walking safaris are on offer in many of the concession areas outside of the park boundaries where many of the safari lodges and tented camps are located. You will either have to join an organized tour by a safari company, or hire or have your own vehicle. Being with a guide is the best option as without one, you will miss a lot of game. There are a huge number of companies offering safaris, which are listed in the relevant chapters. Safaris can be booked either at home or once in Kenya. If you go for the latter it may be possible to obtain substantial discounts, but ensure that the company is properly licensed and is a member of the **Kenya Association of Tour Operators (KATO)** ① *www.katokenya.org*, which represents over 250 of Kenya's tour operators and is a good place to start when looking for a safari. Safaris do not run on every day of the week, and in the low season you may also find that they will be combined, meaning if you are on a six-day safari you could expect to be joined by another party say on a four-day safari. Safaris vary in cost and duration, but on the whole you get what you pay for. The costs will also vary enormously depending on where you stay and how many of you there are in a group. For an all-inclusive safari staying in the large safari lodges that offer twice daily game drives and buffet meals, expect to pay around US$150-250 per person per day (more if you opt for air transfers), and at the very top end of the scale, staying in the most **exclusive tented camps and lodges** and flying between destinations, expect to pay in excess of US$500 per day. At the lower end of the market, a **camping safari** using the basic national park campsites is about US$120-140 per person per day, which given that the park fees alone in some of the parks is US$60 per day, is not unreasonable. These rates include park entrance fees, cost of vehicle and driver, and food.

In total **Kenya Wildlife Services (KWS)** administers 30 national parks and five marine reserves. Some environmentally fragile parks with an overload of visitors, such as Amboseli and Lake Nakuru, charge higher park fees, while those parks with low tourist volume charge less, to encourage a wider spread of tourists around the parks. Entry fees to the most popular parks is by an electronic ticketing system known as Smartcard. If you are on an organized safari your tour operator will organize these, but if you are visiting the parks independently, you need to go to a 'point of sale' and load the card. Assess how much your park entry fees, vehicle costs and camping fees are going to be, depending on how long you will spend in the parks, and how many parks you want to visit, and load up the Smartcard with the relevant amount of money. Anyone over the age of 18 must have their own Smartcard, and under 18s can be paid for with a parent's Smartcard. At the main gates of the parks, you will slide the Smartcard through a machine that will deduct your entry fees, etc off the amount loaded on to the card. Smartcards can be obtained and loaded at: the KWS headquarters at the Main Gate of Nairobi National Park on Langata Road in Nairobi, where the Safari Walk and Animal Orphanage are located; the Main Gate at Lake Nakuru National Park; the Main Gate of the Aberdares National Park; and at the Voi Gate of Tsavo East National Park. They can also be reloaded (but not obtained) at the Mtito Andei Gate of Tsavo West. Money on the cards is not refundable.

National reserves, such as the Masai Mara and the Samburu-Buffalo Springs-Shaba complex, are not administered by KWS and are managed by local councils who set their own prices. These are paid for on arrival at the main gates or lodges in cash, or will be included in the price of an organized safari.

Organizing your own safari

An alternative to going on an organized safari is to self-drive on a do-it-yourself safari. However, because of the entry fees for vehicles this does not necessarily work out cheaper

Parks and reserves: what's what?

National parks National parks are wildlife and botanical sanctuaries and form the mainstay of Kenya's tourist industry. They are conservation points for educational and recreational enjoyment and are managed by Kenya Wildlife Services.

National reserves National reserves are similar to national parks but under certain conditions the land may be used for purposes other than nature conservation. Some controlled agriculture or grazing may be permitted. In marine reserves there may be monitored fishing permitted.

Biosphere reserves These are protected environments that contain unique land-forms, landscapes and systems of land use. There are five in Kenya: Amboseli, Mount Kenya and Watamu-Malindi marine reserves, Mount Kalul and Kiungu Marine Reserve. Specific scientific research projects are attached to them.

World Heritage Sites World Heritage Sites are even more strictly protected. Kenya signed the convention in 1989; as yet only three sites have been inscribed: Mount Kenya, Sibiloi/Central Island national parks, and Lamu old town.

Kenya Wildlife Services park entry fees

Prices as of 1 January 2009. Children's fees are from age 3-18; under 3s go free. Entry is per 24 hours. For further details contact Kenya Wildlife Service, Nairobi, T020-600 800, www.kws.org.

Premier parks
Amboseli and Lake Nakuru
US$60 adults; US$30 children.

Wilderness parks
Aberdares, Tsavo East, Tsavo West, Meru, Chyulu Hills
US$50 adults; US$25 children.

Urban safaris
Nairobi National Park
US$40 adults; US$20 children.
Nairobi Safari Walk
US$20 adults; US$5 children.
Nairobi Animal Orphanage
and Kisumu Impala Sanctuary
US$15 adults; US$5 children.

Nairobi combination ticket
(Nairobi National Park, Nairobi Safari Walk and Nairobi Animal Orphanage)
US$65 adults; US$25 children.

Mountain climbing
Mount Kenya National Park
US$55 adults; US$20 children.
(Residents' rates apply to Kenyan porters and guides.)
Mount Kenya National Park (climbing for the first three days, includes accommodation in KWS mountain huts)
US$150 adults; US$70 children.

Special-interest parks
Mount Elgon, Hell's Gate, Shimba Hills, Arabuko Sokoke Forest, Kakamega Forest
US$25 adults; US$10 children.

Marine parks and reserves
Malindi, Watamu, Kisite, Kiunga
US$20 adults; US$10 children.

Kenya Wildlife Services

The Kenyan government has long been aware that the principal attraction of the country to tourists is its wildlife, and since 1989 has been keen to ensure it is available in abundance for tourists to see. During the 1970s and 1980s Kenya's parks suffered at the hands of poachers and whole populations of wildlife – particularly rhino and elephant – were all but wiped out. But thanks to gallant efforts by the well-organized Kenya Wildlife Services (KWS) and many private ranch owners, today the many species of animal, bird, marine life and plant are far better protected. When the country gained Independence in 1963, there were an estimated 170,000 elephants but by 1989 they numbered just 16,000. In 1989, 12 tons of confiscated ivory was burnt in Nairobi National Park, where today a mound of ash and an information board marks the spot. The fire was lit by then-president Moi and was a symbolic gesture

that declared war on poachers and the mass slaughter of elephants in Kenya. The event, televised across the world, contributed to the CITIES international ban on ivory trading and the establishment of the KWS in 1990, headed up by Richard Leakey. Poaching patrols that were well trained and well equipped with Land Rovers and guns were put in place and extremely stiff penalties for anyone caught poaching were established. All employees of KWS are still armed. The present elephant population in Kenya is around 28,000, and thanks to the anti-poaching efforts by KWS employees, numbers of many more species of large animal have recovered significantly. If visiting the Nairobi National Park, in the car park at the main gate look out for the Conservation Heroes Monument, which lists all the names of KWS employees who have died in the line of duty since the KWS was established.

but it is a good option if you are confident about driving on the poorly maintained tracks within the parks and are prepared to camp. Costs can be favourable compared to an organized safari for a family or group. Some of the parks are better for self-drive than others. For example, Lake Nakuru and Nairobi national parks are easily negotiable in a car and are a pleasure to drive around, whilst others, such as the Masai Mara or Tsavo, have rough roads and there are remote areas where you certainly do not want to get stuck in the event of a breakdown or emergency. On your own safari remember that you will need to budget for vehicle, camping and entry fees and load your Smartcard with the relevant costs. It is a good idea to discuss your itinerary with the staff at the Kenya Wildlife Services head office in Nairobi and they will advise on the fees. In the parks there is also the option to hire a guide from the park HQ for half or a full day to accompany you in your own vehicle.

Special-interest safaris

There are a number of alternative safari options in Kenya. Whilst Kenya has always involved the local communities in park management, in recent years there have been some excellent conservation initiatives in Kenya that have involved and benefited local communities and have proved instrumental in the protection of the wildlife. An excellent example is the Laikipia Plateau where commercial ranches have turned their land into successful game farms and where new tourist lodges provide employment and other benefits to the local people. Many tour operators and lodges have also adopted cultural or environmental policies – worth thinking about when choosing a safari operator. There are a range of tours and establishments to visit away from the national parks that offer more unusual wildlife watching activities, such as tracking rhino and elephant, walking and trekking safaris with camels and Masai or Samburu guides, or horse- or mountain-bike safaris.

Tipping

How much to tip the driver and guide is tricky. It is best to enquire from the company what the going rate is. As a rough guide you should allow about 10% of your safari cost. Always try to come to an agreement with other members of the group and put the tip into a kitty. Remember that wages are low and there can be long lay-offs during the low season. Despite this there is also the problem of over tipping, which can cause problems for future clients being asked to give more than they should. If you are on a camping safari and have a cook, give all the money to the guide and leave him to sort out the split.

Transport

It is worth emphasizing that most parks are some way from departure points, and obviously the longer you spend actually in the parks, rather than just driving to and from them, the better. If you go on a three-day safari by road, you will often find that at least one day is taken up with travelling to and from the park, often on bad bumpy and dusty roads – leaving you with a limited amount of time in the park itself. The easiest option, which is of course the most expensive, is to fly and most parks and reserves have a good network of airstrips and there are daily flights. This gives you the optimum time game viewing in the parks themselves.

Essentials A-Z

Accident and emergency
Police, fire and ambulance T999.

Dress
Travellers are encouraged to show respect by adhering to a modest dress code in public places, especially in the predominantly Muslim areas like Mombasa or Lamu. In the evening at social functions there is no particular dress code although hosts will feel insulted if you arrive for dinner in shorts, sandals or bare feet, and you will be expected to dress up a little in the more upmarket lodges and hotels. On safari, clothes in muted brown and khaki colours are the best. This is certainly true of the more remote parks where seeing unexpected bright colours may startle the animals. But in the Masai Mara, the animals here are so used to seeing a hoards of tourists each day, it is not so important.

Electricity
220-240 volts supply. Square 3-pin plugs in modern buildings. Great variety in older places. An adapter is advised.

Embassies and consulates
Visit www.embassygoabroad.com, for a full list of embassies.

Health
The health care in the region is varied. There are many excellent private and government clinics/hospitals. As with all medical care, first impressions count. If a facility is grubby then be wary of the general standard of medicine and hygiene. It's worth contacting your embassy or consulate on arrival and asking where the recommended clinics are. If you do get ill, and you have the opportunity, you should also ask your medical insurer whether they are satisfied that the medical centre or hospital that you have been referred to is of a suitable standard.

Before you go
Ideally, you should see your GP or travel clinic at least 6 weeks before your departure for general advice on travel risks, antibiotics for travellers' bacterial diarrhoea, malaria and vaccinations. Make sure you have travel insurance, get a dental check (especially if you are going to be away for more than a month), know your own blood group and if you suffer from a long-term condition such as diabetes or epilepsy make sure someone knows or that you have a Medic Alert bracelet/necklace with this information on it.

Basic vaccinations recommended include polio, tetanus, diphtheria, typhoid, and hepatitis A. If you are entering the country overland, you may well be asked for a yellow fever vaccination certificate, and most certainly if you are coming from Tanzania.

A-Z of health risks
Altitude sickness Acute mountain sickness can strike from about 3000 m upwards and in general is more likely to affect those who ascend rapidly (for example by plane) and those who over-exert themselves. Teenagers are particularly prone. On reaching heights above 3000 m, heart pounding and shortness of breath are almost universal and a normal response to the lack of oxygen in the air. Acute mountain sickness takes a few hours or days to come on and presents with headache, lassitude, dizziness, loss of appetite, nausea and vomiting. Insomnia is common and often associated with a suffocating feeling when lying down. You may notice that your breathing tends to wax and wane at night and your face is puffy in the mornings – this is all part of the syndrome.

If the symptoms are mild, the treatment is rest, painkillers (preferably not aspirin-based) for the headaches and anti-sickness pills for vomiting. Should the symptoms be severe and prolonged it is best to descend to a lower altitude immediately and re-ascend, if necessary, slowly and in stages. The symptoms disappear very quickly with even a few 100 m of descent.

The best way of preventing acute mountain sickness is a relatively slow ascent. When trekking to high altitude, some time spent walking at medium altitude, getting fit and acclimatizing, is beneficial. On arrival at places over 3000 m a few hours' rest and the avoidance of alcohol, cigarettes and heavy food will help prevent acute mountain sickness. Other problems experienced at high altitude include sunburn, cracked skin, sore eyes (it may be wise to leave your contact lenses out) and sore nostrils. Treat the latter with Vaseline. Do not ascend to high altitude if you are suffering from a bad cold or chest infection and certainly not within 24 hrs after scuba diving.

Bites and stings Mosquitoes and other insects such as tsetse flies can administer a wicked bite and can carry diseases such as malaria. It is essential to wear long sleeves and trousers in the evening when mosquitoes are at their most prevalent and use a mosquito repellent (see under Malaria, below). Rooms with a/c or fans also help ward off mosquitoes at night.

It is a very rare event for travellers but if you are unlucky enough to be bitten by a venomous snake, spider, scorpion or sea creature, try to identify the creature, without putting yourself in further danger (do not try to catch a live snake). Snake bites in particular are very frightening, but in fact rarely poisonous. Victims should be taken to a hospital or a doctor without delay. Commercial snake bite and scorpion kits are available but are usually only useful for specific types of snake or scorpion. Most

serum has to be given intravenously so it is not much good equipping yourself with it unless you are used to making injections into veins. It is best to rely on local practice in these cases, because the particular creatures will be known about locally and appropriate treatment can be given.

Certain tropical sea fish when trodden upon inject venom into bather's feet. This can be exceptionally painful. Wear plastic shoes if such creatures are reported. The pain can be relieved by immersing the foot in hot water (as hot as you can bear) for as long as the pain persists. The citric acid juice in fruits such as lemon can be useful.

Symptoms include swelling, pain and bruising around the bite and soreness of the regional lymph glands, perhaps nausea, vomiting and a fever. Symptoms of serious poisoning would be numbness and tingling of the face, muscular spasms, convulsions, shortness of breath or a failure of the blood to clot, causing generalized bleeding.

To treat a snake bite reassure and comfort the victim frequently. Immobilize the limb by a bandage or a splint and get the person to lie still. Do not slash the bite area and try to suck out the poison because this can do more harm than good, and the inexperienced should never apply a tourniquet.

Spiders and scorpions may be found in the more basic hotels. If stung, rest and take plenty of fluids and call a doctor. The best precaution is to keep beds away from the walls and look inside your shoes and under the toilet seat each morning.

Dengue fever There is no vaccine against this and the mosquitoes that carry it bite during the day. You will feel like a mule has kicked you for 2-3 days, you will then get better for a few days and then feel that the mule has kicked you again. It should all be over in 7-10 days. Heed all the anti-mosquito measures that you can.

Diarrhoea and intestinal upset   It should be short lasting but persistence beyond 2 weeks, with blood or pain, requires specialist medical attention.

The key treatment with all diarrhoea is rehydration. Try to keep hydrated by taking the right mixture of salt and water. This is available as Oral Rehydration Salts (ORS) in ready-made sachets or can be made up by adding a teaspoon of sugar and a half teaspoon of salt to a litre of clean water. Drink at least 1 large cup of this for each loose stool. You can also use flat carbonated drinks as an alternative. Immodium and Pepto-Bismol provide symptomatic relief.

The standard advice to prevent problems is to be careful with water and ice for drinking. Ask yourself where the water came from. If you have any doubts then boil it or filter and treat it. Food can also transmit disease. Be wary of salads (what were they washed in, who handled them), re-heated foods or food that has been left out in the sun having been cooked earlier in the day. There is a simple adage that says wash it, peel it, boil it or forget it. Also be wary of unpasteurized dairy products as these can transmit a range of diseases.

Diving   If you go diving make sure that you are fit do so. The **British Sub-Aqua Club (BSAC)**, Telford's Quay, South Pier Road, Ellesmere Port, Cheshire CH65 4FL, UK, T0151-350 6200, www.bsac.com, can put you in touch with doctors who do medical examinations.

Protect your feet from cuts, beach dog parasites and sea urchins. The latter are almost impossible to remove but can be dissolved with lime or vinegar. Watch for secondary infection, which you'll need antibiotics for. Serious diving injuries may require time in a decompression chamber.

Check that the dive company knows what it is doing, has appropriate certification from BSAC or **Professional Association of Diving**

Instructors (PADI), Unit 7, St Philips Central, Albert Rd, St Philips, Bristol, BS2 OTD, T0117-300 7234, www.padi.com, and that the equipment is well maintained.

Hepatitis   Hepatitis means inflammation of the liver. Viral causes of the disease can be acquired anywhere in the world. The most obvious symptom is a yellowing of your skin or the whites of your eyes. However, prior to this all that you may notice is itching and tiredness. Pre-travel hepatitis A vaccine is the best bet. Hepatitis B (for which there is a vaccine) is spread through blood and unprotected sexual intercourse: both of these can be avoided. Unfortunately there is no vaccine for hepatitis C or the other hepatitis viruses.

Malaria   Malaria can cause death within 24 hrs and can start as something just resembling an attack of flu. You may feel tired, lethargic, headachy, feverish; or, more seriously, develop fits, followed by coma and then death. Have a low index of suspicion because it is very easy to write off vague symptoms, which may actually be malaria. If you have a temperature, go to a doctor as soon as you can and ask for a malaria test. On your return home if you suffer any of these symptoms, get tested as soon as possible, even if any previous test proved negative, the test could save your life. Remember ABCD: Awareness (of whether the disease is present in the area), Bite avoidance, Chemoprohylaxis, Diagnosis.

To prevent mosquito bites wear clothes that cover arms and legs and use effective insect repellents in areas with known risks of insect-spread disease. Use a mosquito net treated with insecticide as both a physical and chemical barrier at night in the same areas. Guard against the contraction of malaria with the correct anti-malarials. Note that the Royal Homeopathic Hospital in the UK does not advocate homeopathic options for malaria prevention or treatment.

Repellents containing DEET (Di-ethyltoluamide) are the gold standard. Apply the repellent every 4-6 hrs but more often if you are sweating heavily. If a non-DEET product is used check who tested it. Validated products (tested at the London School of Hygiene and Tropical Medicine) include Mosiguard, Non-DEET Jungle formula and non-DEET Autan. If you want to use citronella remember that it must be applied very frequently (ie hourly) to be effective. If you are a popular target for insect bites or develop lumps quite soon after being bitten, carry an Aspivenin kit. This syringe suction device is available from many chemists and draws out some of the allergic materials and provides quick relief.

Rabies Avoid dogs and monkeys that are behaving strangely. Bats also carry rabies in Kenya. If you are bitten by a domestic or wild animal, do not leave things to chance: scrub the wound with soap and water and/or disinfectant, try to at least determine the animal's ownership, and seek medical assistance at once. The course of treatment depends on whether you have already been satisfactorily vaccinated against rabies. It is important to finish the course of treatment.

Sun Long-term sun damage can lead to a loss of elasticity of skin and the development of pre-cancerous lesions. Years later a mild or a very malignant form of cancer may develop.

To prevent burning, use sunscreen. The higher the SPF the greater the protection. However, do not use higher factors just to stay out in the sun longer. 'Flash frying' (bursts of excessive exposure), as it is called, is known to increase the risks of skin cancer. Follow the Australians with their Slip, Slap, Slop campaign: Slip on a shirt, Slap on a hat, Slop on sun screen.

Ticks and fly larvae Ticks usually attach themselves to the lower parts of the body often after walking in areas where cattle have grazed, and swell up as they suck blood. The important thing is to remove them gently, so that they do not leave their head in your skin because this can cause a nasty allergic reaction. Do not use petrol, Vaseline, lighted cigarettes, etc to remove the tick, but, with a pair of tweezers remove the beast gently by gripping it at the attached (head) end and rock it out in the same way that a tooth is extracted. Some tropical flies that lay their eggs under the skin of sheep and cattle also do the same thing to humans with the result that a maggot grows under the skin and pops up as a boil. The best way to remove these is to cover the boil with oil, Vaseline or nail varnish to stop the maggot breathing, then to squeeze it out gently the next day.

Water There are a number of ways of purifying water. Dirty water should first be strained through a filter and then boiled or treated. Bringing water to a rolling boil at sea level is sufficient to make the water safe for drinking, but at higher altitudes you have to boil the water for a few minutes longer to ensure all microbes are killed. There are sterilizing methods that can be used and there are proprietary preparations containing chlorine or iodine compounds. Chlorine compounds generally do not kill protozoa (eg giardia). There are a number of water filters now on the market. Make sure you take the spare parts or spare chemicals with you and do not believe everything the manufacturers say.

Other diseases and risks Fresh water can be a source of diseases such as bilharzia. Avoid infected waters, check the CDC, WHO websites and a travel clinic for up-to-date information. Lake Victoria and many smaller lakes are infected and it's always wise to ask locally about swimming.

Unprotected sex always carries a risk, with an awesome range of visible and invisible diseases including HIV, hepatitis B and C, gonorrhea, chlamydia, herpes, syphilis and warts, just to name a few. You can reduce the risk by using a condom, a femidom or avoiding sex altogether.

Further information

www.bloodcare.org.uk The Blood Care Foundation (UK) will dispatch certified non-infected blood of the right type to your hospital/clinic.

www.btha.org British Travel Health Association (UK). This is the official website of an organization of travel health professionals.

www.fitfortravel.scot.nhs.uk Fit for Travel (UK). A-Z of vaccine and travel health advice requirements for each country.

www.fco.gov.uk Foreign and Common-wealth Office (FCO). This is a key travel advice site, with useful information on the country, people and climate and lists of the UK embassies/consulates.

www.masta.org Medical Advisory Service for Travellers Abroad (MASTA). A-Z of vaccine and travel health advice and requirements.

Local customs and laws

Stand for the national anthem and show respect if the national flag is being raised or lowered. Do not take photographs of military or official buildings or personnel, especially the president. Always ask before photographing local people. In some regions, the Masai are so used to tourists wanting to take pictures of them a fee is definitely expected. Do not tear the local currency, and respect the currency laws of the country. Importing or possession of drugs and guns is prohibited and punished severely. The attitude to *bhangi* (cannabis) and *miraa* (a mild stimulant) is ambivalent: both are illegal but appear to be tolerated by the authorities. However, if you are caught your embassy is unlikely to be sympathetic. If you do get in trouble with the law or have to report to the police, always be exceptionally polite and

relatively humble, even if you are reporting a crime against yourself. The Kenyan police generally enjoy their authoritative status; to rant and rave and demand attention will get you absolutely nowhere. Calling a policeman 'sir' is customary. Respect is accorded to elderly people, usually by the greeting *Shikamoo, mzee* to a man and *Shikamoo, mama* to a woman. In English, it is common for people to use the terms 'my sister' or 'aunt', 'my brother' or 'uncle' (depending on how old they think you are) as greetings. For anyone spending any length of time in Kenya, or returning after a long break, it is a sad day when you have reached the status of aunt or uncle – it means you are getting old!

Money
Currency
→ *US$1=93KSh, £1=152KSh, €1=134KSh (Aug 2011)*

The currency in Kenya is the Kenyan shilling (the written abbreviation is either KSh or using /= after the amount, ie 500/=). Notes are 50, 100, 200, 500 and 1000KSh, coins are 5, 10 and 20KSh. As it is not a hard currency, it cannot be brought into or taken out of the country, however there are no restrictions on the amount of foreign currency that can be brought into Kenya. There are banks with ATMs and bureaux de change at both Nairobi and Mombasa airports. There are inevitable queues but at Nairobi it is marginally quicker to change your money after you go through customs. The easiest currencies to exchange are US dollars, UK pounds and euros. If you are bringing US dollars cash, try and bring newer notes – because of the prevalence of forgery, many banks and bureaux de changes do not accept bills printed before 2000. Sometimes lower denomination bills attract a lower exchange rate than higher denominations.

Departure taxes can be paid in local or foreign currency, but they are usually included in the price of an air ticket.

Exchange Visitors should change foreign currency at banks, bureaux de change or authorized hotels, and under no circumstances change money on the black market, which is illegal. All banks have a foreign exchange service. The government has authorized bureaux de change known as forex bureaux to set rates for buying foreign currency from the public. Forex bureaux are open longer hours and offer faster service than banks and, although the exchange rates are only nominally different, the bureaux usually offer a better rate on traveller's cheques.

Credit cards and traveller's cheques
Traveller's cheques (TCs) are widely accepted, and many upmarket hotels, travel agencies, safari companies and restaurants accept credit cards. Most banks in Kenya are equipped to advance cash on credit cards, and increasingly most now have ATMs that accept Visa, Mastercard, Plus and Cirrus cards. Diners Club and American Express are, however, limited. Increasingly, many of the large petrol stations, such as Caltex and Mobil, are starting to install ATMs, especially in Nairobi and Mombasa. Your bank will probably charge a fee for withdrawing cash. It is quite feasible to travel around Kenya with just a credit or debit card, although it is always a good idea to bring some cash or TCs as a back-up.

Cost of travelling
In upmarket luxury lodges and tented camps expect to pay in excess of US$150 per person per night for a double, rising to US$500 per night per person in the most exclusive establishments. There are a number of places aimed at the very top-of-the-range tourist or honeymooner that charge nearer US$1000 per person per night. For this you will get impeccable service, cuisine and decor in fantastic locations either in the parks or on the coast. In 4- and 5-star hotels and lodges expect to spend US$200-300 a day. Careful tourists can live reasonably comfortably on US$100 a day staying in the mid-range places, however, to stay in anything other than campsites on safaris, they will have to spend a little more for the cheapest accommodation in the national parks. Budget travellers can get by on US$40 utilizing the cheap guesthouses and going on a basic camping safari. However, with additional park entry fees and related costs, organized camping safari costs are at the bare minimum US$200 for a 3-day/2-night excursion to the Masai Mara for example. Commodities such as chocolate and toiletries are more expensive as they are imported but are readily available. Restaurants vary widely from side-of-the-road local eateries where a simple meal of chicken and chips will cost US$2-3 to the upmarket restaurants in the cities and tourists spots that charge in excess of US$60 for 2 people with drinks.

Opening hours
Banks Mon-Fri 0830-1330, Sat 0830-1100.
Embassies Usually mornings only.
Kiosks Often open all hours, as the owner frequently lives on site. **Post offices** Mon-Fri 0800-1700, Sat 0900-1200. **Shops** Generally Mon-Sat 0800-1700 or 1800.

Safety
The majority of the people you will meet are honest and ready to help you so there is no need to get paranoid about your safety. However, Nairobi and Mombasa do have reputations for crime, and the most popular national parks have their fair share of robberies. There is a high rate of street crime not just in Nairobi and Mombasa but also in Kisumu and the coastal beach resorts, especially bag- snatching. Basically, you just have to be sensible and not carry expensive cameras, open bags or valuable jewellery and be careful about carrying large sums of money. Waist pouches ('bum-bags' or

'moon-bags') are very vulnerable as the belt can be cut easily. Day packs have also been known to be slashed, with their entire contents drifting out on to the street without the wearer knowing. Carry money and any valuables in a slim belt under clothing. Also, do not automatically expect your belongings to be safe in a tent. Avoid walking around after dusk, particularly in the more run-down urban areas – take a taxi – and walking alone at night, even on beaches, is dangerous. In built-up areas, lock your car, and if there is an *askari* (security guard) nearby, pay him a small sum to watch over it, although you should still be careful as con-artists have been known to impersonate hotel employees and even police officers. Also be wary of someone distracting a driver in a parked vehicle, whilst an accomplice gets into the car on the opposite side. Always keep car doors locked and windows wound up, and lock room doors at night as noisy fans and a/c can provide cover for sneak thieves. Crime and hazardous road conditions make travel by night dangerous.

Car-jacking occurs and is a particular problem in Nairobi. You also need to be vigilant of thieves on buses and trains and guard your possessions fiercely. For petty offences (driving without lights switched on, for example) police will often try to solicit a bribe, masked as an 'on-the-spot' fine. Establish the amount being requested, and then offer to go to the police station to pay, at which point you will usually be released with a warning. For any serious charges, immediately contact your embassy or consulate. The British High Commission strongly advise against travel in Northeast Kenya (Moyale, Mandera, Wajit and Garissa), because of difficulties with the Somalian unrest, and there is a problem with *Shiftas* (bandits) attacking vehicles on roads in Northern Kenya.

It's not only crime that may affect your personal safety; you must also take safety precautions when visiting the game reserves and national parks. If camping, it is not advisable to leave your tent or *banda* during the night. Wild animals wander around the camps freely in the hours of darkness, and a protruding leg may seem like a tasty take-away to a hungry hyena. This is especially true at organized campsites, where the local animals have got so used to humans that they have lost much of their inherent fear. Exercise care during daylight hours too – remember wild animals can be unpredictable and potentially dangerous.

Telephone

→ *Country code +254.*

Generally speaking, the telephone system is very good. You should be able to make international calls from public call boxes and the easiest way of doing this is with a phone card (available from most post offices). If this is not possible, make your call through post offices where you get your money back if you fail to get through. If you dial through the operator, there is a 3-min minimum charge. Most hotels and lodges offer international telephone and fax services, though they will usually charge double. In larger towns, private centres also offer international services. Calls from Kenya to Tanzania and Uganda are charged at long-distance tariffs rather than international. If you have a mobile phone with a roaming connection, you can make use of Kenya's cellular networks, which cover most larger towns, the length of the coast and the Mombasa to Uganda road and the tourist areas but not some of the parks and reserves or the north of Kenya away from the towns. Sim and top-up cards for pay-as-you-go mobile providers are available almost everywhere; in the towns and cities these often have their own shops, but you can buy cards from roadside vendors anywhere, even in the smallest of settlements. Mobile phones are now such a part of everyday life in Kenya that many establishments have abandoned the local landline services and use the mobile network instead. Quite remarkably, cell phone provider **Celtel**, operates a system called **One Network**, the world's 1st borderless network. It covers 22 African countries from Zambia to Gabon and enables callers to use their phones without roaming and all calls across this vast region are at local (not international) rates. The network now has a staggering 25 million subscribers. If you are travelling on, say to Uganda or Tanzania, it's a good idea to opt for a Celtel Sim card. At the time of writing Celtel was rebranding itself under the Zain telecommunications umbrella so look out for both cards.

Time
GMT+3.

Tipping
It is customary to tip around 10% for good service, which is greatly appreciated by hotel and restaurant staff, most of whom receive very low pay. Some upmarket establishments may add a service charge to the bill. See page 21 for advice on tipping safari guides.

Visas and immigration
Almost all visitors require a visa, with the exception of some African countries. A transit visa valid for 7 days costs US$20 per person; a single-entry visa valid for 3 months costs US$50; a multi-entry visa valid for 12 months costs US$100. Visas are issued at the following entry points: Busia, Lunga Lunga, Malaba, Migori, Moyale, Namanga and Taveta border posts and at Jomo Kenyatta International Airport in Nairobi, Moi International Airport in Mombasa and Eldoret International Airport. Visas can be paid for in US dollars, euros or UK pounds sterling. Multi-entry visas are not available on arrival but only through embassies. As long as your single-entry visa remains valid you are allowed to move freely between Kenya, Tanzania and Uganda without the need for re-entry permits. If you want to get an extension you can stay a maximum of 6 months in the country fairly easily, but at extra cost. In Nairobi this can be done at Nyayo House, corner of Kenyatta Av and Uhuru Highway, T020-222 022, Mon-Fri 0830-1230 and 1400-1530; it can also be done at the Provincial Commissioner's Offices in Embu, Garissa, Kisumu, Mombasa and Nakuru. Do check your visitor's pass as it has been known for people who have overstayed their time in the country to be fined quite heavily. Your passport must be valid for a minimum of 6 months after your planned departure date from Kenya; this is a requirement whether you need a visa or not. For more information visit www.immigration.go.ke. Incidentally, if passengers are transiting through Nairobi and have a couple of hours to kill, they are allowed out of the airport on their transit visas, so there is no reason at all why they can't grab a taxi and go to Nairobi National Park for a game drive.

Weights and measures
Metric. In country areas items are often sold by the piece.

Contents

Southern Kenya

Tsavo National Park

Tsavo is the largest game park in Kenya, and its beautiful landscape and proximity to the coast make it a popular safari destination. It offers tremendous views with diverse habitats ranging from mountains, river forest, plains, lakes and wooded grassland. Because of its open spaces, the animals are fairly easy to spot and elephants, covered in bright red dust, are often seen wandering along every horizon. Its vastness creates a special atmosphere and on these endless plains trampled by thousands of animals it is not difficult to imagine that this is once how all of East Africa looked liked.

Ins and outs → *Phone code: 043.*

→ For listings, see pages 37-39.

Getting there There are no scheduled flights to either Tsavo East or West, although Mombasa Air Safaris (see page 58) will touch down on request and there are several airstrips suitable for chartered light aircraft.

Getting around Both Tsavo East and West are fairly easily navigated with a good map as all tracks are clearly defined, and junctions are numbered. Bring all your own provisions into the park including petrol and water. You should be able to eat or drink at any of the lodges if you so desire. There is a shop at Voi Gate in the east selling (warm) beers, sodas, bread and some vegetables, and another shop in Tsavo West selling basic provisions.

Background

This is the largest national park in Kenya at around 21,000 sq km. It lies in the southern part of the country, halfway between Mombasa and Nairobi and is bisected by the Mombasa–Nairobi railway and road link. For administrative purposes it has been split into two sections; **Tsavo East** (11,747 sq km) lying to the east of the Nairobi–Mombasa road/railway is the part of the park made famous by the 'Man-Eaters of Tsavo', and **Tsavo West** (9065 sq km). The Waliangulu and Kamba tribes used to hunt in this area before it was gazetted. The remoteness of much of the park means it has had serious problems with poaching in the past. As a consequence, much of the northern area (about two thirds of Tsavo East) used to be off-limits to the public in an attempt to halt poaching here, which had decimated the rhino population from 8000 in 1970 to around 100 in 1990. Recent anti-poaching laws have been particularly successful in Tsavo; the number of rhinos and elephants are increasing and the northern area of Tsavo East is once again open to the public. In 2007, the Kenya Wildlife Service did a census of the elephant population in Tsavo and the number was 11,696.

The first European to visit this part of Kenya was Doctor Krapf, who journeyed on foot and crossed the Tsavo River in 1849 on his way to Kitui. Captain Lugards, the explorer, also passed through this area – the rapids on the Galana River are named after him.

Tsavo East

Tsavo East is the much less-visited side of the park where you will be able to see the wildlife without the usual hordes of other tourists. It mainly consists of vast plains of scrubland home to huge herds of elephants. The landscape is vast, and empty of any sign of humans, dotted with baobab trees.

Ins and outs

ⓘ *Gates open 0630-1830. US$50, children US$25, vehicle US$4.50 per day.*

The park HQ is at Voi Gate (where you can obtain and reload Smartcards) just north of Voi on the Nairobi–Mombasa road, where there is a small educational centre. Other gates off the main road are Manyani Gate, 25 km north of Voi, and Buchuma Gate at the extreme southeast corner of Tsavo East. It is also possible to enter the park on the C103 road from Malindi via Sala Gate on the eastern boundary of the park. This route, which runs alongside the Galana River between Manyani Gate and Sala Gate, may be impassable during the rains.

Sights

Wildlife includes all of the Big Five, plus zebra, giraffe, impala, gazelle, eland and cheetah, and there are over 500 bird species. The **Kanderi Swamp**, not far from Voi Gate, has the most wildlife in the area. The main attraction is the **Aruba Dam** built across the Voi River where many animals and birds congregate. **Mudanda Rock**, about 30 km north of Voi, is a 1.6-km long outcrop of rock that towers above a natural dam and at times during the dry season draws hundreds of elephants. The **Yatta Plateau**, at about 290 km long is the world's largest lava flow. The **Lugards Falls** on the Galana River, 40 km northeast of Voi are pretty spectacular. They are a series of rapids rather than true falls. The rocks have been sculpted into fascinating shapes by the rapid water flow channelled into a gorge so narrow that it is possible to stand with legs spanning the cleft, overlooking the falls.

Tsavo West

Tsavo West is the more developed part of the park combining easy access, good facilities and stunning views over the tall grass and woodland scenery. The area is made up from recent volcano lava flows, which absorb rainwater that reappears as the crystal-clear Mzima Springs 40 km away, and supports a vast quantity and diversity of plant and animal life.

① Tsavo East National Park

Sleeping 🛏		
Ashnil Aruba Lodge 11	Galdessa Camp 4	Rock Side Camp 6	Voi Wildlife Lodge 7
Crocodile Camp 3	Kilalinda Lodge 1	Sagala Lodge 10
	Ngutuni Lodge 9	Satao Camp 5	Camping △
	Patterson's Safari Camp 13	Tarhi Camp 12	Ndololo 8
	Red Elephant Safari Lodge 8	Voi Safari Lodge 2	

② Tsavo West National Park

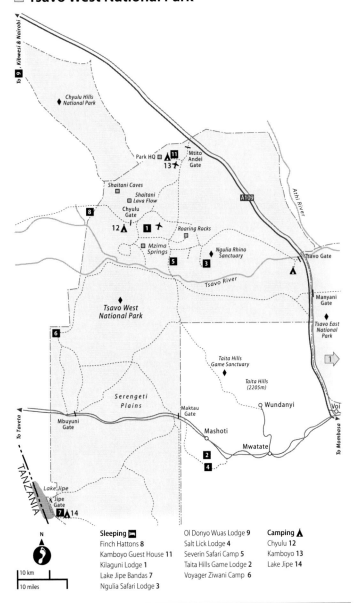

Sleeping 🛏
Finch Hattons **8**
Kamboyo Guest House **11**
Kilaguni Lodge **1**
Lake Jipe Bandas **7**
Ngulia Safari Lodge **3**

Ol Donyo Wuas Lodge **9**
Salt Lick Lodge **4**
Severin Safari Camp **5**
Taita Hills Game Lodge **2**
Voyager Ziwani Camp **6**

Camping ⛺
Chyulu **12**
Kamboyo **13**
Lake Jipe **14**

Ins and outs

ⓘ Gates open 0630-1830. Adults US$50, children US$25, vehicle US$4.50 per day. Smartcards can be reloaded (but not obtained) at the Mtito Andei Gate.

There are several entrance gates into Tsavo West. Two are on the Nairobi–Mombasa road: Tsavo Gate, 320 km from Nairobi and 5 km north of Voi, and Mtito Andei Gate, 30 km north of Tsavo Gate, 240 km south of Nairobi and 249 km north of Mombasa. Buses from Nairobi to Mombasa pass near both, and hitching to these gates is fairly easy, but since walking inside the park is not allowed, visitors without vehicles may have a very long wait. Chyulu Gate in the northwest corner of the park is used by vehicles coming into Tsavo West from Amboseli National Park. 4WD and high-clearance vehicles are required for this route, especially in wet weather. Other entries are at Ziwani Gate, Jipe Gate and Kasigau Gate all to the south of the park. Buses also run between Voi and Taveta on the Tanzanian border (and then on to Moshi) through the south of the park via Maktau and Mbuyuni gates.

Sights

The main attractions at Tsavo West are the watering holes by **Kilaguni** and **Ngulia** lodges that entice a huge array of wildlife particularly in the dry season. During the autumn the areas around **Ngulia Lodge** are a stopover for hundreds of thousands of birds from Europe in their annual migration. Not far from the Kilaguni Lodge is the **Mzima Springs**, a favourite haunt of hippos and crocodiles. There is an underwater viewing chamber, but the hippos have obviously decided against being watched by moving to the other side of the pool. Also around the lodges are the spectacular **Shaitani lava flow** and cones, as well as caves that are well worth visiting. You will need to bring a good torch. **Chaimu Crater** to the south of **Kilaguni Lodge** can be climbed and although there is little danger of animals here, it is best to be careful. At the extreme southwest of the park, bordering Tanzania, is the beautiful **Lake Jipe**, which is fed by underground flows from Mount Kilimanjaro. Here are found pygmy geese and the black heron along with many other species of bird. Wildlife you are likely to spot include hyrax, agama lizards, dwarf mongooses, marabou storks, baboons, antelope, buffalo, zebra, giraffe, jackals and hyenas, crocodiles, hippos, leopards, lions and cheetahs. If you're very lucky you might see wild dogs. There are some black rhino although most have been moved to the **Ngulia Rhino Sanctuary** *ⓘ daily 1600-1800*, which is close to the Mzima Springs and is a fenced area of 62 sq km containing about 60 rhinos.

Chyulu Hills National Park

This was established in 1983 as an extension to Tsavo West. Previously a game conservation area, the park is virtually untouched by humans. The long mountain range is home to lion, giraffe, zebra and oryx. Described as being the youngest mountain range in the world, it is made up of intermingled volcanic cones and lava flows that are considered only to be around 500 years old. Many of the cones are covered with grass and there are extensive forests. There is no permanent water supply in this mountain range except for a small spring at Ngungani. Kilimanjaro is clearly visible from the crest of the Chyulu Hills.

Taita Hills Game Sanctuary

In the south Tsavo West more or less surrounds the privately run Taita Hills Game Sanctuary which is actually south of the Taita Hills about 15 km west of Mwatate. There is a wide variety of game present here including lion, cheetah, elephant and plains game. Prolific bird life includes the extremely rare Taita Falcon, a bird recorded in early Egyptian hieroglyphics. **Mount Vuria** at 2205 m is the highest point in the Taitas, and from the summit there are excellent views of the plains of Tsavo below. The Taita are in fact three groups of hills, the **Dabida**, **Sagalla** and **Kasigau**. The Chyulu Hills can be seen if it is not misty. Road access to Taita Hills is on the road from Voi to Taveta. You'll need your own transport, or to be part of a safari, to reach this region.

Tsavo National Park listings

For Sleeping and Eating price codes and other relevant information, see pages 11-16.

● Sleeping

Tsavo East *p33, map p34*

$$$$ Galdessa Camp, reservations Galdessa Camp, Ukunda, T040-320 2630, www.gald essa.com. 10 km upstream from Lugards Falls on the Galana River are 12 *bandas* with river frontage. The camp is divided into down- stream and upstream camps, with their own central facilities that can also be booked for exclusive use. The central mess areas house dining areas, bars, and large, comfortable lounges. Price includes full board (excluding alcohol), game drives, and walking safaris.

$$$$ Kilalinda Lodge, reservations **Private Wilderness**, Nairobi, T020-882 598, www.kilalinda.com. The 6 luxury cottages overlook the river, and the largest has its own plunge pool and jacuzzi. Facilities include central split-level bar, lounge, dining room, library and swimming pool. The highlight is the twin Victorian bath tubs in a private *boma* with open roof. Game drives in both Tsavo East and West national parks, fishing, game walks and fly camping on offer.

$$$ Ashnil Aruba Lodge, reservations, **Ashnil Hotels**, Nairobi, T020-556 946, www.ashnil hotels.com. Newly opened in 2008, each of the 40 partly canvas rooms have wide terraces overlooking the Aruba Dam and safari-style decor and 2 have disabled facilities. There's a curio shop, ice-cream parlour, restaurant and bar, rates are full board, and in the evening are wildlife and cultural talks and African dancing shows. An affordable option aimed at overnight visitors from the coast.

$$$ Crocodile Camp, 3 km from the Sala Gate and usually accessed from Malindi on the C103, reservations **African Safari Club**, UK T+44 (0)20-8466 0014, www.africansafari club.com. Overlooking the Galana River in an exceptionally fertile area. There are fixed tents on a solid base or wooden bungalows with veranda and chairs, all covered by *makuti* thatched roofs. All have twin beds, a private shower and wc, a/c and hot water. Meals are served in the thatched dining room and there is a cosy bar and small swimming pool. This is principally used by guests on safari from the African Safari Club package resorts on the coast but it does accept independent bookings.

$$$ Patterson's Safari Camp, on the Athi River in the north of the park, 8 km from the Tsavo Gate, reservations Nairobi T020-202 1674, www.pattersonsafaricamp.com. There are 20 spacious and shady en suite tents, some sleeping 4 people, with nice views over the sludgy brown river, which attracts a lot of game. The name derives from railway worker John Patterson who shot the 'man-eaters' of Tsavo when the railway was being built. There's a pleasant thatched bar and restaurant and a bonfire is lit in the evening.

$$$ Voi Safari Lodge, reservations, Mombasa, T041-471 861, www.safari-hotels.com. Slightly cheaper than the lodges of equivalent standard in West

Tsavo and much less crowded, with 52 rooms, each with 2 beds, but they are starting to look dated and are overdue for a refurbishment. There's a swimming pool, the animal hide by the waterhole gives very good close-up views at eye level and baboons and rock hyrax wander through the hotel and gardens. Not recommended for the unfit or elderly as there are lots of steps between the buildings.

$$$ Satao Camp, reservations **Southern Cross Safaris**, Mombasa T041-243 4600, www.satao camp.com. Permanent tented camp with 20 double tents, 2 with disabled facilities, constructed of sisal and *boroti* poles topped with a *makuti* roof, very nice bathrooms with stone features and hot showers. Overlooks a waterhole with resident hippo, where elephant, lion, zebra, etc drink at night. Lovely thatched bar and restaurant with atmospheric lighting, very good food, safari chairs out front around a bonfire. Game drives and sundowner trips into the bush on offer, although many animals come right into the camp. Well organized and professional, very good value.

$$$ Tarhi Camp, 12 km from Voi Gate, reservations, Mombasa, T041-548 6378, www.camp-tarhi.de. Not in as scenic a location as some of the other lodges, but an affordable option within the park, this German-run tented camp has simple permanent tents each with toilet, shower and fan, and there's a rustic bar and a mess tent for meals. Rates are US$60 per person full board and US$50 per person half board, children are half price. You can arrive here in a normal car, and then go on game drives in a 4WD from the camp for US$20 per person.

Camping

$ Ndololo Campsite, near Voi Gate, about 7 km into the park, has water and pit latrines and firewood is available. You pay for camping at the gates.

Tsavo West *p34, map p35*
$$$$ Finch Hattons, 65 km from the Mtito Andei Gate, reservations Nairobi, T020-553 237/8, www.finchhattons.com.
Award-winning luxury camp that oozes atmosphere, which accommodates up to 50 people, in large safari tents with twin beds, each with minibar, wooden Swahili chest, bookshelves and an antique writing desk, large deck balconies with chairs, tables and daybed. Elegantly appointed bar and restaurant and a comfortable private lounge, extensive library of books and an excellent range of classical music including Denys Finch Hatton's favourite selection of Mozart, swimming pool, dinner is very formal with 6 courses, fine china and crystal glasses.

$$$ Kamboyo Guest House, 8 km from the Mtito Andei Gate, reservations **Kenya Wildlife Service**, Nairobi, T020-600 800, www.kws.org. Self-catering cottage with 3 rooms with double beds and 1 room with a single bed, 10 people maximum, must be taken as a unit for US$200 per night, towels, bed linen and kitchen utensils are provided, you just need to bring food, firewood and drinking water.

$$$ Kilaguni Lodge, 20 km from the Mtito Andei Gate, T045-622471, www.serena hotels.com. Good-quality lodge from the Serena chain, blends well into the landscape, 56 spacious rooms, lots of wooden decks for game viewing, decorated with wooden sculptures of animals, a rock-hewn bar, swimming pool, excellent buffet meals with a wide variety of choice, rates are full board. This was the first lodge to be built in any of Kenya's parks. Mt Kilimanjaro can be seen on a clear day.

$$$ Ngulia Safari Lodge, 55 km from the Mtito Andei Gate, reservations, Mombasa, T041-471 861, www.safari-hotels.com. Slightly cheaper than the others at about US$100 per person full board, but still very good, with 52 rooms, a swimming pool and in a good location. The waterhole, again, is a big draw both for the animals and tourists.

Staff are very knowledgeable on the wildlife and are extremely helpful. The lodge overlooks the Ngulia Rhino Sanctuary and rhinos can be viewed through the binoculars that are set up especially. The lodge is renowned as a haven for bird lovers every year Oct-Dec, who come to be involved in the bird 'ring' of migrating birds escaping the harsh winter conditions of the northern hemisphere. It is the only place in Kenya where this activity takes place.

$$$ Severin Safari Camp, 50 km from Mtito Andei Gate, reservations Mombasa, T041-548 7365, www.severin-kenya.com. Thatched central area with good restaurant and bar, and a pleasant fire pit for bonfires with traditional safari chairs overlooking the plains, spacious octagonal tents with very high ceilings and mosquito nets under thatch with good views.

$$$ Voyager Ziwani Camp, reservations Nairobi, T020-444 6651, www.heritage-east africa.com. A Heritage Group's Voyager resort, of good standard and aimed at families and 1st-time safari goers. At the western boundary of the park on the edge of a small, secluded dam on the Sante River, with full-size permanent tents and excellent food. Of the camp's 25 tents, 16 sit on the southern bank of the Sante River and 9 on the northern. Offers game drives and walks with highly qualified naturalists, and there is an Adventurer's Club for children. Rates vary depending on season.

$$ Lake Jipe Bandas, reservations through the Warden 045-22483, or **Kenya Wildlife Service**, Nairobi, T020-600 800, www.kws.org. In total they sleep 5 people, have a kitchen but no utensils and you need to bring your own firewood, drinking water, food and bedding. Come here completely self-sufficient. Cost is US$50, regardless of the number of people, payable at the park gates.

Camping
There are also campsites (**$**) close to each of the gates at Tsavo: **Kamboyo Campsite**

8 km from the Mtito Andei Gate, and **Chyulu Campsite** 1 km from the Chyulu Gate. There are no facilities but water and pit latrines so you will need to be completely self-sufficient. Another campsite is available on the shores of Lake Jipe. Campers share the outdoor cooking area and ablutions block with guests at the **Lake Jipe Bandas** (see above).

Chyulu Hills National Park p36
$$$$ Ol Donyo Wuas Lodge, in the Chyulu Hills, www.oldonyowuas.com, reservations **Bush and Beyond/Bush Homes of East Africa**, Nairobi, T020-600 457, www.bush-and- beyond.com and www.bush-homes.co.ke. 7 individual 2- or 4-bedroomed enormous luxury thatched cottages, some with private swimming pools, and a beautiful, central dining room. All cottages have en suite bathrooms, lounge with an open fireplace and a veranda with panoramic views of the plains and Mt Kilimanjaro and there is also the option of sleeping outside on the roof. All-inclusive of food, drinks, day and night game drives, and guided bush walks. You can also go horse riding or mountain biking with armed guards. Most guests fly in using **Safarilink** (page 7).

Taita Hills Game Sanctuary p36
The 2 Sarova-run lodges here are quite close together, but they are both rather odd-looking structures, given that they advertize themselves as game lodges.

$$$ Salt Lick Lodge, outside of the park in the Taita Hills, reservations **Sarova Hotels**, Nairobi T020-276 7000, www.sarova hotels.com. This is noted for its strange design, basically a group of 96 rooms in huts on elevated stilts that are connected by open-air bridges over a number of water-holes. All rooms have a balcony. The lodge is resplendent with African wooden tables and batiks and rugs. The area is lit by floodlights for game viewing at night, and there is an underground tunnel and chamber allowing guests to watch wildlife safely at ground level. Tour packages offered range from 2-4 days and generally include transport from Nairobi or Mombasa, sanctuary fees, game-drives and full-board accommodation. **$$$ Taita Hills Game Lodge**, reservations **Sarova Hotels**, Nairobi T020-2767000, www.sarovahotels.com. This is a rather unusual stone building covered with ivy, with 62 ordinary but comfortable rooms with balconies and wicker furniture, but the decor in the public areas is a little old fashioned. Rates include sanctuary fees and all buffet meals, there's a bar and enormous stone fireplace, plus tennis courts and a pool.

Contents

Footprint features

The Coast

Ins and outs

Getting there and around

The gateway to the coast of Kenya is Mombasa, although some visitors fly directly to Malindi or Lamu and there are daily scheduled services between these and Nairobi. The coastal highway runs north of Mombasa all the way to Kenya's northern frontier. Driving your own car or hired car as far as Malindi is very easy, and there are regular buses and *matatus*. Many hotels and resorts in this area have Mombasa shuttles or can arrange vehicle transfers. Private taxis from Mombasa will also take you to the north coast beaches for an agreed fare. Services are less regular north of Malindi, although there are daily buses to Lamu. To the south of Mombasa, the Likoni car ferry links the city with the coastal road that runs to the border with Tanzania. Once off the ferry there are regular *matatus* to Ukunda, the village at the turn-off for the beach road to the resorts along Diani Beach, where you can swap *matatus* or take a taxi. Again many of the southern resorts arrange shuttle services between Mombasa and the beach. Larger buses run daily between Mombasa, Moshi and Dar es Salaam in Tanzania, crossing the border at the extreme south of the coast road at Lunga Lunga. Another slower option for reaching the coast is to take the overnight train from Nairobi to Mombasa that runs three times a week. Many people book week-long package holidays to the resorts, but independent travellers may want to consider hiring a car to explore the coast as the roads from the southern tip of Diani Beach to Malindi are good and most of the resorts accept walk-in guests (often for discounted rates) if they have room, although this would be inadvisable in high season.

Best time to visit

The climate on the coast is markedly different to that in Nairobi and the Kenyan Highlands, and if driving down the main Nairobi–Mombasa road, you will feel the rise in temperature and humidity as you get nearer to the coast. The average temperature is 28-30°C, and days are long and sunny just about all year round. Despite this, there is a down season on the coast during the rainy season from April to June, when it is often overcast and muggy, and many of the resorts and hotels offer discounts and some even close altogether out of season. If you can put up with a few afternoon showers, this is not a bad time to visit, and you are likely to have the beach to yourself, but on the downside, many other facilities such as restaurants and watersports centres also close. By contrast, during high season, especially around Christmas and New Year, the beaches are very busy with European package-holiday makers and room rates are at their premium.

Mombasa

With a history going back 2000 years, Mombasa is the oldest town in Kenya. Although the town is centred on an island about 4 km long and 7 km wide, it has now begun to sprawl on to the mainland. It owes its development to its location, for the island forms an ideal natural deep-water harbour. Today goods are sent from the port to not only Kenya but to Uganda, Burundi, Rwanda and Sudan.

Mombasa has large communities of Indian and Arabic origin. It has the greatest concentration of Muslims in Kenya and their influence on the culture is strong. There are some ancient, Arab-inspired houses with elaborately carved doorways in narrow streets and passages, and a few other worthy distractions such as Fort Jesus and the city's most famous landmark: two pairs of crossed concrete elephant tusks created as a ceremonial arch to commemorate the coronation of Elizabeth II in 1952. Despite these, Mombasa is not a terribly attractive place and rubbish here is quite a problem, as is the traffic and pollution. Most visitors do not stay in the town itself – the city's hotels are not especially nice – and instead stay in one of the beachside locations to the north or south of Mombasa and visit on a day trip. It is now linked by causeways to the mainland at three points as well as by the Likoni Ferry.

Ins and outs → *Phone code: 041. Population: 70,000. For listings, see pages 51-60.*

Getting there

Mombasa is easily accessible and **Moi International Airport** ① *T041-433 221, www.kenyaairports.com*, is 10 km west of the city centre on the mainland. There are several direct charter flights from Europe bringing people out on package holidays, as well as several daily scheduled flights from Nairobi on **Kenya Airways**, **Fly 540**, and **Air Kenya**. Shop around but generally flights are good value; from US$110 return with Fly 540 for example. **Kenya Airways** code-shares with Tanzania's **Precision Air**, and there are now flights between Mombasa, Zanzibar and Dar es Salaam. **Mombasa Air Safaris** links Mombasa to airstrips in the Masai Mara and Amboseli. Arriving at Moi International from Nairobi is quite a pleasant experience as you emerge into the balmy sunny weather. There are desks for the car-hire companies, and stands for various taxi firms that offer transfers into town, and further afield to the north and south-coast beaches. For those arriving on international flights, visas are processed quickly at immigration.

The overnight train from Nairobi runs three times a week and there are several bus services a day with various different companies. Although on the coast, there are no boat links to anywhere else in Kenya or to neighbouring countries, and travelling by *dhow* is illegal for foreigners, but cruise ships pull into the port from time to time and there is the option of seeing Mombasa from the water on the *Tamarind dhow* (see page 53). ▶▶ See Transport, page 57.

Getting around

The city is bisected by two main roads: Moi Avenue, which runs from the industrial area to the west of the island, and then becomes Nkrumah Avenue to Fort Jesus in the east, and Digo Road that crosses it in the centre of the city around the Old Town. Numerous *matatus* run up and down Digo Road going to the Likoni Ferry to the south and Nyali Beach and other points in the north. Taxis can be found all over town parked on street corners. *Tuk-tuks* are beginning to feature on the city's streets and are considerably cheaper than regular taxis. You can walk around the centre of Mombasa but the heat and humidity will tire you out quickly if you are too energetic. The traffic fumes are also particularly bad. Moi International Airport is located on the mainland about 10 km out of the centre of town. To get from the airport to the centre of town, you will need to take a taxi, which should cost in the region of US$10-12 depending on the time of day. Inside the airport are several taxi and shuttle bus desks that can arrange not only lifts into town but direct shuttles to most of the beach resorts. Prices are clearly marked on their boards.

Tourist information

There's no official tourist office as such but there is a clutch of tour operators along Moi Avenue that can give out information and display a variety of leaflets. They will of course want to book you on to something.

Safety

Although there's nowhere in the city centre that is considered a no-go area as such, petty theft does occur so don't flash valuables or walk down dark alleyways. Be particularly wary on the crowded Likoni Ferry. Also by contrast to Nairobi and other towns where streets empty after 1800, on the coast, and because of climatic conditions, many businesses close for a siesta in the middle of the day. As such the city stays awake longer, and the streets are still busy in the early evening and shops stay open later. Nevertheless, when they do close and people go home, do not wander the streets and take a taxi.

Background

The seasonal monsoon wind known as the Kazkazi blows down the coast from the northeast between October and April, as it has done for thousands of years bringing trade to Mombasa. Between May and September this monsoon wind becomes the Kuzi, when it turns through 180° and blows back up the coast towards the Arabian Gulf. The Kazkazi and the Kuzi winds were the key to the foreign exploitation of Kenya and the rest of East Africa for thousands of years: the earliest known reference to Mombasa dates from AD

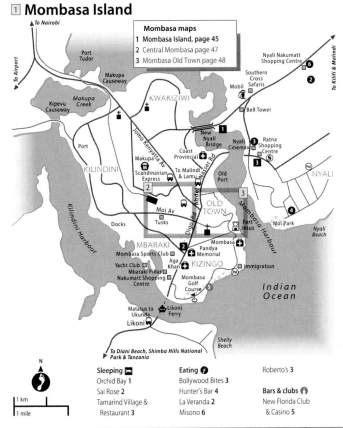

1 Mombasa Island

Mombasa maps
1 Mombasa Island, page 45
2 Central Mombasa page 47
3 Mombasa Old Town page 48

Sleeping
Orchid Bay 1
Sai Rose 2
Tamarind Village & Restaurant 3

Eating
Bollywood Bites 3
Hunter's Bar 4
La Veranda 2
Misono 6

Roberto's 3

Bars & clubs
New Florida Club & Casino 5

150 when the Roman geographer Ptolemy placed the town on his map of the world. Roman, Arabic and Far Eastern seafarers took advantage of the port and were regular visitors, and the port provided the town with the basis of economic development and it expanded steadily.

By the 16th century Mombasa was the most important town on the east coast of Africa with a population estimated at 10,000. A wealthy settlement, it was captured by the Portuguese who were trying to break the Arab trading monopoly, particularly in the lucrative merchandising of spices. The town first fell to the Portuguese under the command of Dom Francisco in 1505. He ransacked the town and burnt it to the ground. It was rebuilt and returned to its former glory before it was ransacked again in 1528. However, the Portuguese did not stay and, having again looted and razed the town, they left.

The building of Fort Jesus in 1593, the stationing of a permanent garrison there, and the installation of their own nominee from Malindi as Sultan, represented the first major attempt to secure Mombasa permanently. However, an uprising by the townspeople in 1631 led to the massacre of all the Portuguese. This led to yet another Portuguese fleet returning to try to recapture the town. In 1632 the leaders of the revolt retreated to the mainland leaving the island to the Europeans. Portuguese rule lasted less than 100 years and they were expelled by the Omanis in 1698. The Omanis also held Zanzibar and were heavily involved in the slave trade. Their rule was supplanted by the British in 1873.

The British efforts to stamp out the slave trade, and anxiety about German presence in what is now Tanzania, led in 1896 to the beginning of the construction of the railway that was to link Uganda to the sea. The first rail was laid at Mombasa Railway Station on 13 May 1896 and the railhead reached Port Florence (Kisumu) on Lake Victoria on 20 December 1901, having ascended the Great Rift Valley western wall and crested the Mau Summit at some 2700 m above sea level, making it the highest metre-gauge railway in the world. One of the railway camps that was established before the construction of the line across the Rift Valley was at Nairobi. This town grew so rapidly that by 1907 it was large enough for the administrative quarters to move inland. The climate of Nairobi was considered to be healthier than the coast, and because of its elevation was too high for malaria-bearing mosquitoes to survive. Meanwhile, with the railway, the importance of the port of Mombasa increased rapidly and it became known as the Gateway to East Africa, serving Kenya, Uganda, Rwanda and Burundi.

In more recent history, Mombasa was the scene of a terrorist attack in 2002 when a hotel on one of the northern beaches, popular with Israelis and the only Israeli-owned hotel in the Mombasa area, was car bombed by suicide bombers, leaving 10 Kenyans and three Israeli holidaymakers dead. At the same time an Israeli plane was fired at as it was taking off from Mombasa Airport. Although the attacks to this day still haven't been confirmed as the work of al-Qaeda, if they were, it would have been their first attack on Israelis, despite their alleged hostility towards Israel.

Sights

Fort Jesus

ⓘ *Nkrumah Rd, T041-312 839, www.museums.or.ke, US$11.50, children (under 18) US$5.75, daily 0930-1800, guides are available for a tip or buy the information booklet at the entrance.*
Mombasa Old Town's major attraction, Fort Jesus dominates the entrance to the Old

Harbour and is positioned so that, even when under siege, it was possible to bring supplies in from the sea. There's nothing to see as such in the harbour itself – there may be a few boats but long gone are the days when ocean-going *dhows* docked here. The Portuguese built the fort to protect their trade route to India and their interests in East Africa and it was designed by Italian architect Jao batisto Cairato. The fort was his last assignment as chief architect for Portuguese possession in the east. Today it's hailed as one of the best examples of 16th-century Portuguese military architecture. It's believed that since the Portuguese sailed under the flag of the Order of Christ, Jesus was an obvious choice of name.

Despite this apparently secure position the Portuguese lost possession of the fort in 1698 following an uprising by the townspeople who had formed an alliance with the Omanis. The fort had been under siege for 15 months before it finally fell. The British took control of the fort in 1825 and it served as a prison from then until 1958, when it was restored and converted into a museum.

At the main gate are six cannons from the British ship the *Pegasus* and the German ship the *SS Konigsberg*. The walls of the fort are particularly impressive being nearly 3 m thick at the base, though the fort feels much smaller inside than it looks from the outside. Look

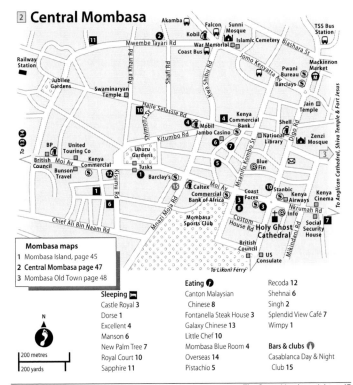

2 Central Mombasa

Mombasa maps
1 Mombasa Island, page 45
2 Central Mombasa page 47
3 Mombasa Old Town page 48

N

200 metres
200 yards

Sleeping
Castle Royal 3
Dorse 1
Excellent 4
Manson 6
New Palm Tree 7
Royal Court 10
Sapphire 11

Eating
Canton Malaysian
  Chinese 8
Fontanella Steak House 3
Galaxy Chinese 13
Little Chef 10
Mombasa Blue Room 4
Overseas 14
Pistachio 5

Recoda 12
Shehnai 6
Singh 2
Splendid View Café 7
Wimpy 1

Bars & clubs
Casablanca Day & Night
  Club 15

out for what is effectively the oldest graffiti in Mombasa, inscribed by early Portuguese sentries. In the late 18th century the Omanis built a house in the northwest corner of the fort in what is known as the **San Felipe Bastion**. The Omanis also razed the walls of the fort, built turrets and equipped it with improved guns and other weaponry to increase its defensive capabilities. Since then the Omani House has served various purposes including being the prison warden's house, and today it houses a small exhibition of Omani jewellery and artefacts. You can climb up on to the flat roof for good views of Mombasa. Close to the Omani house you'll see one of the trolleys that used to be the mode of transport around town. Nearby is a ruined church, a huge well and cistern, and an excavated grave complete with skeleton. The eastern wall of the fort includes the Omani Audience Hall and the Passage of the Arches, a passage cut through the coral to give access to the sea.

The **museum** is situated in the southern part of the fort in the old barracks. Exhibits include a fair amount of pottery as well as other interesting odds and ends donated from private collections or dug up from sites along the coast. Also displayed are finds from the Portuguese frigate Santo Antonio de Tanna which sank near the fort during the siege in 1698, and the far end of the hall is devoted to the fascinating culture and traditions of the nine coastal Mijikenda tribes, including a map of sacred forests. The diversity of the exhibits is a good illustration of the wide variety of influences that this coast was subject to over the centuries.

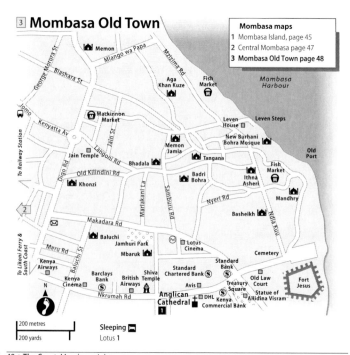

③ Mombasa Old Town

Mombasa maps
1 Mombasa Island, page 45
2 Central Mombasa page 47
3 Mombasa Old Town page 48

Sleeping
Lotus 1

200 metres
200 yards

Old Town

While Mombasa's Old town doesn't quite have the medieval charm of Lamu or Zanzibar, it's still an interesting area to wander around, preferably early morning or late afternoon (out of the midday sun). The Old Town is not in fact that old, as most buildings are little more than 100 years old, though their foundations and some walls go back many centuries, and you'll get a clearer idea to the age of the town from its 20-odd mosques. The earliest settlement was probably around Mzizima Road, from where pottery dating from the 11th-16th centuries has been discovered but there's no other evidence left of this early settlement. However, the Old Town does have a few exceptional houses characteristic of Swahili coastal architecture, with fretwork balconies and ornately carved doors, which were once considered a reflection of the wealth and status of the family; the wealthier the merchant of the house was the bigger and more elaborate his front door. Sadly, many of these old houses have been destroyed but there are now preservation orders on the remaining doors and balconies, so further losses should hopefully be prevented.

Ndia Kuu (Great Way) Leading from Fort Jesus into the Old Town, this road is one of the oldest in Mombasa; it existed during the Portuguese period and formed the main street of their settlement. Today some of the road's older houses have been restored and now serve as souvenir shops to visitors to the fort. Further north **Mzizima Road** was the main route between the Portuguese town and the original Arab/Shirazi town. One of the older buildings on the island is **Leven House** located just off the top end of Ndia Kuu. This was built around the beginning of the 19th century and has served many different purposes since then. It was originally occupied by a wealthy trading family and later was the headquarters of the British East Africa Company. It also housed a German Diplomatic Mission and more recently has been used by the Customs Department. Among its most famous visitors were the explorers and missionaries Burton, Jackson and Ludwig Krapf. In front of Leven House are the Leven steps – here a tunnel has been carved through to the water's edge where there is a freshwater well. Burton actually mentions climbing up through this tunnel but you do not need to follow his example; there are steps nearby. Close to the Leven Steps and the Fish Market is **New Burhani Bohra Mosque**, with a tall minaret, built in 1902, and is the third mosque to have been built on this site. On Mbarak Ali Hinawy Street, to the east of Ndia Kuu, close to the Old Port is **Mandhry Mosque**, built of coral rubble and finished with lime plaster with a white minaret. This is thought to be the oldest mosque on the island dating from around 1570 and originally was only one storey but another two storeys were added in 1988 and 1992 because of the need of a madrasa and women's prayer gallery. To the west of here, there are many more mosques and elderly houses in the cramped winding alleyways ways linking the Old Town to Digo Road, which are wonderfully lively, with market traders selling everything from *kangas* and cell phone accessories to baobab seeds and fried taro roots. It's not a very big area and most of these lanes eventually lead to a main road, so it's not easy to get lost. On Langoni Road, the Jain Temple has an intricate icing-sugar exterior in dozens of pastel shades. It was built in 1963 and was the first Jain Temple to be built outside India. Jainism is a Hindu religion closely related to Buddhism, and inside are ornamental painted figurines of deities in niches, each with a drain so they can be easily cleaned and rinsed off. You may be permitted to go inside (mornings only) but ensure you remove shoes and anything made of leather as the Jain faith is strictly vegetarian.

Nkrumah Road and around

At the eastern end of Nkrumah Road near Fort Jesus is the administrative centre of the British colonial period. The main buildings surround **Treasury Square**, with the handsome **Treasury** itself on the east side. In the square is a bronze statue of Allidina Visram, born in 1851 in Cutch in India. In 1863, at the age of 12, he arrived in Mombasa and became a prosperous merchant and planter, encouraging education and prominent in public life. He began trading in cloves and ivory, but when the building of the Uganda railway started, he opened up shops to supply food and other necessities to the workers of the railway. When the railway was finished, he had over 100 shops in Kenya and Uganda. He died in 1916.

The **Old Law Court** on Nkrumah Road dates from the beginning of the 20th century, and is well worth a visit, as it is now a library and also a gallery where there are often historic photograph exhibitions. It houses the collections of some scholars who have studied the Swahili Coast. Near the Law Court on Treasury Square is another building of approximately the same age. This was the **District Administration Headquarters**. The roof is tiled and there is a first-floor balcony.

Proceeding west from Treasury Square, on the left is the **Anglican Cathedral**, built in 1903 and with a plaque to mark 150 years of Christianity in Mombasa, celebrated in 1994. The cathedral itself is a mixture of European and Mediterranean influences, whitewashed with Moorish arches, slender windows, a dome reminiscent of an Islamic mosque, with a cross, and two smaller towers topped by crosses. On the right, just behind the main road and set in lovely gardens with ponds, is the spectacular, modern, Hindu **Shiva Temple**, which is topped with a gold spire and guarded by statues of lions and the Hindu god Ganesh with its elephant head.

Before the intersection with Moi Avenue is the **Holy Ghost Cathedral**, an elegant structure of concrete rendered in grey cement. Cool and airy inside, it has a fine curved ceiling of cream and blue, *fleur de lis* designs and stained-glass windows.

Moi Avenue and around

This is Mombasa's main road with a two-lane carriageway and is about 4 km long and runs from east to west from Digo Road to the port area at Kilindini. Along it are many shops that the tourist will want to visit including souvenir shops travel agencies and tour operators offices. The **Tusks** are found on Moi Avenue and were built in 1952 to commemorate a visit by Queen Elizabeth (Princess Elizabeth as she was then). They are actually rather disappointing close up. There are curio shops for about 50 yards in both directions – the goods are not very good quality and are rather expensive, although do look out for the fabulous beaded sandals.

Near the Tusks are **Uhuru Gardens**. It is difficult to get in from Moi Avenue as curio kiosks block most of the entrance. Inside are some handsome trees, a fountain (not working), a café, and a brass cannon worn smooth from serving as a makeshift seat.

To the north of Moi Avenue, on the corner of Haile Selassie and Aga Khan is the **Swaminaryan Temple**, an exotic confection in powder blue and pink, and in front of the Railway Station, the neglected **Jubilee Gardens**, which were laid out to mark the 60th anniversary of Queen Victoria's reign in 1897. Finally, there is the **War Memorial** on Jomo Kenyatta near the bus company offices, with bronze statues dedicated to the African and Arab soldiers who served with the East African Rifles in the First World War.

Kizingo

Kizingo area, in the southern part of the island around the lighthouse and Mombasa Golf Club, is considered to be one of the prime residential areas of the city. It has some very fine buildings whose style has been called **Coast Colonial**. These buildings are spacious and airy with wide balconies and shutters designed to take advantage of every breeze. Hardwoods were used and many of the building materials were imported from Europe and Asia. Along Mama Ngina Drive it is possible to look over the cliffs that rise above Kilindini Channel and out towards the sea.

Mbaraki

To the south of the island at Mbaraki just to the west of the Likoni Ferry roundabout is the **Mbaraki Pillar**, which is an 8-m-tall coral stone hollow pillar that is tapered and leans at a slight angle and stands next to a small mosque, which was rebuilt in 1988. It's thought to be about 300 years old but not much is known about it. Theories suggest it might be a tomb, or a house built for a powerful spirit, or even a navigational mark and lighthouse. Old Portuguese maps show that there was an anchorage at the Mbaraki Creek and perhaps the pillar was a shipping mark indicating the entrance and as it has vertical window slits on all sides, maybe a lantern was placed at the top.

Nyali

To the northwest of the island, Nyali is across the New Nyali Bridge, which was built in 2002 to replace an older one, which along with the Makupa and Kipevu causeways is one of the three road crossings on to the island. It was in this area that newly freed slaves settled, and a bell tower is erected in their memory, which can be seen at the junction of the main road north and Nyali Road. Today, Nyali is one of the wealthier suburbs of Mombasa, dominated by large houses where many of Mombasa's expat community live. There are a number of good restaurants here including the excellent Tamarind as well as the Ratna Shopping Centre, the Nyali Cinemax Centre, and the Nyali Nakumatt Complex, which has a number of shops, restaurants and a very large branch of **Nakumatt** supermarket. Only a few kilometres to the north of Nyali along the main coast road begins the strip of north coast hotels and restaurants.

Mombasa listings

For Sleeping and Eating price codes and other relevant information, see pages 11-16.

🛏 Sleeping

Mombasa *p43, map p45, p47, p48*

There is no upmarket accommodation in Mombasa and very little reason to stay in the city itself. It is much better to stay at a far more attractive beach hotel and visit Mombasa Old Town for the day.

$$$ Tamarind Village, adjacent to the Tamarind Restaurant, Nyali, T041-474 600, www.tamarind.co.ke. This is a collection of 1- to 3-bedroom self-catering apartments (you can also order food from the restaurant) in a Swahili-style whitewashed building with turrets and curved archways in a lovely waterside setting, with 2 swimming pools, a squash court, gym and pleasant gardens. Each spacious, light apartment has Swahili furnishings, a/c, kitchenette, veranda and satellite TV.

$$$ Orchid Bay, Nyali, immediately after you cross Nyali Bridge turn left at the petrol station and then follow the road back under the bridge, T041-473 238, www.orchidbay hotel.741.com. An attractive fairly new Moorish-style block with 42 rooms with a/c, hot water, TV, and patios or balconies with good views back across to Mombasa Island, set in lush tropical gardens right next to the water, though there's no beach. Secure parking, restaurant and pleasant mosaic swimming pool. Popular local conference venue.

$$$ Royal Court Hotel, Haile Selassie Rd, T041-222 3379, www.royalcourt mombasa.co.ke. Spacious and luxuriant entrance hall decorated in Swahili style, central position, 8-storey modern hotel with modern en suite rooms, a/c, electronic door locks and balconies. Good rooftop bar/ restaurant (see Eating), downstairs bar and casino, and a swimming pool. Well run and offers good value.

$$ Castle Royal Hotel, T041-222 2682, www.680-hotel.co.ke. Lovely white colonial building and historic hotel built in 1909 that was completely refurbished and reopened in 2005 after lying derelict for several years. All 60 double, single and family rooms have nice modern furniture, cool tiled floors, satellite TV, electric safes, a/c, high-speed internet, sound proofing and the front ones have balconies. Very good terrace restaurant and bar (see Eating). Recommended as the best place to stay in the city centre.

$$ Hotel Sai Rose, Nyrere Av, T041-222 0932, www.sairosehotel.com. Next to the Ex-Telcom House this odd-looking narrow building has a spacious reception area and restaurant and 23 self-contained rooms, curiously some of which are in the basement. It's worth paying a little extra for the upstairs executive rooms, some of which have Swahili-style decor, fridges and a/c.

$$ Lotus, Cathedral Lane off Nkrumah Rd, close to Fort Jesus, T041-231 3207, www.lotushotelkenya.com. Recently renovated, this has a charming central courtyard shaded by tropical plants and a lovely atmosphere with wood panels and Oriental arches, single, double or triple rooms, all have a/c and hot water. There is a good bar and restaurant that serves buffet lunches. Recommended.

$$ Sapphire Hotel, Mwembe Tayari Rd, T041-494 893. In a handy location for the railway station, this has 110 comfortable modern rooms with marble decor, a/c, balconies and satellite TV, although saying that it hasn't been maintained very well. **Mehfil** restaurant, terrace BBQ, buffet lunch, also has a swimming pool and a gym.

$ Excellent Hotel, Haile Selassie Rd, T041-222 7683. In a central location, just a short walk from the railway station or a moderate walk to bus terminals, spacious rooms have fans and bathrooms with lots of hot water. Friendly staff, well run, clean with good security, rooftop bar and the price includes breakfast. One of the best budget options and deservedly popular.

$ Hotel Dorse, Kwashibu Rd, T041-222 252, hoteldorse@africaonline.co.ke. Very modern block, all 34 rooms have a/c, bathroom, phone and TV, secure parking around the side, nothing unique but high quality for the area, everything is very new and fresh, standard hotel dining room and conference hall.

$ Manson Hotel, Kisumu Rd, T041-222 2419. Located in a fairly quiet residential area, some of the 80 rather dark rooms in this modern hotel have fans, others a/c, all rooms have hot water and mosquito nets. Restaurant, TV lounge with pool table, reasonable value and a cooked breakfast is included.

$ New Palm Tree, Nkrumah Rd, T041-315 272. Rather striking whitewashed old building, reception area has a high ceiling and gallery with comfy sofas, simple, quiet but rather faded hotel, fans, bathrooms but no hot water, there is a cosy relaxed bar and the restaurant serves basic dishes.

Mombasa *p43, map p45, p47, p48*

There are a number of eating places to choose from apart from hotel restaurants. With its large Indian population there is a lot of excellent Indian food as well as fresh fish and shellfish. At the budget end of the scale there are numerous canteens around the city centre that sell sausage or chicken and chips, samosas and pies, especially popular during the day with office workers. Also look out for the outdoor stalls selling Swahili snacks, which are all over the place especially in the Old Town, along Haile Selassie Road, and to the southeast of the island along Mama Ngina Drive. At these you might get egg chapatti, as the name suggests, a chapatti cooked with an egg inside it, *kachri bateta*, a potato, tomato, chutney and chilli mix, *mshikaki*, grilled beef or mutton kebabs served with chapattis and a bit of salad, and *mogo* (roasted cassava), *makai* (maize meal) or *guvaji* (sweet potatoes). Also look out for fresh coconut juice.

$$$ Hunter's Bar, near the **Tamarind** in Nyali, T041-231 1156. Open 1200-1500,1800-late, closed Tue. Secluded international restaurant popular with Nyali's expats, in a rather attractive Mediterranean style with a bar and tables arranged around a well-manicured courtyard offering a wide variety of seafood and meat dishes, but its speciality is its mouth-watering steaks. Other popular items offered include game meat, chicken Kiev and even apple pie.

$$$ Roberto's, in the Nyali Cinemax, Nyali, T041-471 110. Daily 1000-2300. Traditional Italian trattoria with murals of Italian village life on the walls and one of the most extensive Italian winelists in Kenya. The long menu uses imported ingredients and features Italian classic cuisine and is strong on interesting fish dishes, jumbo prawns and wood-fired pizzas. Desserts include tiramisu and ice-cream with a shot of espresso coffee.

$$$ Shehnai, Fatemi House, Maungano St, T041-222 2847. Open 1200-1400, 1900-2230, closed Mon. Superb cuisine, specialities are *mughlai* and tandoori dishes, very professionally run where the quality and taste of food is paramount, elegant furniture, soothing music, pleasant decor, although no alcohol, but there is a terrace bar at the **Jambo Casino** a few doors along if you want to have a drink before or after. Recommended.

$$$ Tamarind, Silo Rd, Nyali, T041-474 600-2, www.tamarind.com, www.tamarind dhow.com. Daily 1230-1430, 1900-2230. This beautiful restaurant has marvellous views overlooking a creek that flows into the ocean, and the Moorish design of the building is well thought out, cool and spacious with high arches, while the food and service are both excellent. It specializes in seafood. It also offers cruises around Tudor Creek on the 2 luxurious *Nawalikher* and *Babulkher*, *dhows* where you can sip *dawa* cocktails (vodka, lime, honey and crushed ice) and eat lobster, whilst watching the moon rise over Mombasa Old Town and Fort Jesus, and listening to the strains of a traditional Swahili band. The set meals on the *dhow* include seafood hors d'oeuvres to start, followed by grilled lobster or seafood in coconut sauce. There are 2 sailings a day for lunch (US$40) and dinner (US$70). The lunchtime option is exclusive to package-day tours, while the evening option departs at 1830. Reservations essential. This is a memorable eating experience and thoroughly recommended for any visitor to the coast.

$$$-$$ Misono, at the Nakumatt Shopping Centre, Nyali, T041-471 454. Mon-Sat 1230-1430, 1900-2230. Restaurant offering not too expensive and authentic sushi, sashimi and tepanyaki dishes, the chefs are well trained and offer an authentic 'show' while cooking, the decor has a Japanese feel and diners receive a Japanese greeting at the door accompanied by the sound of a 'bong'.

$$$-$ Castle Terrace, at the **Castle Royal Hotel**, T041-222 0373. Daily 0600-1000,

1230-1500, 1900-2300, all day for snacks and drinks. Lovely refurbished terrace but rather unfortunately it looks straight at the traffic on Moi Av. Nevertheless this is a social place for a drink and the food is very good. Inventive menu, steaks and grills, some pasta, African specials such as 1 kg of fillet beef served with *ugali*, seafood platters for 2, sandwiches and ice cream. Recommended.

$$ Bollywood Bites, at the **Nyali Cinemax** in Nyali opposite Ratna Sq, on the way to the **Tamarind**, T041-470 000. Mon-Sat 1800- 2300, Sun 1200-1500, 1800-2300. Authentic vegetarian Indian cuisine, modern restaurant uniquely decorated in a Bollywood theme, a wide selection of mughlai and tandoori dishes, specialities include Indian ice cream, *kulfi*, Indian milkshake, *faluda*, and freshly squeezed juice. Go and see a Bollywood movie at the cinema and eat here for rather a different night out.

$$ Canton Malaysian Chinese, in the car park behind the Castle Hotel, T041-222 7977. Daily 1100-1500, 1800-2300. An upstairs formal restaurant, though the decor is rather plain, bar with some wine and spirits, good food including crispy duck with pancakes and deep-fried crab claws, good choices for vegetarian and lychee for dessert.

$$ Galaxy Chinese Restaurant, Archbishop Makarios St, T041-231 1256. Daily 1100-1430, 1800-2300. Popular Chinese restaurant and is probably one of the best in town. It has especially good seafood dishes including excellent ginger crab and a good range of 'sizzling' dishes. Good service and refreshing a/c. There are other branches on the north and south coasts.

$$ La Veranda, Mwea Tabere St, behind the **Nakumatt Shopping Centre**, Nyali, T041-548 5452. Daily 0900-late. Good traditional Italian restaurant and bar, home-made pasta with a variety of sauces, pizza oven, homely atmosphere, wide range of drinks including Italian wines.

$$ Overseas, Moi Av just west of the Tusks, T041-227 801. Daily 1100-2200. Popular

Chinese and Korean with a bar, it is family-run, friendly and the food is pretty cheap and good and it's particularly known for its seafood. Look out for the red lanterns hanging outside. It is next door to a Chinese herbal clinic.

$$ Rooftop Restaurant, in the **Royal Court Hotel**, Haile Selassie Rd, T041-222 3379. Daily 1130-1430, 1730-late. High-quality food in balcony restaurant with great views of Mombasa's rooftops with pleasant decor of green plants and blue and white linen, with a good range of continental dishes, predominately Italian, plus some creamy Indian curries and tandoori dishes. The casino and bar on the ground floor of the hotel is open until 0600.

$ Books First is an excellent chain of bookshops. There are branches at the **Nakumatt Complex** near the Likoni Ferry, and at the **Nyali Shopping Centre**. They also double up as very good cafés for coffees, pizza, snacks, some Indian and Mexican dishes and offer internet access.

$ Fontanella Steak House, on corner of Moi Av and Digo Rd. Mon-Sat 0900-1800. Nice relaxing courtyard workers' café off the street surrounded by plants, red and white checked tablecloths, attentive service, popular meeting place, very large menu with daily specials, everything from chicken masala, *nyama choma* and fried liver to simple fare such as ice cream, fresh juice and plenty of cold beer.

$ Little Chef, Digo Rd. Centrally located, very busy canteen open all day until 2300, African food, burgers, chicken and chips on plastic tables, no booze, popular at lunchtime.

$ Mombasa Blue Room Restaurant, Haile Selassie Rd, T041-222 4021, www.blueroom online.com. Daily 0900-2200. Established in 1952, this excellent bright, clean, and bustling cafeteria seats over 140 people and is somewhat of a Mombasa institution. A family- run, a/c self-service restaurant, it offers Indian snacks, like samoosas, bhajia, kebabs, as well as fish and chips, chicken, burgers and pizzas, and everything is homemade. The delicious ice cream is made with filtered water; in fact they produce ice cream that is suitable for people with diabetes. It also doubles up as a DVD hire shop, and has the nicest and quickest internet café in town. Popular with locals and a good place to meet people. Recommended.

$ Pistachio Ice-Cream and Coffee Bar, Msanifu Kombo St. Open 0800-1700. Wonderful ice cream and fruit juices, home-made cakes and excellent coffees, it serves snacks and you can also have proper meals – including a buffet lunch, pleasant decor, well-run. Thoroughly recommended.

$ Recoda, Moi Av near the Tusks, T041-222 3629. Daily 1830-2400. This canteen serves traditional Swahili cuisine and is one of the oldest restaurants in Mombasa (it opened in 1942). The food is basic but cheap with large portions, and it's only open in the evenings and closed during Ramadan. The menu features dishes such as fish with coconut rice and puréed beans, *mahamri* (a staple bread), and *mshikaki* (a type of kebab).

$ Singh, Mwembe Tayari Rd, T041-493 283. Open 1200-1430, 1900-2230, closed Mon. Good modern a/c restaurant with chunky furniture run by the Sikh Temple. Although the menu is not very extensive the food is authentic, freshly prepared and tasty, in particular the butter chicken is excellent and there's a good choice for vegetarians. Serves alcohol.

$ Splendid View Café, Maungano Rd. Mon-Sat 1100-2230. Very good, cheap Indian meals, plus some prawns and steaks – huge portions. Nice variety of dishes for US$4-10 in a clean canteen environment, look out for the daily lunchtime specials.

$ Wimpy, next to the **Tusks**. Standard burgers and shakes, Wimpy breakfasts are not that bad if you are looking for a traditional fry-up.

Bars and clubs

Mombasa *p43, map p45, p47, p48*
Casablanca Day and Night Club, Mnazi Moja Rd, T0722-847 792, www.casablanca mombasa.com. Daily 24 hrs. A huge venue on 2 floors with several bars, 2 dance floors, restaurant, varied music from 1970s disco to Kenyan rap and hip hop, exotic floor shows, sports on giant TVs in the afternoons. It's popular but it can get crowded so watch your valuables and be aware that it's working girls' territory.

New Florida Club and Casino, Mama Ngina Drive, T041-220 9036, www.floridaclubs kenya.com. Disco from 2100 daily, casino and bars 24 hrs. A branch of Nairobi's raucous Florida clubs, in huge premises, with several bars and dance floors, on the waterfront with ocean views, cabaret live shows at midnight, also casino and restaurant serving *nyama choma* and other snacks. Again gets absolutely packed and men will get a lot of attention from prostitutes.

Entertainment

Mombasa *p43, map p45, p47, p48*
Golden Key Casino, at the Tamarind Restaurant, Nyali, T041-471 071, www.tamarind.co.ke. Daily 1800-0400. Mombasa's most sophisticated and elegant casino in a lovely setting on the roof of the restaurant with great night time views of Mombasa Island from the terrace with a full range of gaming tables and modern slot machines, cocktails and snacks.

Lotus Cinema, Makadara Rd, and the **Kenya**, opposite the Social Security House on Moi Av, both have fairly up-to-date Hollywood and Bollywood movies.

Nyali Cinemax, located in Nyali opposite Ratna Square, T041-470 000, www.nyali cinemax.com. This is an ultra-modern a/c cinema that plays the latest box-office releases. There is also the **Scorpian Sports Bar** here, a couple of restaurants, a casino and a 10-pin bowling alley and a casino.

○ Shopping

Mombasa *p43, map p45, p47, p48*
The souvenirs that you will find in Mombasa are wooden carvings including Makonde carvings from Tanzania, soapstone carvings and chess sets, baskets, batiks and jewellery. There are lots of stalls in and around the market and around the junction of Digo Rd and Jomo Kenyatta Av. There are also lots more along Msanifu Kombo St; along Moi Av from the Castle Hotel and down to the roundabout with Nyerere Av; and around Fort Jesus. For *kikois*, *kangas* and other material or fabric go to Biashara St, which runs off Digo St parallel to Jomo Kenyatta Av. The Indian tailors here can also make up clothes to order from the cloth. Avoid buying seashells. As a result of killing the crabs, molluscs and other sealife that live inside the shells to sell them to tourists, populations have declined dramatically and many are seriously threatened. Vendors may tell you they have a licence, but don't encourage this trade.

Markets
Mackinnon Market is a lively, bustling and colourful market on Digo Rd and was named after Dr W Mackinnon, a colonial administrator at the turn of the 20th century. The main section of the market is situated in an enormous shed but numerous stalls have spilled out on to the streets. Apart from an excellent range of exotic fresh fruit and vegetables, you will be able to buy baskets, jewellery and other souvenirs. If you are prepared to haggle and bargain in a good-natured manner you can usually bring the price down quite considerably.

Shopping centres
In Nyali is the **Ratna Shopping Centre**, the **Nyali Cinemax Centre**, and the **Nyali Nakumatt Shopping Centre**, which has a number of shops, restaurants and a very large branch of **Nakumatt** supermarket. There is also another vast branch of **Nakumatt**, with a number of other shops and cafés near to the Likoni Ferry.

Out of town on the road to the airport is the **Akamba Handicraft Cooperative**, off Port-Reitz Rd, Changamwe, T041-343 4396, www.akambahandicraftcoop.com. Daily 0800-1730. This sells a vast range of curios from animal statues and decorated spoons to walking sticks and wooden bowls. It was established in 1963 with 100 carvers and now promotes and distributes the work of about 3000 carvers. They are presently establishing a nursery of fast-growing neem wood trees to provide renewable resources of wood for the carvers (ebony now is very rare). The showroom is a popular stop for tourists as they are bussed in and out of the airport, or on city tours, you can watch the carvers at work, and reasonably low prices are fixed and 80% goes to the carver, while 20% goes to the cooperative.

▲ Activities and tours

Mombasa *p43, map p45, p47, p48*
Sports clubs
Mombasa Golf Club, Mama Nginga Dr, T041-228 531. This 9-hole course was established in 1911 and sits on top of coral cliffs with good ocean views. Day membership is available and clubs and caddies can be hired.
Mombasa Sports Club, Mnazi Mosi Rd, T041-222 4226, www.mombasa sportsclub.co.ke. There's an old colonial saying that you can't put more than 3 Englishmen in a foreign country without them forming a club, and this is the country's oldest sporting club. Established in 1896, the same year the building of the Uganda Railway started, it hosted celebrations of Queen Victoria's Jubilee in 1897. There are facilities here for cricket, squash, tennis, basketball and football, among other sports, and there's a gym.

Tour operators

Mombasa's tour operators act as booking agents for the beach hotels and most can also organize day or overnight safaris to the parks close to the coast such as Tsavo or Simba Hills, as well as tours of the city and other local attractions. For example, expect to pay around US$35 for a ½-day city tour, US$75 combined with lunch on the Tamarind Dhow (see page 53), US$110 for a day trip up to Malindi and the Gedi Ruins, and US$130 for a day tip to Tsavo East. Some also offer car hire and transfers to the beach. For more Mombasa-based tour operators, visit **Kenya Association of Tour Operators**, www.katokenya.org.

African Quest Safaris, Palli House, Nyerere Rd, T041-227 052, www.africanquest.co.ke. City tours and day trips to attractions on the north coast, plus longer safaris.

African Route Safaris, 2nd floor, Old Cannon Towers, Moi Av, T041-230 322, www.african routesafaris.com. Offers 1- to 2-night safaris to Tsavo East and 3-night trips to Tsavo and Amboseli, plus ½-day city tour and full-day Gedi Ruins tour.

Bunson Travel Service, Southern House, Moi Av, T041-231 1331, www.bunsonkenya.com. A good, reliable, well-established travel and tour agent. Flight and rail bookings, safaris and hotel bookings, and day tours to Shimba Hills, Gedi Ruins, Wasini Island and overnight trips to Tsavo.

Distance Car Hire and Tours, Wimpy Building, next to the Tusks, Moi Av, T041-222 2869, www.distancetours.com. 1- to 4-day tours to Tsavo, and a longer 6-day safari from Mombasa to the Masai Mara, Nakuru and Tsavo. Also can arrange tours of Tanzania's northern circuit from Mombasa.

Kenya One Tours, Nkrumah Rd, T041-202 2311, www.kenyaonetours.com. Good all-round operator offering safaris across the country, plus day trips from Mombasa, overnight safaris to Tsavo and Shimba Hills and fly-in safaris from Mombasa to the Masai Mara.

Ketty Tours, Travels & Safaris, Ketty Plaza, Moi Av, T041-231 2204, www.kettysafari.com. Combined Tsavo East, Tsavo West and Amboseli 4-day safaris, city tours, and day trips to Shimba Hills and Malindi and the Gedi Ruins.

Pollman Tours and Safaris, Taveta Rd, Shimanzi, T041-210 6000, www.poll mans.com. General park excursions and safaris starting in Nairobi and finishing in Mombasa, has a large fleet of vehicles.

Southern Cross Safaris, Nyali Bridge Rd, T041-475 074, www.southerncrosssafaris.com. Established award-winning operator with over 40 years' experience, runs a daily trip to its own camp in Tsavo East, **Satao Camp**, has a fleet of safari vehicles and its own plane, is a specialist for safaris for disabled clients and agents for beach resorts. It also runs the excellent www.kenyalastminute.com, where you can pick up some bargain last-minute holidays to Kenya. Highly recommended.

Special Lofty Safaris, Nkrumah Rd, T041-222 0241, www.lofty-tours.com. City tours, Mombasa by night tours, half-day trips to Shimba Hills, and 1- to 3-day safaris to Tsavo.

United Touring Company (UTC), UTC Building, Moi Av, T041-222 9834, www.utc.co.ke. Another professional operator offering safaris across Kenya and beach hotel reservations.

⊖ Transport

Mombasa p43, map p45, p47, p48
Air
Moi International Airport is on the mainland about 10 km out of the centre of town, T041-433 211, www.kenya airports.com. Airport tax for domestic flights is US$4 but this is included in the price of scheduled airline tickets and is only payable on charter flights. Some of the airlines are now flying between Mombasa and Tanzania, but remember you will need to show a yellow fever vaccination certificate on arrival in Tanzania. **Mombasa Air**

Safaris, links Mombasa to airstrips in the parks and reserves.

Air Kenya has 1 daily flight to **Nairobi**'s Wilson Airport (1 hr 5 mins) that departs at 1105. In Nairobi you can link on to their scheduled services to the airstrips in the parks and reserves. **Fly 540** has 5 daily flights to **Nairobi** (1 hr) from US$69 1 way, at least 2 daily flights to **Malindi** (15 mins) from only US$30 1 way, and 1 daily flight to **Zanzibar** (45 mins) in Tanzania, which from US$99 1 way is especially good value. **Kenya Airways** has about 10 flights a day to **Nairobi** (1 hr) between 0600 and 2300. They don't fly directly to Malindi or Lamu, so you'll have to back track via Nairobi or take another airline. **Kenya Airways** code shares with Tanzania's **Precision Air**, and there are now flights to **Zanzibar** and **Dar es Salaam** on Tue, Thu, Fri and Sun. **Mombasa Air Safari** uses small planes and operates a daily scheduled 'Beach to Bush' service between Mombasa, and the airstrip at Diani Beach, to **Amboseli**, **Tsavo**, and the **Masai Mara**. It also has daily scheduled flights to **Malindi** and **Lamu**.

Airline offices **Air Kenya**, Wilson Airport, Nairobi, T020-605 745, www.airkenya.com. **Fly 540**, T041-343 4822, www.fly 40.com. **Kenya Airways**, Wilson Airport, T041-350 5500, town office, Electricity House, Nkrumah Rd, www.kenya-airways.com. **Mombasa Air Safari**, Moi International Airport, T041-343 3061, www.mombasaairsafari.com.

Bus
On all buses seats can be booked and there is no overcrowding with standing passengers anymore. There are lots of bus companies that go to **Nairobi** and their kiosks are on Jomo Kenyatta Av opposite the Islamic Cemetery and near the market. They usually leave early morning and evening, take 9-11 hrs and cost about US$15. **Akamba Bus**, T041-349 0269, www.akambabus.com, is on Jomo Kenyatta Av. Buses and *matatus* depart for **Malindi** frequently throughout the day and take about 1½ hrs. They leave Mombasa when full from Abdel Nasser Rd outside the New People's Hotel. There are daily buses to **Lamu**, which also pick up in **Malindi**, 7 hrs, US$10, and the **Pwani Tawakal Bus Company**, T041-222 975, http://pwani tawakal.com, is recommended for the Lamu service, which has 3 daily departures between 0600-0800. The bus will take you to the Mokowe Jetty on the mainland from where you get a ferry across to Lamu (see page 114).

The bus service to Lamu has been targeted by bandits in past years, with some fatalities, and for many years the service was not recommended. However, there has not been an incident for quite some time and it is reasonably regarded to be safe. Despite this, armed escorts get on the bus on the last stretch of the road to Lamu at either Garsen or Witu. Heading south to **Tanzania**, **Scandinavian Express**, is a very good Tanzanian bus company, Arrow Plaza, Jomo Kenyatta Av, T041-490 975, www.scandinaviagroup.com. It runs a daily service at 0800, which takes about 4 hrs to **Tanga**, US$13 and 10 hrs to **Dar es Salaam**, US$23. There is an identical daily service in the opposite direction that departs Dar es Salaam also at 0800. Other buses to Tanzania also go from Jomo Kenyatta Av. The border is at **Lunga Lunga**, see page for border-crossing information. If not going all the way to Dar es Salaam, then from Tanga there are bus connections on to **Moshi** and **Arusha**.

Car hire
Avis, airport, T041-432486, Nkrumah Rd, T041-222 0465, www.avis.com.
Budget, airport, T041-343 3211, Associated Motors Complex, Kenyatta Av, T041-249 0047, www.budget-kenya.com.
Distance Car Hire and Tours, Wimpy

Building, next to the Tusks, Moi Av,
T041-222 2869, www.distancetours.com.
Europcar, Makena House, Nkrumah Rd,
T041-311 994, www.europcar.com.
Hertz, airport, T041-434 4020,
www.hertz.com.
Special Lofty Safaris, Nkrumah Rd,
T041-222 0241, www.lofty-tours.com.

Ferry

The Likoni Ferry docks at the southeast
of the island. The two 24-hr ferries cross
simultaneously and depart about every
15 mins from about 0400-0100, and every
hour in the middle of the night and are free for
pedestrians and cyclists (cars US$0.60 and
motorbikes US$0.30). There is always a throng
of people waiting to board or disembark from
the boat – keep your hands tightly on your
possessions and beware of pickpockets and
thieves. The waters are said to contain sharks
although this is debatable. *Matatus* to the ferry
leave from outside the post office on Digo Rd –
ask for Likoni. In fact it is possible to get a
matatu to the Likoni ferry from just about
anywhere in the city even if the taxi drivers tell
you otherwise. When the ferry docks, the
matatus for Ukunda (the turn-off to Diani
Beach) are located at the top of the slipway
from the ferry.

Taxi

Taxis leave from **Moi International Airport**
to local destinations. Prices are fixed and are
posted up on boards and vary depending
on whether you choose a small private car
or minibus. Into town expect to pay around
US$10, to **Nyali Beach** about US$20, to
Shanzu Beach about U$35, and to **Diani
Beach**, which includes the crossing of the
Likoni Ferry, about US$60.

You can also organize shuttles from
Mombasa's Moi International Airport to
all the north coast resorts through the
resorts themselves or with the taxi
companies in the arrivals hall.

Train

Mombasa Railway Station, T041-433 211,
is at the end of Haile Selassie Av at Jubilee Sq.
There are services 3 times a week between
Mombasa and Nairobi. The train is
notoriously late so don't book onward travel
on the same day as the arrival of the train.

❶ Directory

Mombasa *p43, map p45, p47, p48*
Banks There are many banks on Nkrumah
Av and Moi Av with ATMs. The 3 branches
of **Barclays Bank**, Digo Rd, Moi Av, and
Nkrumah Av, have efficient foreign-exchange
facilities and will give cash advances off cards.
Courier companies DHL, Nkrumah Av,
T041-222 3933, www.dhl.com. Currency
exchange **Pwani Bureau de Change**,
opposite Mackinnon Market on Digo Rd, is
fast and efficient and good rates are offered,
while **Coast Forex Bureau** is on the corner of
Moi Av and Digo Rd on the opposite corner
to the Stanbic Bank. Internet There are
many cybercafés or small businesses offering
email and internet access in Mombasa.
However, access is compromised by frequent
interruptions to the power supply. The best
are the **Info Café**, Ambalal House, opposite
the Kenya Airways office on Nkrumah Av,
which also serves snacks and juices, and the
internet café at the back of the **Mombasa
Blue Room Restaurant**, Haile Selassie Rd.
Blue Fin Cyber Cafe, Meru Rd, also sells fresh
sugarcane juice. **Books First** is an excellent
chain of bookshops that also double up as
internet cafés, and there are branches at the
Nakumatt Complex near the Likoni Ferry,
and at the Nyali Shopping Centre. Cultural
centres **Alliance Française**, Freed Building,
Moi Av, T041-340 079, www.amba
france-ke.org. **British Council**, Jubilee
Insurance Building, Moi Av just west
of the Tusks, T041-222 3076, www.british
council.org. Immigration The visa office is
on Mama Ngina Rd next to the police station,
T041-231 1745. Medical services Aga

Khan Hospital, Vanga Rd, T041-222 7710, www.agakhanhospitals.org. **Mombasa Hospital**, Mama Ngina Rd, T041-231 2191, www.mombasahospital.com. **Pandya Memorial Hospital**, Dedan Kimathi St, T041-231 3577, www.pandyahospital.org.

Coast Provincial General Hospital, Kisauni Rd, T041-231 4201. There are plenty of well-stocked pharmacies in the city centre. **Post office** Digo St, Mon-Fri 0800-1800, Sat 0900-1200.

South coast

The beaches on the south coast are some of the best in the world. The sand – coral that has been pounded by the waves over the centuries – is fine and very white. There are a few well-developed areas, but you don't need to go far to find a quiet spot. The most popular beach is Diani – it is also the most built up and not surprisingly is now the most expensive. However, most of the buildings are well designed and local materials have been used so they do not intrude too much. The hotels all have their own restaurants and bars and most of them arrange regular evening entertainment such as traditional African dancers and singers or acrobats. They also organize watersports and day trips to sights in the region including Mombasa city tours, and day trips to Wasini Island and the Kisite-Mpunguti Marine National Park, as well as longer overnight safaris to some of the parks, so it is feasible to stay in one hotel for your entire holiday, and take organized local excursions from there.

Ins and outs ➡ For listings, see pages 70-80.

Once across the Likoni Ferry the A14 heads south on a reasonably good tarred road. It runs about 300 m parallel to the coast, although you cannot see the sea from the road. The turn-off to Tiwi Beach is about 20 km south of the ferry and the turn-off to Diani Beach is at Ukunda about 25 km. There are plenty of *matatus* running up and down between the township of Likoni where the ferry docks and Ukunda, but these are less frequent south of Ukunda. About 12 km from Likoni is the turn-off to the right to Kwale and the Shimba Hills National Reserve and Mwaluganje Elephant Sanctuary.

Likoni and Shelley Beach → *Phone code: 040.*

Likoni is a sprawling (and none too clean with piles of unsightly rubbish everywhere) township on the southern side of the Likoni Ferry and is effectively a creek-side suburb of Mombasa. The road that leads from the ferry is lined with market stalls. Shelley Beach just to the east of the ferry is the closest beach to Mombasa, and can be visited for a day trip if you are staying in the town and are not too bothered by the proximity of the urban sprawl. However, it is narrow and uninviting and swimming here can be problematic due to excessive seaweed and there is the need to watch carefully over your belongings.

Tiwi Beach → *Phone code: 040.*

The next resort, Tiwi Beach, is about 20 km from Likoni Ferry and 3 km off the main coastal road down a very bumpy track (turn left at the supermarket). Never walk down this road as muggings can occur. This beach is wider than that at Shelley but not as nice as Diani and for a number of years was particularly popular with families and with budget travellers. Its popularity has waned in recent years however in favour of the hotels at Diani, and **Twiga Lodge**, once a firm favourite on the backpacker circuit through East Africa, is a shadow of its former self.

   However, the beach is ideal for children; the waves are smaller than those at Diani, and hundreds of rock pools are exposed when the tide is out, all with plenty of marine life in them. There is also some quite good snorkelling here and it is possible to scuba dive too. However, it is prone to large amounts of seaweed in April and May. If you walk up the beach in the direction of Shelley Beach for about 1.5 km you come to 'Pool of Africa', a rock pool in the shape of the African continent where you can swim, and even dive through a small tunnel to another pool aptly named **Madagascar**. Before you go exploring on the beach and reef check up on the tides (local people will be able to advise) and set out with plenty of time. It is very easy to get cut off when the tide comes in and it turns quite rapidly. Also be sure you have a good pair of thick rubber-soled shoes to protect your feet against the coral and sea urchins. It is possible to walk south to Diani Beach at low tide, but again it is important to ensure you check the times of the tides to avoid getting stranded.

Diani Beach → *Phone code: 040.*

The beach itself is the longest commercially used beach in Kenya with about 20 km of dazzling white sand, coconut trees, clear sea and a coral reef that is exposed at low tide. It has acquired a whole string of hotels over the years, although most of these have been sensitively built, often out of thatch and local materials. Diani is the place to come if you want a traditional beach holiday; the climate and scenery are marvellous, accommodation and food is of a very high standard, and activities on offer include windsurfing, kitesurfing, sailing, snorkelling and scuba-diving. You can also go waterskiing or parascending, or hire a bike or motorbike and there is the additional option of combining time on the beach with a safari to one of the closer national parks and game reserves inland. Increasingly, a number of shopping centres have mushroomed on the 'strip' geared towards tourists, as well as numerous informal souvenir stalls, and

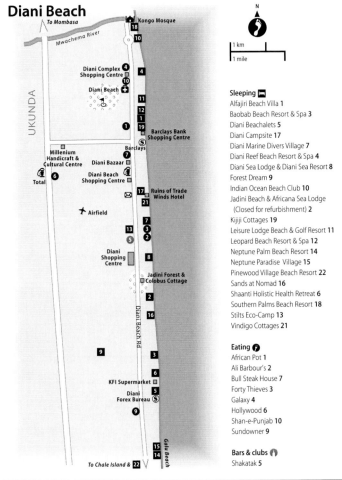

Diani Beach

Sleeping 🛏
Alfajiri Beach Villa 1
Baobab Beach Resort & Spa 3
Diani Beachalets 5
Diani Campsite 17
Diani Marine Divers Village 7
Diani Reef Beach Resort & Spa 4
Diani Sea Lodge & Diani Sea Resort 8
Forest Dream 9
Indian Ocean Beach Club 10
Jadini Beach & Africana Sea Lodge
  (Closed for refurbishment) 2
Kijiji Cottages 19
Leisure Lodge Beach & Golf Resort 11
Leopard Beach Resort & Spa 12
Neptune Palm Beach Resort 14
Neptune Paradise Village 15
Pinewood Village Beach Resort 22
Sands at Nomad 16
Shaanti Holistic Health Retreat 6
Southern Palms Beach Resort 18
Stilts Eco-Camp 13
Vindigo Cottages 21

Eating 🍴
African Pot 1
Ali Barbour's 2
Bull Steak House 7
Forty Thieves 3
Galaxy 4
Hollywood 6
Shan-e-Punjab 10
Sundowner 9

Bars & clubs 🍸
Shakatak 5

On the sea bed

The 80-m ship *MV Dania* spent 45 years plying the waters off the African coast, mainly as a live cattle transporter. In 2002 her life on the waves ended as she was sunk below the ocean just north of Mombasa. But the Dania has a new life as one of Africa's finest wreck dives and Mombasa's newest reefs, and the cattle pens and cabins already have become home to all kinds of sea life. The ship now lies in around 30 m of water just off Bamburi Beach and when she was sunk landed perfectly upright. She was fully prepared for sinking and had her engines removed and hull cleaned to minimise any environmental impact. The interior was fully cleared for safe penetration by divers, and all potentially dangerous objects, such as wiring and doors were removed, as have all but three of the original brass portholes, allowing divers and marine life to move freely in and out of the control room and the hull with ease. Many artificial reefs have been created around the world from wrecks; some as a result of natural disaster and some, as in Dania's case, intentionally. A variety of materials, ranging from military tanks to naval ships, have been used and over the years, extensive research has been carried out to monitor and quantify the success of these artificial reefs. The result has been that artificial reefs develop into thriving coral communities, almost indistinguishable from their natural counterparts. The solid structure that an artificial reef provides facilitates the attachment of algae, sponges, benthic organisms and gorgonia to its surface, organisms that would otherwise float around aimlessly, which are vital for coral production. Over time the vessel slowly transforms into a functioning reef; coral is produced, sea turtles and pelagic fish seek refuge amongst the protective overhangs, and as the reef matures it attracts larger sharks, groupers and moray eels. Artificial reefs also enhance the development of rare coral species that are not often found in natural reefs. In addition to the environmental aspect that artificial reefs bring, coral reefs, both natural and artificial, are also taking on an increasingly important role in supplying compounds for use in medicines. AZT is used in the treatment of HIV-infected patients and its chemical composition is derived from that of a Caribbean reef sponge. Furthermore, 50% of all new cancer drug research is conducted upon marine organisms.

With thanks to Bruce Phillips from Buccaneer Diving, www.buccaneer diving.com.

other facilities include the golf course and casino at the Leisure Lodge, a number of independent restaurants and nightclubs outside the confines of the resorts, and many of the resorts have added wellness spas and/or fitness facilities to their ever growing list of things to do.

Diani is mostly geared to big-spending package tourists from Europe, which generates some disadvantages: intrusive beach touts or 'beach boys' that hound visitors trying to sell curios, camel rides along the beach or trips on glass-bottomed boats, as well as offering themselves as models for photos (some of the Masai who come round are not Masai at all but are of other tribes). Most of the goods are poor quality and hugely overpriced, although you can try bargaining the quoted prices down. Additionally, over the years Diani has gained a bit of a reputation as a bit of a pick-up place for European female tourists looking for sex with Kenyan men. Even if no payment for 'company' is exchanged, there are many hopeful young men in the area that seek to befriend a European woman in the hope of a passage to Europe.

Getting there
From Likoni the A14, the main Kenya–Tanzania coastal road goes south and all the turnings off are well signposted. For Diani, go as far as Ukunda village (25 km) where there is the turning off to the smaller road that runs along Diani beach. At the T-junction, some hotels are to the left, while all the others are to the right. The hotels and other facilities surrounding this junction are commonly referred to as the Diani 'strip'. Most of the large resorts at Diani will collect you from Mombasa's Moi International Airport or the train station for a charge of around US$35 per person, and transfers are usually included in package holiday rates. *Matatus* run frequently from Likoni to the south coast.

Sights
It is worth going out to the reef at low tide at least once when the very top is exposed to look at the myriad of fish. You'll need to take a boat if you want to go out to the main reef, although you should be able to wade out to the sand bank which is not too far. Of course this depends on the tides. At full moon and new moon there are **spring tides**, which means very high high tides and very low low tides, while in between there will be **neap tides** with low highs and high lows. Wind and kite surfers can go out for longer at neap tides, while those wanting huge waves will do better at high tide.

At the far north of Diani beach just past the **Indian Ocean Beach Club**, is the **Kongo Mosque** (also known as the Diani Persian Mosque). It is rather a strange place, very run-down but not really a ruin, and still has some ritual significance. The mosque is believed to date from the 15th century and is the only remaining building from a settlement of the Shirazi people who used to live here. There are a number of entrances and you should be able to push one of the doors open and have a look inside.

Jadini Forest
ⓘ *T040-320 3519, www.colobustrust.org, Mon-Sat 0800-1300, 1400-1700, US$7.50, children under 12 free.*
This is a small patch of the forest that straddles the main beach road and used to cover the whole of this coastal area. It is great for birdwatching, and many species of butterflies occupy the clutches of hardwood trees, but it's especially good for spotting primates. The forest is home to troops of baboon, a large population of vervet monkey and the endangered Angolan black and white colobus monkey. There are only an estimated 2000 colobus in Kenya, 400 of which are at Diani. Local group the **Colobus Trust** is devoted to the conservation of these rare primates and their habitat. Many of the primate species of this area are threatened both by traffic on the main coastal road, and by hand-feeding by tourists, which encourages anti-social and unnatural behaviour. The **Colobus Trust** works to build aerial bridges, known as 'colobridges' across the roads to prevent traffic casualties, and works to educate tourists against feeding monkeys. Another major problem is that the creatures get electrocuted on the many un-insulated power lines around Diani. The main electricity lines can carry up to 22,000 volts, which can be fatal,

whilst the domestic power lines, which carry around 240 volts, can severely stun an animal and cause loss of a limb and/or secondary infections. Trees that allow access to the power lines have been cut back so the monkeys have reduced contact with them and the trust sends a team out weekly to keep vegetation trimmed. It has also been involved with rehabilitating vervet monkeys that were kept as pets and re-releasing them back into the wild at Shimba Hills. It has a centre called Colobus Cottage with plenty of information, nature trails, and can give good advice on local wildlife. It also offers a one-hour guided primate walk.

Shimba Hills National Reserve

ⓘ *US$25, children US$10, car US$4.30.*

This small reserve, 56 km southwest of Mombasa, is very easy to access on a day trip from the coast as it is less than an hour's drive from Diani Beach. The 300 sq km are covered with stands of coastal rainforest, rolling grasslands and scrubland. Due to strong sea breezes, the hills are much cooler than the rest of the coast making it a very pleasant climate. The rainforest itself is totally unspoilt and opens out into rolling downs and gentle hills and the flora ranges from baobab trees on the lower slopes nearer the coast to deciduous forests on the hills and vestigial rainforest along the watercourses. Two of Kenya's exquisite orchids are found here.

Ins and outs

The main route to Shimba Hills and Mwaluganje is through the small town of Kwale, on the C106, which branches off the main A14 coast road 12 km south of the Likoni ferry. The main gate is 3 km beyond Kwale. The road is well tarred as far as Kwale. It is also possible to enter the park through the Kivunoni (eastern) Gate, which is located about 1 km south of the C106 3 km from Kwale. It is possible to take a half-day trip from Mombasa and Diani for around US$50 through one of the tour operators or resorts.

Sights

There are a number of Roan antelope, waterbuck, reedbuck, hyena, warthog, giraffe, leopard, baboon and bush pig in the reserve. The altitude and the damp atmosphere also attract countless butterflies and birds around the grassy hills and on the edges of the forest. However, it is famed for being the only place in Kenya where you might see the Sable antelope found in the same habitats as several large herds of buffalo. There are also about 300 elephant in the reserve who favour the refreshing fruit of the borassus palm, which is abundant here, and close-range elephant viewing is virtually guaranteed. The best place to see the wildlife is near the spectacular **Sheldrick Falls** and on the **Lango Plains** close to Giriama Point. Picnic sites on either side of the escarpment provide an entrancing view of the Indian Ocean to the east, and on a clear day, the imposing mass of Mount Kilimanjaro rising behind the Taita Hills to the west.

Adjacent is the **Mwaluganje Elephant Sanctuary** set up to provide access for the elephants between the Shimba Hills and the Mwaluganje Forest Reserve, and it protects 2500 ha of their traditional migratory route. The sanctuary is an innovative concept due to the fact that the local cultures, the Duruma and Digo people, have become involved along with other local landowners, the Kwale County Council, local politicians and the

Kenya Wildlife Service, and a fee is payable to the local community from every visitor to the reserve. This has helped to build school classrooms and improved the water supply in the region. There is only one tented camp in the sanctuary and you can visit here either on a day or overnight trip arranged with the resorts on the coast.

South of Diani

Chale Island

About 10 km at the southern end of Diani is a small bay and Chale Island, which lies about 600 m offshore and measures just 1.2 km long and 800 m wide. Chale refers to the name of an old warrior of the Digo tribe who is buried on the island, and on certain days of the year his descendants still come to celebrate religious rituals. During February and March, giant turtles lay their eggs on the beaches. When they are hatched, the baby turtles are helped back to sea by the local people and staff at the only hotel on the island, which is centred around a particularly fine half-moon shaped white-sand beach. Despite being off-shore, the forest behind the hotel is home to some wildlife including vervet monkeys and baboons and good birdlife. There are also some inland mangrove forests situated on lakes fed by the tides.

Gazi

Gazi is a village at the southern end of Diani, once significantly more important than it is now as it was once the district's administrative centre. Here you will see the **House of Sheik Mbaruk bin Rashid**. There are said to be the bodies of eight men and eight women buried in the foundations of the house to give the building strength. He was also notorious for torturing people, and suffocating them on the fumes of burning chillies. In the Mazrui Rebellion of 1895 Mbaruk was seen arming his men with German rifles and flying the German flag. British troops did eventually defeat him and he ended his days in exile in German East Africa (Tanzania). The rather run-down house is now used as a school. It once had a very finely carved door but this has been moved to the Fort Jesus Museum. Ask directions for Gazi as it is not signposted on the main road.

Msambweni

About 50 km south of Likoni is the village of Msambweni which is home to what is one of the best hospitals on the coast as well as a famous leprosarium. The beach is really lovely with coral rag-rock cliffs and there are some ruins in this area that are believed to have been a slave detention camp. **Funzi Island** is a private island located just off the coast from here at the mouth of the Ramisi River where there is a luxury lodge, and again like Chale Island it is blessed with swaying palms, mangrove forests and sugar-white beaches.

Shimoni

This is a small fishing village about 75 km south of Likoni whose name means 'Place of the Hole' and is derived from the method of entry to the system of **Slave caves** ⓘ *to the west of the village, nominal entry fee (collected directly by the local people to help pay for the dispensary and educate the children), daily 0830-1030, 1330-1730.* 'Shimo' means cave in Kiswahili and the vast network opens directly on to the beach. There are several caves, once joined together and reputed to extend some 5 km inland. Due to silting, the floor has risen, blocking off access to the further caves, and what you now see is only the main entrance cavern. The next cavern, immediately behind this one, which is now only accessible via a hole in the roof of the cave, has a spring of completely fresh water in it. It is said that the caves were used by slave traders to hide the slaves, before they were shipped out to the slave market on Zanzibar. The other story associated with these caves is that they were used as a secret place of refuge by the Digo people during their intermittent battles with various marauding tribes, including the Masai, through the ages. Archaeological findings indicate that these coral caves, with their lovely stalactites, have been inhabited for several centuries. Today they are home to a thriving population of bats.

To reach the caves take the path that begins opposite the jetty and walk up through the forest. When you get to the entrance take a ladder down through a hole in the ground. Immediately opposite the entrance to the cave are the remains of the Imperial East Africa Company's old headquarters. It is now unfortunately a ruin.

Shimoni is best known as the take-off point for snorkelling excursions into the Kisite-Mpunguti Marine National Park and Wasini Island (see below) and for deep-sea fishing trips into the Pemba Channel, which is a 35-mile stretch of the ocean that separates Tanzania's island of Pemba from the mainland. It reaches depths of 823 m, and is home to three varieties of marlin – black, blue and striped – as well as sailfish, spearfish, swordfish, yellowfin tuna, tiger shark, mako shark and virtually every game fish popular with anglers. A gentle north current runs through the channel, acting much like a scaled-down version of the Gulf Stream, which is forced up by the lip in the north of the channel, also referred to locally as the Sea Mountain, which creates rips and eddies that bring nutrients to the surface that concentrate the fish in a very tight area. The fishing season is usually from August to the end of March. See under Activities and tours (page 80) for fishing operators.

Kisite-Mpunguti Marine National Park and Wasini Island
ⓘ US$20, children US$10.

To the far south is this marine park, which has superb coral gardens and lots of sea life. It covers 39 sq km on the southernmost part of the Kenyan coastline and is managed and protected by the Kenya Wildlife Service. The small islands dotting the coastline have old established trees including baobabs with their thick gnarled trunks and the coral seas of turquoise and dark green stretch away. Mountains rising straight up in the south over the ocean mark the Tanzanian/Kenyan border. Kisite-Mpunguti is a flat little marine park, an atoll, with a dead coral shelf in the middle rising up off it like a table. Unremarkable on the surface, what is truly amazing is what is in the waters around it: it is said to be the best snorkelling in Kenya. The protected areas have a high diversity of marine life with fringing reef, channels, islands and offshore reefs. Hard and soft corals are a common feature. Green and Hawksbill turtles and seven species of dolphins are present and are both sighted by visitors on a virtually daily basis. Humpback whales are sighted regularly on their yearly migration in October/November, sometimes as early as July. This stretch of the coastline is also a birdwatchers' paradise. Every morning, visitors are bussed in from the coastal resorts and the little convoy of *dhows* string out in a line and drop anchor. The water is pure, warm and turquoise in colour, and is so salt-saturated that it is difficult to swim in initially, as it seems to suspend you. There are thousands of fish, in a dazzling array of sizes, shapes and colours, just below the surface. There are also several dive spots here, and the reefs are excellent for drift diving. The bottom is a combination of sand flats and reef outgrowths. Sting rays and turtles are commonly seen, as are parrot fish, trumpet fish, bat fish, grouper, Napoleon wrasse, clown fish and Spanish dancers. One of the better reefs is **Nyulli Reef**, which lies at 30 m and drops to over 80 m. This reef is spectacularly long and a large quantity of large pelagics as well as reef fish are found here. This is also home to a family of very large groupers up to 68 kg in size.

Wasini Island falls within the Kisite-Mpunguti Marine National Park. It is a wonderful place, 1 km wide and 6 km long, totally undeveloped with no cars, no mains electricity and no running water. There is no reliable freshwater supply on the island, only rainwater. Some of the proceeds of the tourist trade have been used to build large culverts where they can store rainwater. A small village on the island includes the remains of an Arab settlement. There are also the ruins of 18th- and 19th-century houses as well as a pillar tomb with Chinese porcelain insets that have, so far, survived. The beach is worth exploring as you might well find bits of pottery and glass. Also interesting are the dead coral gardens behind the village, which you can explore from a boardwalk. They are above the sea although during the spring tide they are covered as they are linked to the sea 30 m below through a series of caverns. Some of the coral formations are said to resemble animal shapes (they call one the elephant). There's also a good variety of birds including brown-headed parrots, sunbirds, palmnut vultures and African fish eagles, and animals include monitor lizards, Sykes monkeys and wild goats.

Most people visit the park on a tour. They depart daily from all the hotels along the north coast, Mombasa and Diani Beach. Included is transport, boat tours with snorkelling and lunch at the **Wasini Island Restaurant** (better known as **Charlie Claw's**). The day begins with collection from the hotels and a transfer to Shimoni. Then guests go snorkelling by *dhow*, or glass-bottomed boats are available for those who do not wish to swim. There is no shade or protection from the burning sun and wearing a shirt/long sleeved T-shirt whilst snorkelling is a wise precaution. Masks and snorkels are available but fins are not permitted to minimize damage to the reef. Lunch at **Charlie Claw's** includes steamed crabs in ginger with claws the size of your fist, along with fresh lime and baked coconut rinds for dipping in salt, followed by barbequed fish and rice steamed in coconut, and a fresh fruit platter and *sim sim* (ginger spiced coffee with balls of sugared sesame seed). This goes down well with cold Kenyan beer, but the wise drink water first. This restaurant has been going for 25 years. There is not much of a beach on Wasini Island, as it gets covered by the incoming tide, so the afternoon is spent lazing away on day beds in the restaurant gardens, or there are optional visits to the Wasini Village, the Shimoni Caves or diving. Prices for the full day trip are around US$100 from the north coast and US$90 from the south, although these prices come down depending on the season. All the hotels and resorts can book this excursion.

South coast listings

For Sleeping and Eating price codes and other relevant information, see pages 11-16.

🛏 Sleeping

Hotel prices vary with the season. Low is Apr-Jun; mid is Jul-Nov; high is Dec-Mar. There's a wide choice of accommodation along the beach and a number of all-inclusive resorts where rates include all meals, usually buffets, and some watersports, which are favoured by package holidaymakers on 1- to 2-week stays. Nevertheless most of these accept direct bookings, and out of the high season, walk-in guests. A family or group may want to consider renting a good-value cottage or villa where you can cook for yourself. If you are self-catering at Tiwi Beach, it's a good idea to pick up a few provisions at the large branch of **Nakumatt** supermarket near the Likoni Ferry in Mombasa. At Tiwi itself, there is only a small shop for basic provisions at the turn-off to the beach. The next shops are at Ukunda and Diani further south.

Tiwi Beach *p62*
$$$ Sheshe Baharini Beach Hotel, reservations, Nairobi, T020-856 2025, www.sheshebeach.com. A fairly upmarket place with 24 cool, spacious rooms with a/c and ceiling fans, patios or balconies, some with 4-poster beds, 4 of which overlook the beach, while the rest are located in the gardens or by the swimming pool. There are 2 bars and a good restaurant for seafood, which also has a pizza oven and a fairly good selection of wine. Trips on a glass-bottomed boat can be arranged and you can walk along the beach to the mangrove forest at the mouth of the Mwachema River.
$$$ Tiwi Beach Resort, T040-330 0190, www.tiwibeachresort.com. An attractive thatched resort with 210 rooms, all with queen-size bed and 1 single bed, a/c, TV,

wooden floors, arranged in 2-storey blocks with either balcony or patio. Of the 3 restaurants, the Indian one **Shere e Punjab**, is among the best on the coast. There are several bars and cafés, business centre, all watersports can be arranged, rates are half board. It has an exceptional swimming pool, 250 m long, connected by channels and slides.
$$$ Coral Cove Cottages, T040-320 5195, www.coralcove.tiwibeach.com. 9 self-catering *bandas* that vary in price – the 6 most expensive 2-bedroom cottages have bathrooms and cost about US$100 per night. All are attractively decorated. It is a lovely location, a beautiful white-sand beach, with swaying palm trees in a private cove. A personal cook/house-help/laundry-man/woman can be hired for an additional cost, and local people come round daily selling fish and vegetables. Excellent value.
$$ Maweni and Capricho Beach Cottages, T040-330 0012, www.mawenibeach.com. Located on a small cliff overlooking the beach, which is about 5 mins' walk away down a flight of steps, there are 26 simple but comfortable 1- to 3-bed thatched self-catering cottages, either sea-facing or in the tropical gardens where there's a small swimming pool. If you don't want to cook yourself, you can hire a cook or eat simple seafood dishes in the **Dhow Restaurant**.
$$ Sand Island Cottages, T040-330 0043, www.sandislandtiwi.com. Quiet and a little remote, 1- to 3-bed self-catering low-rise thatched cottages in a grove of palms, 30 m back from the beach, similar set-up to the Coral Cove Cottages above, in that you can hire a cook/maid at extra cost and local people do the rounds with fish and vegetables. Snorkelling equipment available.

Diani Beach *p62, map p63*
There are plenty of all-inclusive large beachside resorts along the Diani 'strip', and

most allow non-guests (for a fee) in for the day to use the facilities such as swimming pools and sun loungers. 2 of these, south of the Diani Shopping Centre, Jadini Beach Hotel and Africana Sea Lodge, managed by **Alliance Hotels** (www.alliancehotels.com), were at the time of writing closed for a complete refurbishment. If you are self-catering at Diani, there are plenty of supermarkets and local people come round the self-catering resorts each morning with a delicious selection of fish and seafood, and sometimes fruit and vegetables, for sale strapped to the back of their bicycles. Surprisingly for this inclusive stretch of prime holiday coastline, there are also a couple of good options for backpackers and campers.

$$$$ Alfajiri Beach Villa, T0733-630 491, www.alfajirivillas.com. An exclusive retreat aimed at families or groups, 3 beautiful Italian-owned double-storey thatched villas with wide verandas and balconies. Each has 2-4 en suite bedrooms with additional rooms under the *makuti* roof for children, vast beds swathed in mosquito nets, decorated with exquisite objet d'art from around the world, and rim-flow pools almost on the beach. Mediterranean-influenced food with olive oils, parma ham and cheeses flown in weekly from Europe. With 20 staff, Alfajiri was listed in 2005 by *Harpers and Queen* magazine as one of the world's top 100 places to stay. Very stylish but at a price, full board rates start from US$850 per person, half for children. Included is a vehicle for excursions, butlers and trained nannies for children. Closed Apr-Jul.

$$$$ Baobab Beach Resort & Spa, T040-320 2623, www.baobab-beach-resort.com, on the cliff at the southern end (to get to the beach you have to climb down the steep steps). This is a large recently renovated and extended resort popular with German package holiday-makers, with almost 300 a/c rooms with views over the gardens,

ocean or the 3 swimming pools. Open-air disco, several bars and restaurants, fitness centre and spa, loads of activities from bicycle hire to windsurfing. Rates are full board and meals are mostly buffets, but there is the option to eat in the à la carte restaurant for additional cost.

$$$$ Diani Reef Beach Resort and Spa, T040-320 2723, www.dianireef.com. Refurbished in 2005, a super luxurious and comfortable hotel with 300 m of beach frontage, all the 300 rooms are a/c with satellite TV, mini bars, internet, and safes. The hotel has a full range of facilities including a craft shop, 5 bars, 6 restaurants, 2 swimming pools, kids' club, casino and disco, floodlit tennis courts, squash courts, a diving school, golf-putting course, and landscaped lagoons with boating facilities and sun bathing islands. The spa has a gym, steam rooms, jet baths, saunas, treatments, etc.

$$$$ Shaanti Holistic Health Retreat, T040-320 2064, www.shaantihhr.com. This is a new Ayurvedic sanctuary with just 8 sea-facing a/c rooms with attractive stone bathrooms and patios arranged in a long white block. Facilities include various beauty treatments and massages, yoga on a large yoga terrace under thatch overlooking the beach, jacuzzi, swimming pool, open-air bubble baths, and a meditation room where you can listen to soothing music on headphones. It has a good vegetarian restaurant in a thatched wooden tower and is also the location of the **Buddha on the Beach** restaurant (see under Eating).

$$$ Diani Marine Divers Village, just to the north of **Forty Thieves restaurant**, T040-320 2367, www.dianimarine.com. A small, friendly place with a combination of rooms including a simple permanent tent under thatch on a wooden deck that sleeps 4, a self-catering honeymoon cottage with additional hot-tub on the roof, and 2 4-bedroom self-catering villas where a cook can be hired. All rooms are spacious and airy, with large Swahili-style beds with mosquito nets and overhead fans. The Village offers breakfast and in the vicinity there are many restaurants. The dive centre is based here and most people stay on a dive package (see under Activities and tours).

$$$ Diani Sea Lodge and Diani Sea Resort, T040-322 114. Dianisea@africaonline.co.ke. 2 large slightly faded all-inclusive resorts next to each other on the beach popular with German visitors. The rooms in the Lodge are in cottages and have balconies or terraces and a/c, but are simple and small. Better are the a/c rooms at the Resort, which are arranged in blocks with fridge, TV, and balcony. Both have swimming pools, mini- golf, kids' playgrounds and tennis courts. Diving and watersports can be arranged.

$$$ Forest Dream, near Baobab Beach Resort & Spa, T040-320 3224, www.forest dreamcottages.com. 7 large 3- to 6-bed cottages with kitchen, cook and cleaner, ideal for groups and families of 4-12 people, some have jacuzzis and a/c, all set in established gardens and each cottage is quite private, though they are some walk from the beach. Very hi-tech swimming pool with underwater music, massage jets, a nice waterslide and a waterfall that cascades from a huge rock.

$$$ Indian Ocean Beach Club, T040-320 3730, www.jacarandahotels.com. Moorish-style arched main building with smaller *makuta* thatched-roof buildings in secluded 10-ha grounds with old coconut and baobab trees. 100 rooms with a/c, fans, phones, 3 restaurants, 3 bars including the **Bahari Beach Bar**, which is reputed to have the best view on Diani Beach. Facilities include a 200 m swimming pool and 3 smaller pools and tennis courts, and wind-surfing, sailing, snorkelling, scuba-diving, glass-bottomed boat trips and deep-sea fishing can be arranged.

$$$ Leisure Lodge Beach & Golf Resort, T040-320 3624, www.leisurelodge

resort.com. Over 200 rooms in standard hotel block with balconies or in villas clustered around private pools, many restaurants, casino, several swimming pools, tennis courts, health club, dive school and windsurfing school. The 18-hole, 72-par championship golf course, home to the Diani Beach Masters, is recognized as 1 of the best golf courses in East Africa.

$$$ Leopard Beach Resort & Spa, T040-320 2721, www.leopardbeachresort.com. A popular newly refurbished luxury resort, set amidst 10 ha of lush tropical gardens, with 70 standard rooms, 20 superior garden rooms, 48 sea-facing rooms, plus some private cottages and villas. Several restaurants and bars, boutiques, diving, disco and live music, and swimming pool. The luxurious spa is set in a lovely patch of peaceful forest where massages, etc. can be taken outside. Closed end Apr to mid-Jun.

$$$ Neptune Palm Beach Resort, T040-320 2350, www.neptunehotels.com. Together with its sister hotel (below) these are the most southerly of the large hotels, more than 2 km south of **Baobab Beach Resort & Spa** and actually on Galu Beach. 60 newly refurbished en suite rooms with balconies, set in attractive large gardens, all-inclusive rates, watersports available. Shared facilities with the Paradise Village below.

$$$ Neptune Paradise Village, T040-320 2350, www.neptunehotels.com. 258 rooms set in 10 ha of gardens, organized in 2-storey cottages with 4 rooms in each, 2 restaurants serving buffet meals and 2 à la carte restaurants, several bars, rates include all meals. Watersports available, and there's a kiddie's club and a very large swimming pool.

$$$ Pinewood Village Beach Resort, T040-3203131, www.pinewood-village.com. Excellent accommodation in 58 newly renovated rooms and suites incorporating Swahili-style and home-made furniture set in cottages on Galu Beach, almost as far south as Chale Island and therefore at one of the quietest stretches of beach. Each has a/c, minibar, balcony/terrace, and internet and the more expensive suites have additional living rooms and kitchens with their own chef for private dining. Facilities include several restaurants and bars, an attractive swimming pool, gym and spa, a dive base, tennis court and gift shop. A popular venue for weddings.

$$$ The Sands at Nomad, T040-320 3643, www.thesandsatnomad.com. This used to be a standard package resort but recently went under a complete refurbishment and now markets itself as a boutique hotel. The 37 stylish rooms and suites are decorated in Swahili style, and have a/c and minibars, and some have jacuzzis and 4-poster beds. The **Nomad Beach Bar and Restaurant** is one of the most popular along the 'strip', and there's an additional sushi bar, plus a lovely 5-m deep pool surrounded by established overhanging trees, a spa, an internet café and watersports centre. Dive operators **Diving the Crab** and **H2O Extreme** have outlets here (see under Activities and tours), hence the deepness of the pool as it's used for practice dives.

$$$ Southern Palms Beach Resort, T040-320 3721, www.southernpalmskenya.com. Quality resort with over 300 rooms arranged in 4-storey blocks with thatched roofs, with a/c, DVD players, minbars, and 4-poster beds, the additional 'day-bed' can be used by children or there are adjoining rooms. Facilities include 4 restaurants, 5 bars, hair and beauty centre, internet café and there are plenty of activities and entertainment on offer. The highlight here is the vast area of interconnecting swimming pools with 2 swim-up bars.

$$ Diani Beachalets, T040-320 3180, www.dianibeachalets.com. A range of chalets from fully equipped houses with bathrooms and kitchens suitable for families or groups,

to cheap backpackers' *bandas* with shared facilities, the larger units overlook the beach. Tennis court but no pool or restaurant so you will have to stock up before you get here, although there is a supermarket in walking distance, fishermen come round in the mornings with fresh seafood and you can buy cold beers at reception. This is one of the cheapest options on the south coast and accommodation can work out as little as US$9 per person sharing.

$$ Kijiji Cottages, T040-330 0035, www.kijiji cottages.com. These are some of nicest cottages in the Diani area, well looked after, rates include a cleaner, and for an additional expense, a cook. They have 2-3 spacious en suite bedrooms, broad terraces and are set in gardens, the sea-facing ones cost a little more. There's also an attractive swimming pool.

$$ Vindigo Cottages, T040-320 2192, www.vindigocottages.com. These 7 simple self-catering *bandas*, sleeping 2-8 people work out very cheap if shared by a family or group, and the *banda* sleeping 8 is only US$100 a night. All cottages are basically equipped with bed linen, mosquito nets, crockery, cutlery and saucepans but no towels. Set in 4 ha of gardens, a little way away from any other development, giving the cottages a more secluded feel than many other places in Diani.

$ Diani Campsite, T040-320 3192, www.dianicampsite.com. Located near the now defunct ruins of the former Trade Winds Hotel, this self-catering resort has been tidied up in recent years and now offers 10 simple thatched *bandas* with kitchens, and a grassy campsite with a 'camphouse' with cookers, fridges and lockers, plus clean washing facilities and tents can be hired. There's a restaurant and bar where you can order simple seafood meals and pizzas and the beach is a short stroll away.

$ Stilts Eco-Camp, T0722-523 278, stilts@barboursafaris.com. On the opposite side of the main road from the Ali Barbour's Restaurant in a lush tract of forest inhabited by monkeys and bushbabies, here are a clutch of basic cheap tree *bandas*, which as the name suggests are built on stilts, with beds, mosquito nets and balconies and a campsite, all with shared toilets and showers with solar-heated water. There's a pub and restaurant, which has day beds for lazing around, and the beach is a 5-min walk away.

Shimba Hills National Reserve *p66*
$$$ Shimba Lodge, reservations **Aberdare Safari Hotels**, T040-222 9608, www.aberdaresafarihotels.com. A well-designed timber lodge overlooking a waterhole illuminated at night for viewing, which offers similar 'cabin' accommodation to that of Treetops in the Aberdares National Park, with small wooden rooms with shared bathrooms and verandas looking straight into the forest. A 100-m boardwalk has been constructed at tree level giving good views of the forest canopy and you can walk to the Sheldrick's Falls where there is a natural pool for swimming. The dining room is open air, there is a pleasant bar and several secluded decks for game viewing well into the night. There's an excellent opportunity to spot elephant, forest antelope, maybe leopard and bushbaby, and optional early-morning game drives into the park offer the opportunity to see Shimba's famous Sable antelope. Half-board rates are in the region of US$240 for a double, children under 5 are not permitted. Day and overnight excursions can be arranged through the Mombasa tour operators or from the coastal resorts.
$$ Sable Bandas, Kenya Wildlife Service, Nairobi, T020-600 800, www.kws.org. Located 3 km from the main gate to the reserve, this has 4 *bandas* with 2 double beds in each with linen and towels, shared showers and toilets, solar power, shared kitchen with gas cooker and tap (not drinking) water. There's also a well-maintained and peaceful campsite here

with excellent views over the surrounding forested areas. Drinking water, firewood and food must be brought; US$35 per person in the *bandas* and US$10 per person camping.

Mwaluganje Elephant Sanctuary
$$$ Travellers Mwaluganje Elephant Camp, reservations through the **Traveller's Beach Hotel & Club** in Bamburi on Mombasa's north coast, T041-548 5121, www.travellers beach.com. Set on a small hill overlooking a waterhole in the Elephant Sanctuary, there are 20 tents, each with 2 beds, though there is room for a 3rd bed to be added, bathroom and private veranda with views over a well-used elephant trail. Again, excursions here are usually arranged from Mombasa and the coastal resorts and include transfers, entry fees, meals and game drives.

Chale Island *p67*
$$$$ The Sands at Chale Island, T040-3330 0269, www.thesandsatchaleisland.com. Luxury all-inclusive resort, with 55 rooms centred around a beautiful white crescent- shaped sandy beach, comprising roomy and elegant tented bungalows, or apartments and penthouses in round multi-storey blocks topped with thatch, and a couple of water suites that are actually built over the ocean on stilts and reached by boardwalks, all furnished with African/Arabic antiques. The 2 restaurants offer local and international cuisine, diving and deep-sea fishing are on offer and there's a swimming pool, spa and gym.

Msambweni *p67*
$$$$ Funzi Keys, Funzi Island, south of Msambweni, T0733-900 446, www.thefunzi keys.com. Very exclusive tented camp situated on a beautifully secluded island, furnished to a very high standard. 10 spacious cottages set along the high-water line and

constructed of stone and thatch with large netted windows and hand-carved king-sized 4-poster beds, a perfect honeymoon venue. Facilities for many watersports are available and included in the price, as are all meals, drinks (except champagne) and transport. Rates are US$240-690 per person depending on season. This is a very special place and the management report that some guests have been in tears on departure. Closed Apr-Jul.

$$$$ Msambweni Beach House, on Msambweni Beach, reservations Nairobi, T020-357 7093, www.msambweni-house.com. Set in a commanding position on a small cliff with great ocean views, this is a super luxury family-run establishment with 6 spacious rooms in the main house with lovely all-white decor and Swahili furniture, in front of which is a stunning 25-m infinity swimming pool, plus 2 private villas with their own pool, jacuzzi cook and butler. Excellent cuisine including some French and Belgium dishes as well as seafood.

Shimoni *p67*

$$$ Betty's Camp, near the jetty, T0722-434 709, www.bettys-camp.com. A small simple and a little over-priced place with no beach as such but overlooking the ocean with either tented rooms under thatch with own shower/toilet or en suite rooms within the main house, can accommodate 10-12 people in total, swimming pool, poolside terrace restaurant and bar open to all with a good range of seafood, can arrange fishing and trips to Wasini Island.

$$$ Mwazaro Mangrove Lodge, T0722-711 476 (mob), www.keniabeach.de. About 8 km north of Shimoni, there is a sign to Mwazaro Beach, turn right there and the camp is another 1 km. Run by a friendly German man Hans, accommodation is in either thatched *bandas* on the beach with sand floors and lit by hurricane lamps, or en suite rooms in the main coral-rag house with solar and wind-powered electricity. The restaurant

serves excellent affordable Swahili-style food, there's a comfy lounge and bar where you can play chess or backgammon, and tea is served all day. A guide will take you on an interactive tour to a local fishing village or on a boat tour to a nearby mangrove forest. You can also negotiate to camp here. A lovely remote, laid-back spot and a far cry from the larger holiday resorts.

$$$ Pemba Channel Lodge and Fishing Club, T0722-205 020, www.pembachannel lodge.com, www.pembachannel.com. Just 6 simple white *bandas* set in tropical gardens, with many trees indigenous to the Shimoni area. Each *banda* has a small veranda – all with sea views and there's a pool. The Clubhouse has an attractive, homely lounge filled with wicker sofas and overstuffed cushions, marlin trophies and fishing photos adorn the walls. There is a great camaraderie amongst the fishermen around the very 'Hemingway-esque' bar at the end of the day.

$$$ Shimoni Reef Lodge, reservations, Mombasa, T041-471 771, www.shimonireef lodge.com. Wonderful location, overlooking Wasini Island, high standards catering almost exclusively to keen anglers, 10 open-plan cottages with ocean views and private verandas, each is on 2 levels and sleeps 4 people. There is a sea water swimming pool made up of multi levels that is good for kids, an open-air terrace restaurant overlooking the ocean where seafood is a speciality, and fishing, diving and snorkelling are on offer.

$$ Shimoni Gardens, 2 km west of the village, T0727-247 100, www.shimoni gardens.com. A quiet spot, not quite on the beach but not far away nestled in a patch of jungley forest, there are 16 small, clean en suite whitewashed thatched cottages, and 6 simple rooms built of reed and thatch with shared facilities, set in nice gardens full of palms and flowering shrubs. There's a small restaurant for basic meals and beers, and they run their own *dhows* to Wasini Island for the snorkelling excursion.

Diani Beach *p62, map p63*

Most of the large resorts have buffet meals, particularly for all-inclusive guests, and although these vary in quality, they are usually of a fairly high standard. Some also have individual specialist restaurants, which are also open to non-guests. The best choice is probably in the **Leisure Lodge Beach & Golf Resort**, which has both the upmarket Cascada's Mediterranean restaurant and the Fisherman's Cove seafood restaurant, and the **Diani Reef Beach Resort & Spa**, which has the Sake Oriental Japanese restaurant and the very good Fins, which again specializes in seafood. There are also a number of individual places along the Diani 'strip'. All offer very good fish and seafood and you can rely on it being very fresh. If you are on holiday on the south coast and have the cash to splash, ensure you visit both the **Tamarind** in Mombasa (page53) and **Ali Barbour's** (below).

$$$ Ali Barbour's, just north of the Diani Shopping Centre, T040-320 2033. Open daily from 1900. Diani's most popular restaurant, which is set in an underground cave that has various chambers that go 10 m below ground level, a stone floor has been fitted and a sliding roof that comes across if the weather is bad. Lights have been set in niches in the walls and it's very atmospheric. It does excellent seafood including an expensive but expansive platter, as well as French food. If staying on Diani Beach they will provide free transport. A very unique experience and most people who holiday in Diani visit. Casual, but beachwear is not permitted.

$$$ Buddha on the Beach, at **The Shaanti Holistic Health Retreat**, T040-320 2064, www.shaantihhr.com. Daily 1200-1400, 1800-2300. A fairly new seafood restaurant with a small but excellent menu of inventive dishes such as lobster medallions grilled in honey and soy sauce, whole crab steamed in chilli and ginger, and Cajun blackened red snapper. There's an extensive winelist and tables are set in an attractive whitewashed thatched building overlooking the beach. On Fri and Sat 1800-2000, they run an oyster bar on the beach and serve fresh Kilifi oysters with a glass of wine.

$$$ Forty Thieves, next door to **Ali Barbour's**, and under the same management, T040-320 3003. Daily 0900-late. Lively bar and restaurant open all day from breakfast serving good food and snacks, the steamed crab and Swahili prawns with coconut rice are especially good and the comfortable lounge-style tables are set under thatch right next to the beach where you can kick off your shoes in the sand. It's also a popular night spot and meeting place for many of the local residents who affectionately call it 'Forties', with pool tables, live entertainment, satellite TV, and discos on Wed, Fri and Sat nights. Also good live music and buffet lunch on a Sun. Provides free transport in the evening.

$$$ Nomads Beach Bar & Restaurant, at **The Sands at Nomads**, T040-320 3643. Open 0900-late. Right on the beach on wooden decks and under canvas with good service and atmosphere. It does a very popular Sun buffet lunch with live jazz, which is good value, and the à la carte menu features pizzas, excellent and imaginative pastas, risottos, seafood and grills.

$$$ Shan-e-Punjab, Diani Complex Shopping Centre, opposite **Diani Reef Beach Resort & Spa**, T040-320 2116. Daily 1000-2400. Good-value Indian dishes, specializes in Punjab and tandoori cuisine, tikka and masala with a full range of seafood, more expensive continental dishes available, open-air beer garden and cocktail menu, provides free transport from the hotels.

$$ Bull Steak House, behind the petrol station just north of the **Diani Beach Shopping Centre**. Daily 1200-late. Informal restaurant and bar under a conical thatched roof, plus rooftop terrace, popular with Germans for the very large steaks from 250 gram fillets to 1 kg T-bones, good cuts of prime Angus beef, and also offers a German bratwurst that's a metre long!

$$ Galaxy, opposite **Diani Reef Beach Resort & Spa**, T040-300 018. Daily 1100-1430, 1800-2300. Part of a chain that also has branches in Mombasa and Bamburi Beach, this offers tasty Chinese cuisine, a small menu but with quality items such as grilled lobster, roast duck, and ginger crab, and is set on a nice open terrace surrounded by lush tropical gardens. Offers free pick-ups from the hotels.

$$ Sundowner, a 5-min walk from the **Diani Beach Chalets**, T040-320 2138. Serves excellent Kenyan food and local beers at low prices, one of the best-value places to eat, curries, grilled and fried fish, very good English breakfasts, sometimes has seafood such as lobster, simple decor in outside thatched bar and restaurant but nice atmosphere.

$ African Pot, near the **Barclay's Bank Shopping Centre**, T040-320 3890. Daily 1000-late. Good value, tasty local food, served in the traditional way in (as the name suggests) big earthenware pots, such as *nyama choma* (charcoaled meat), masala curries, *chipati*, *matoke*, *ugali* and pilau rice, all washed down with cold Tusker beer. Good place for a group to share dishes

$ Hollywood, Ukunda opposite the **Total** petrol station, T040-320 2562. Daily 0900-2300. A rather odd combination of tasty Kenyan and German food at good prices, including chicken stew, fish and chips and the like, and German items like bratwurst and schnitzel, plus fresh juices (the mango is delicious), beer and some wines. Tables are set on a pleasant terrace bedecked with plants.

🎵 Bars, clubs and entertainment

Diani Beach *p62, map p63*
Most of the large resorts put on some kind of evening entertainment for guests, which in Kenya is referred to as 'animation' and is usually a troupe of male dancers putting on a display of acrobatics (at which Kenyans seem to be uncannily good), or perhaps traditional drumming or Masai dancing. Almost all the resorts have nightclubs and many have discos on the beach, which are of varying quality and in the family resorts usually feature lots of children running around. Along the Diani Beach Rd there are also a couple of independent nightclubs.

Shakatak, www.shakatak-kenya.com, on the opposite side of the road and just south of Ali Barbour's, is the biggest is nightclub, which is German-run with a restaurant and beer garden. It's very popular, expect to queue to get in during high season, with a large dance floor and floor shows that start daily at 2100, and although it's a little seedy and prostitutes abound, it can be a lot of fun. The website (which is in German) very generously explains that in Kenya, men over 40 go to nightclubs! They make their ice from mineral water and there are plenty of taxis outside.

Probably the nicest place to go dancing is **Forty Thieves**, next door to **Ali Barbour's** (see under Eating), which has pool tables, live entertainment, satellite TV, and on Wed, Fri and Sat nights the restaurant tables are pushed back for a disco.

There's a **Casino**, located in the **Leisure Lodge Beach & Golf Resort**, which is open daily from 1200-0300 and has many slot machines, a few gaming tables and a bar.

🛍 Shopping

Diani Beach *p62, map p63*
Curios
There are many curio stalls dotted along Diani Beach Rd, and they are usually grouped near the entrance to the resorts. Additionally

'beach boys' wander around selling items, who you'll have to be assertive with to leave you alone as they can be fairly aggressive with their sales tactics. There are also several upmarket curio shops in the shopping centres (see below).

Food

If you are self-catering it is worth buying most of your supplies in Mombasa where it is cheaper. Try the large **Nakumatt** supermarket just near the Likoni Ferry; it sells everything imaginable. There are a number of places closer to the beach. At the small village of **Ukunda** on the main road at the Diani turn-off, where you can get most things from stalls or small local shops. On Diani Beach Rd itself, there are now 4 shopping centres: opposite Diani Reef Beach Resort and Spa is **Diani Complex**, the smallest of the 4, while further south the **Barclays Bank Shopping Centre** is next to Barclays Bank and has a small supermarket, a shop selling booze, an internet café and a couple of top-end curio shops that among other items sell *kikoys* and the beautiful beaded leather sandals that are made on the coast. **Diani Shopping Centre** and **Diani Beach Shopping Centre** are close to each other to the north of Diani Beach post office. Unfortunately the latter was almost destroyed in a fire in late 2007, so it remains to be seen if it will re-open again. The **Muthaiga Mini Market** in Diani Shopping Centre is a very well-stocked supermarket with many chilled items and imported goods and there is also a shop here for the Kikoy Company. There's another good supermarket just up from the Diani Beachalets that also sells booze. For fresh fruit, vegetables and fish you will be able to buy off the vendors who come round all the self-catering places with their stock on their bicycles.

▲▲ Activities and tours

Diani Beach *p62, map p63*
Most of the resorts will help organize

dhow and glass-bottomed boat trips, safaris and diving.

Deep-sea fishing

Expect to pay in the region of US$600-700 per boat per day including all equipment for 4-6 people, and trips go out to the Pemba Channel off-shore from Shimoni (see page 80).
Blue Marlin Fishing Club, to the south of the beach close to the Neptune hotels, T040-320 2799, www.bluemarlinfishingclub.com.
Fisherman's Paradise, also near the Neptune hotels, T0728-705 447, www.fishermansparadise-kenya.nl.

Golf

Leisure Lodge Beach & Golf Resort, T040-320 3624, www.golfinginkenya.com. This attractive 18-hole championship course is open to all guests of Diani Beach hotels and resorts. Expect to pay in the region of US$70 for 18 holes with club hire and for keen golfers, there are weekly packages. The par 72 course has 85 bunkers and a large lake which is home to a resident crocodile who is inexplicably named Colin, and golfers may spot monkeys around the course. There's a club bar and restaurant, lessons available in English, German or Italian, and caddies and golf carts can be hired. To play the course men must have a handicap of at least 28 and ladies 36, or a playing certificate from a recognized club. Beginners welcome on the driving range. The course is home to the Diani Beach Masters.

Tour operators

There are several tour agencies, mainly in and around the shopping centres, otherwise all the large resorts organize local tours and activities. The popular day trip for snorkelling by *dhow* in Kisite-Mpunguti Marine National Park and lunch on Wasini Island (see page 68) includes transport to and from the north beach and south beach hotels, snorkelling equipment, marine reserve entrance fees, soft drinks, beer, wine and lunch. The times of pick-ups vary depending on how far away you are, but they are generally fairly early to get to the *dhows* at Shimoni by around 0900.

Adventure Tours & Safaris, Barclays Bank Shopping Centre, T040-320 3759, www.kenya-wildlife-safaris.com. Day trips plus overnight and longer to Tsavo and other parks.

DM Tours & Safaris, Diani Shopping Centre, T040-320 4015, www.dmtours.net. Day tours, and longer safaris including a 3-day Tsavo and Amboseli combination.

Malibu Tours & Safaris, Diani Shopping Centre, T040-320 3164. A large fleet of taxis and other vehicles and can arrange day trips and safaris.

Pilli Pipa Dhow Safaris, Colliers Centre, near Barclays Bank Shopping Centre, T040-320 3599, www.pillipipa.com. Operates the excursion to Wasini and also offers diving.

The Diani Beach Safari Company, Diani Beach Shopping Centre, T040-320 4012, www.dianitours.com. Wasini Island, Mombasa, city tours, Shimba Hills day trips and overnight stays to Tsavo.

Wasini Island Restaurant, T040-320 2331, www.wasini-island.com. This company owns the famous Charlie Claw's restaurant on Wasini Island, and offers that day trip as well as diving.

Watersports

There is a wealth of watersports on offer along the beach. With warm water and cross- and side-shore winds, Diani has good conditions for wind- and kitesurfing along the wide uncrowded beach and the flat water inside the reef is perfect for beginners. Windsurfers cost around US$50 for a half a day, while kitesurfing gear costs in the region of US$90 per half day, and hourly and daily instruction for both is available. Snorkelling of course can be done by simply walking into the sea, or from *dhows*. There are over 30 dive sites within a 20-25 minute boat trip from Diani Beach, which with 15-30 m depths, offer excellent visibility and a diverse amount of marine life. There are also 2 wrecks for experienced divers to explore – the *HMS Hildasay* sank in 1945, while the *MV Funguro* sank in 2002 and both lie at a depth of just over 20 m. Expect to pay in the region of US$55 for an individual dive and US$470 for a 4-5 day PADI Open Water course. As well as below, Pilli Pipa Dhow Safaris and Wasini Island Restaurant above also offer diving.

Aqualand, Pinewood Village, T040-320 2720, www.southerncrossscuba.com. Watersports centre at Galu Beach offering kite- and windsurfing courses, sailing, kayaking, jet-skiing, banana boats, diving and snorkelling. A very professional company with a whole range of activities on offer and now have other branches known as **Ocean**, in the Diani Reef Beach Resort & Spa, and **Sx Scuba**, in the Indian Ocean Beach Club. Aqualand is also the base for the **East African Whale Shark Trust** (www.giantsharks.org). There has recently been an increase of whale shark numbers in Kenyan waters and the trust was established in 2005 to raise awareness about protection of whale sharks, and is involved in collecting and analyzing data on the local whale shark population.

Barakuda Diving, www.barakuda.50megs. com. Has a dive centre at **Tiwi Beach Resort** and at some of the resorts north of Mombasa.

Diani Marine, T040-320 2367, www.diani marine.com. A well-established operator with over 25 years' experience at Diani with several dive packages and also a unique 'bubble maker', which is a special pool for introductory dives for children over 8. Clients can stay in the Diver's Village (see under Sleeping).

Diving The Crab, at **The Sands at Nomad**, T040-320 3400, www.divingthecrab.com. Established operator with over 20 years' experience on the Kenya coast with a very comprehensive website, has over 150 sets of dive equipment and cylinders, 8 custom-built dive boats, and 10 PADI instructors.

H2O Extreme, offices at **Leisure Lodge Golf & Beach Resort, Leopard Beach Resort & Spa**, and **The Sands at Nomad**, T0721-495 876, www.h2o-extreme.com. A professionally run wind- and kitesurfing school that rents out equipment to experienced surfers. Also hires out pedalos and sea kayaks.

Shimoni *p67*

Pemba Big Game Fishing Club, T0722-205 020, www.pembachannel.com. Can arrange fishing in the Pemba Channel and has 3 fully equipped boats, and liveaboard, which can sleep up to 10 people and frequently does a multi-day run to Pemba Island in Tanzania. The fishing club has a reputation as Africa's premier marlin destination and has attracted many illustrious guests.

Sea Adventures, reservations Mombasa, T020-217 0208, www.bigame.com. Run by experienced skippers Pat and Simon Hemphill, this offers deep-sea fishing charters into the Pemba Channel plus 4- to 8-day safaris to Pemba Island for small groups of up to 4 people. It also takes children over 8 years old and Simon's son and daughter both caught their first marlin under the age of 11.

⊖ Transport

Diani Beach *p62, map p63*
Air
A small airfield at Ukunda is used for small planes – usually charters for safaris. **Mombasa Air Safari** (see page 58) will touch down here on request to pick up passengers for its flights between the coast and the parks.

Bus and matatus
For **Diani** by *matatu* you have to change at Ukunda village. The fare from Likoni to **Ukunda** costs about US$1 and from from Ukunda to Diani US$0.40. There is also a large fleet of brightly coloured *tuk-tuks* operating between Ukunda and all along the beach road that you simply flag down, if the drivers themselves do not drive right up to you. These cost little more than a US$1 for any journey and take up to 3 people. There used to be a number of places along the beach to hire cars, but the *tuk-tuks* have replaced the need for car hire. Rather amusingly the Diani *tuk-tuks* have wobbly arms and hands that wave at you as they drive along and some even have giant hats on their ro

❻ Directory

Diani Beach *p62, map p63*
Banks All the banks have ATMs and foreign-exchange facilities. **Kenya Commercial Bank**, main road in Ukunda, **Barclays Bank of Kenya**, Diani Beach, at the head of the road to Ukunda. **Diani Forex Bureau**, in a white building near Diani Beachalets. **Internet** Good but expensive café in the **Barclays Bank Shopping Centre** and many of the hotels offer access. **Medical services** Diani Beach Hospital, south of **Diani Complex Shopping Centre**, T040-320 2435, www.dianibeachhospital.com. This is a private, modern hospital and 24-hr pharmacy with very high standards and is used to dealing with European patients. Since early 2008, it has been offering a growing list of cosmetic procedures to holiday-makers. **Post office** Opposite the ruins of the **Trade Winds Hotel**.

North coast

There is a whole string of beaches along the north coast including Nyali, Kenyatta, Bamburi and Shanzu, with lots of hotels on the seashore immediately north of Mombasa. North of Mtwapa Creek are Kikambala and Vipingo beaches. The major attractions of Watamu Marine Park, Malindi and Lamu are further north. At these latter places there is much more choice for the budget traveller and anyone who wants to avoid the package tours. There are major historical sites at Kilifi, Malindi and Lamu. The north coast is also the location of the Malindi Marine Biosphere Reserve. This strip along the coast is 30 km long and 5 km wide and was gazetted in 1968, and covers an area of 213 sq km. It lies about 80 km north of Mombasa, and includes the Malindi Marine Park, the Watamu Marine Park and Mida Creek. The vegetation includes mangrove, palms, marine plants and various forms of algae that are home to crabs, corals, molluscs, cowrie and marine worms. Coral viewing is popular here, as are boat trips and watersports.

Nyali, Kenyatta and Bamburi beaches → *Phone code: 041.*

Nyali, Kenyatta and Bamburi beaches are well developed and there are lots of hotels. Most of them cater for package tours from Europe and usually each hotel caters for a particular nationality. None of them are cheap. All have facilities such as swimming pools, tennis courts, watersports and they tend to look after their guests very well, organizing all sorts of activities and trips. Here the coast is lined with pristine palm-fringed beaches and the offshore reefs. Both outer and inner reef walls offer world-class diving with spectacular coral gardens and drop-offs, and Kenya's best wreck diving on the *MV Dania* (see box, page 64).

Mombasa Marine National Park (10 sq km) was established in 1986 for the protection of the area's coral reefs. It can be accessed by snorkelling or glass-bottomed boat trips from the resorts along the beaches and there are also diving sites.

Mamba Village ① *Links Rd, Nyali, behind Nyali Beach and the hotels, US$9.50, children US$5, daily 0800-1830, feeding is at 1700,* is the biggest crocodile farm in Kenya and is a habitat for over 10,000 crocodiles of all ages and sizes from newborns to huge fully grown adults. A film explains some of the conservation efforts as well as the financial side of the venture. However it's fairly run down now and the pools where the crocodiles live are rather dank and the display of 'deformed' crocodiles is not a pleasant sight. Of more interest is the small adjacent **Botanical Garden** and **Aquarium**.

Wild Waters ① *Links Rd, Nyali, Next to the Mamba Village, T041-470 408, www.wildwaterskenya.com, US$22, children (under 18) US$10, Mon-Fri 1100-2200, Sat-Sun 1000-2200, water slides close at 1800,* a new water park, is set in manicured gardens and features 11 slides for adults, another five for children, and each is named after a Kenyan river. A 300-m 'lazy river' encircles the whole complex and other facilities include fairground rides, bouncy castles, a video game arcade and a food court. There are also a couple of bars here that stay open late.

Bombolulu Workshops and Cultural Centre ① *about 4 km north of Nyali Bridge on the Malindi road, T041-447 4077, US$6.50, Mon-Sat 0800-1700, the shop stays open until 1800,* is where you might want to do some souvenir shopping and there's a selection of wooden carvings, leather products, textiles and jewellery. Founded in 1969, the crafts are produced by a team of 150 local handicapped people (mostly polio victims) and are generally of reasonable quality and good value. There is also a cultural centre with eight traditional homesteads from different ethnic groups, where guides demonstrate traditional dance, music and theatre. You can do a tour of the workshops and Swahili food is available in the **Ziga** restaurant.

Haller Wildlife Park

① *8 km north of Nyali Bridge on the Malindi Rd, T041-548 5901, daily 0800-1700, adults US$9, children US$4.50.*

This park started out life as the Bamburi cement factory, which began quarrying coral to make lime for the cement around Mombasa in the 1950s. When quarrying stopped in 1971 an effort was made to reclaim the land by reforestation and a nature trail was created. The reclamation scheme was ahead of its time and it attracted the attention of ecologists from all over the world. The nature park has been renamed Haller Wildlife Park

Owen and Mzee

One of the newer residents of the Haller Wildlife Park is Owen the hippo. Just before Christmas in 2004, the Sabaki River to the north of Malindi flooded after heavy rains and washed a number of hippo into the sea, which local people tried to coax back. Then the tsunami hit on Boxing Day making the sea swell dramatically and temporarily the hippo were forgotten as people were absorbed with rescuing local fisherman. The next day the hippo all made it back to the mainland except for Owen who was stranded on a reef. He was less than a year old at the time. After a remarkable rescue by the Kenya Wildlife Service that was watched by hundreds of people he was brought to Haller Wildlife Park. His story is made even more remarkable as when he was released into an enclosure already occupied by some giant tortoises, he was adopted by one of them named Mzee (meaning 'old man' in Kiswahili) who is believed to be about 130 years old. Owen arrived exhausted, confused and extremely frightened and immediately ran to Mzee and cowered behind him as he would have done with his mother. Within days the tortoise and the hippo were eating and sleeping together, and the hippo licked the tortoise's face and followed him everywhere. Owen and Mzee remained inseparable until 2007 when Owen was removed to another enclosure with another hippo. A number of children's books have been written about them, and they have their own website: www.owenandmzee.com.

after the Swiss agronomist who turned the lunar quarry landscape into luxuriant tropical forest. Part of the process included the introduction of hundreds of thousands of millipedes that helped convert the infertile sand into soil, able to support the forest in which the centre is now situated.

There are all manner of things to do and see including a fish farm producing tilapia, a luxuriant palm garden, 3.6 km of forest trails with exercise points and equipment along which you can either walk, jog or cycle, a crocodile farm, a butterfly pavilion and a reptile house. Visitors have the unique opportunity of close-up contact with the variety of animal species, such as various antelope, monkeys, warthog, giant tortoises and lots of different birds. Tours are in English, French, German, Italian or Swahili. You can watch the hippos being fed daily at 1600, and can feed a number of Rothschild giraffes from an elevated platform at 1100 and 1500 daily. Children in particular will thoroughly enjoy this excursion. Finally the **Whistling Pines** restaurant is an excellent place for lunch.

Mtwapa and Shanzu Beach

Mtwapa is a small, bustling, chaotic and extremely friendly town, and is the main service point for Shanzu Beach. The main settlement is just north of the creek, which is busy with boats serving the big-game fishing industry. The beach itself is sheltered and bordered by palms and glass-bottomed boat rides out to the reefs are on offer. There are a number of resorts, most interlinked with one another so guests can use all the facilities.

Ngomongo Villages ① *10 km north of the Nyali Bridge and 1 km east of the main Mombasa–Malindi road, clearly signposted, T041-548 7063, www.ngomongo.com, daily*

0900-1700, US$9, children US$4.50, set in 6.5 ha of another reclaimed quarry in Shanzu, might be described as a theme park of traditional rural Kenyan lifestyles. There are nine villages, one for each of the tribes represented, complete with hut, cultivated crops, domestic and wild animals, village witch doctor and villagers. Visitors can walk around the site to see anything from subsistence farming methods to Akamba wood carving. There is an emphasis on participation, thus you can plant a tree or try many of the activities yourself, such as maize pounding or harpoon fishing whilst trying to balance on a raft. There is also a market selling jewellery and other ethnic items, and the **Kienyenji Restaurant**, built in traditional style, serves a range of African dishes and you can sample the local beer. This won an award from the United Nations Education Programme in 2001.

Jumba la Mtwana ① *www.museums.or.ke, daily 0930-1800, US$7.50, children (under 18) US$3; you can buy a short guidebook to the site or hire a guide*, is a national monument about 15 km from Mombasa and 1 km north of the Mtwapa Creek. The name means the 'house of the slave' and may have been a slave-trading settlement in the 15th century, although it was not mentioned in this capacity in either Arab or Portuguese sources. It is a lovely setting, close to the beach with shade provided by baobabs. To reach the site ask to be dropped off at the sign about 1 km beyond Mtwapa Bridge and from there it is a walk of about 3 km. However, you will probably be offered a lift as you walk down the track. Many of the houses have been rebuilt and undergone frequent changes and it has been suggested that Jumba la Mtwana could have been a meeting place for pilgrims on their way to Mecca. The site is one of Kenya's least-known sites and has only fairly recently been excavated. It is now run by the National Museums of Kenya. Within the site, which is spread over several hectares, there are three mosques, a number of tombs and eight houses. You will notice that architecturally they look little different from the houses of today in the area. This is due to it being such a successful design, there has been no need to change it. The people appear to have been very concerned with ablutions for there are many remains showing evidence of cisterns, water jars, latrines and other washing and toilet facilities. Building with coral rag (broken pieces of coral) was something reserved for the more privileged members of the community, and it is their houses that have survived. Those that belonged to the poorer people would have been built of mud and thatch.

Kikambala Beach → *Phone code: 041.*

Beyond Mtwapa, and 27 km north of Mombasa, the last feasible beach to be reached from Mombasa on a day trip is Kikambala Beach. The turn-off is 8 km north of Mtwapa and the beach is 3 km from the main road. Backed by palms and clutches of thick forest, this is an 11-km long stretch of reef-protected white beach where the sand is so fine in places it squeaks underfoot. There are only a few resorts here, making it much less busy than the strip immediately north of Mombasa. In fact this is the location of the Israeli-managed Paradise Hotel that was bombed by terrorists in 2002, and it's never really recovered from the subsequent tourist slump. If you go for an isolated walk you may notice shells of abandoned once-fashionable holiday cottages with emerald moss growing on the interior walls. Nevertheless, **Sun 'n' Sand** remains popular and is one of the largest resorts on the north coast. The disadvantage here is that it's very flat in this area, which means the sea goes out for nearly a kilometre so swimming is only feasible at high tide and it's not the best destination for watersports. On either side of the road for about 40 km beyond Kikambala lie vast sisal estates.

Kilifi → *Phone code: 041.*

The town of Kilifi is situated to the north of the Kilifi Creek, 60 km north of Mombasa, while Mnarani village is to the south. In the time of the Portuguese, the main town was located to the south of the creek at Mnarani. This popular boating and sailing centre is in an absolutely glorious location – the shore slopes steeply down to the water's edge and the view from the bridge is spectacular. The town has an interesting mix of people with quite a number of resident expatriates. The main industry in the town is the cashew nut factory which employs about 1500 people. To the south there are the Mnarani Ruins. It is an easy-going town with an attractive beach, which is fairly untroubled by the hassle of beach boys associated with some of the beaches closer to Mombasa.

Mnarani Ruins ① *www.museums.or.ke, 0930-1800, US$7.50, children (under 18) US$3.* These were first excavated in the 1950s and it was the place of one of the ancient Swahili city-states that are found along this coast. It is believed that the town was inhabited from the latter half of the 14th century until about the early 17th century, when it was ransacked and destroyed by a group of Galla tribesmen. The inhabitants of the town are thought to have locked themselves into the Great Mosque as they were attacked.

The ruins include one of the deepest wells (70 m) along the coast, two mosques, part of the town wall and city gates and a group of tombs including a pillar tomb decorated with engravings of a wealthy sharif. Note the tomb of the doctor, which is easily the most ornate. At the ruins of the larger or **Great Mosque** can be seen the *mihrab* (which points towards Mecca) surrounded by carved inscriptions. There are many niches in the walls. To the left of the entrance, the smaller mosque is believed to date from the 16th century. There is a huge baobab tree nearby with a circumference of over 15 m. The ruins are best known for the inscriptions carved into them – many of them remaining untranslated. However, in general they are much smaller and less impressive than the ones at Gedi.

To get to the ruins, turn left off the main road to the south of the creek (signposted Mnarani Ruins) and go through Mnarani village. Turn right when you reach the tarmacked road and stop when you can see the creek. There is a signposted path to the left, and the ruins are a few hundred metres down this path and then a climb of about 100 steps. You also get a wonderful view of the creek from the ruins.

Arabuko-Sokoke Forest Reserve

① *The main gate is on the Malindi Rd on the left if heading from Mombasa, 1.5 km before the turnoff to Watamu and Gedi, T042-32462, sokoke@africaonline.co.ke, open 0630-1800, US$25, children US$10.*

Don't expect tropical rainforest as you approach the Arabuko-Sokoke Forest Reserve – from the road the only discernible difference is that the scrub disappears and the trees are closer together. The forest runs for about 40 km north from Kilifi and is 20 km wide at its widest point. It is home to many species of rare bird and is the most important bird-conservation project in Kenya. There are over 40 km of rough driving tracks and a network of walking paths to explore and well-trained and knowledgeable local guides are available to take visitors on educational walks. A well-equipped visitor centre is open daily for information.

Over 260 species of bird have been identified in the forest, and Clarke's weaver is endemic to this area: the 16-cm Sokoke Scops owl is only found here and in a small area in eastern Tanzania, in the Usambara Mountains. The reserve also contains rare species of amphibian, butterfly and plant. It is said to be the largest-surviving stretch of coastal forest in East Africa and covers an area of 400 sq km. The forest is home to rare mammals too, such as the very small Zanzibar duiker (only 35 cm high and usually seen in pairs), the Sokoke bushy-tailed mongoose and the rare golden-rumped elephant shrew. There are four endemic plant species and five endemic butterfly species. The forest was gazetted as a Forest Reserve in 1943 and managed by the Forest Department until 1991, when the Kenya Wildlife Service became a partner in its management and opened it up for tourists. Kenya Forest Research Institute and the National Museums of Kenya joined the management team more recently and in recent years projects such as butterfly pupae production and bee keeping have been started in an effort to help local people make a legitimate living from the forest. Local farmers harvest butterfly pupae, for sale to the Kipepeo project in Gede, and for live export to overseas exhibitions. Efforts to prevent the forest being cut down completely are being made, but the constant needs for fuel and land in a country where the population is increasing so rapidly makes this difficult.

Mida Creek

There is good birdwatching at Mida Creek, which covers 32 sq km of tidal inlet that stretches inland for about 6 km, and it is a key stopover site for migrating birds. It offers the ideal resting and feeding location for birds migrating from Europe, Asia and the Middle East to eastern and southern Africa. The birds refuel on the variety of invertebrate food items buried in the muddy sandflats at low tide and roost on the exposed sandbanks and on the mangroves at high tide. Young corals and fish also start their lives in these nutrient-rich waters, before the tides sweep them into the Indian Ocean. To reach the head of the creek, leave the Mombasa–Malindi road opposite the entrance to the Arabuko-Sokoke Forest and make your way down to the creek's shores. The creek is composed of extensive mudflats and mangrove forests that attract a wide variety of flora and fauna. The best time for birdwatching is the incoming tide, when all creatures are busy feeding. A telescope is very useful. You are likely to see crab plovers with their distinctive crab-crunching bills, curlews, sandpipers, stints, terns, spoonbills and flamingos. There is a suspended walkway that leads 260 m through a progression of mangrove species and a bird hide here. You can also visit by boat on organized excursions from the resorts.

Watamu

Watamu Village → *Phone code: 042.*

In recent years this small fishing village has been seeing some fairly rapid tourist development and is certainly feeling the impact. The atmosphere is mixed, but Watamu still maintains quite a lot of traditional village charm and remains reasonably hassle free, despite the proximity of the tourist hotels. The village has several small supermarkets, a number of curio and souvenir dealers, a butchers, fishmongers and a post office. Watamu is known for its spectacular coral reef, and the coast splits into three bays: Watamu, Blue Lagoon and Turtle Bay, divided by eroded rocky headlands. Each bay becomes a broad white strand at low tide, and it is possible to walk across to the small offshore islands. Like the southern resorts, Watamu is inundated with seaweed at certain times, but the sand is

Turtle watch

Watamu Turtle Watch was formed in 1997 to continue and further develop the marine turtle conservation efforts of a local naturalist Barbara Simpson, which she had been undertaking in the area since the 1970s. Watamu has a small but nationally important nesting population of sea turtles, with 60 nests a year. There is a nest protection programme, which works in cooperation with local people and Kenya Wildlife Services to protect all nests laid on Watamu and Malindi beaches. Daily patrols check for nesting turtles and tracks in the sand that indicate new nests. Nests are allowed to incubate in situ unless they have been laid in an area threatened by sea wash, in which case they are carefully relocated to a safe area. Watamu Turtle Watch is also involved in a project to encourage fishermen to release, rather than slaughter, turtles that get accidentally caught in their fishing gears. For more information about visit www.watamu turtles.com. There are placements on offer for volunteers.

usually clear from December to April. Most resorts are south of Watamu, on the road that runs down to the Kenya Wildlife Services HQ. The setting is attractive, and Turtle Bay is quite good for snorkelling (but watch out for speed boats ferrying fishermen to the large game boats). The water is much clearer here than at Malindi during the wet season. The most exciting way to the reef, 2 km offshore, is to go in a glass-bottomed boat, and at low tide, and especially Spring low tide, a number of eroded corals protrude from the surface, which resemble giant Swiss cheeses. Due to the high concentration of plankton in the sea around Watamu, the marine life is superb and it's also an excellent place for scuba-diving. In particular manta rays and whale sharks are common. Watamu is also a good place to hire bikes as an alternative way of exploring the surrounding area, including the Gedi Ruins. There are a number of shops in the village, with reasonable rates.

Bio-Ken Snake Farm → *Phone code: 042.*
ⓘ *T042-32303, www.bio-ken.com, daily 0900-1200 and 1400-1700, US$10.*
Some 3 km north of the village is a research centre primarily dealing with reptiles, especially snakes and snake-bite venom. Bio-Ken is a registered international advisor on the handling of snake-bite victims and holds snake-bite seminars attended by experts from all over the world. There are over 200 snakes at the farm and a variety of species. Bio-Ken also offers a free 'remove-a-snake' service for people in the Watamu area. Any snakes removed from a property are relocated or brought back to the farm depending on the species. It also runs a snake-spotting day safari with a picnic lunch for visitors to show snakes and reptiles in their natural habitat. The project was established by the late James Ashe, who was appointed Curator of Herpetology at the National Museum of Kenya in Nairobi in 1964. There are about 127 different snake species in Kenya. Of these only 18 have caused human fatalities and only another 6 could kill. Another 10 could cause a lot of pain and the remaining 93 or so are non-venomous and not dangerous.

Watamu Marine Park → *Phone code: 042.*

ⓘ *www.kws.go.ke, US$20, children US$10.*

Along this coast close to Watamu village there is an excellent marine park that has been made a total exclusion zone. Obviously this change of status met with mixed feelings by some fishermen, but they seem to have adapted well, and the influx of tourists has increased the income of the village. The park headquarters are some way south of Watamu at the end of the peninsula that guards the entrance to the creek. Unfortunately the road goes a little inland, hiding views of the sea. The park covers 30 km of coastline, with a fringing reef along its entirety, as well as numerous patch reefs. The fringing reef forms several lagoons, some of which are rich in coral and fish species, while part of the beach within the park is a key turtle-nesting ground. It also encompasses Mida Creek, a diverse and rich ecosystem consisting of mangroves, coral, crustacea, fish and turtles. There are approximately 700 species of fish in the marine park and there are estimated to be over 100 species of stony coral. You go out in a glass-bottomed boat to the protected area and some of the hundreds of fishes come to the boat to be fed. The boats may seem rather expensive but really are well worth it. Trips can be arranged at any of the resorts, or else at the entrance to the actual park. You can also swim or snorkel amongst the fish, which is a wonderful experience and there are lots of shells and live corals that are a splendid range of colours. The water temperature ranges from 20-30°C. If you are short of time, try the islands just offshore from **Hemingways**.

Gedi Ruins

ⓘ *www.museums.or.ke, 0930-1800, US$7.50, children US$3.60. If you come by matatu you will have to walk the last 1 km.*

The Gedi Ruins are about 4 km north of Watamu and are signposted from the village of Gedi. This is one of Kenya's most important archaeological sites and is believed to contain the ruins of a city that once had a population of about 2500. It was populated in the latter half of the 13th century, and the size of some of the buildings, in particular the mosque, suggests that this was a fairly wealthy town for some time. However, it is not mentioned in any Arabic or Swahili writings and was apparently unknown to the Portuguese although they maintained a strong presence in Malindi just 15 km away. It is believed that this was because it was set away from the sea, deep in the forest. Possibly as a result of an attack from marauding tribesmen of the Oromo or Galla tribe, the city was abandoned at some time during the 16th century. Lack of water may have also been a contributing factor as wells over 50-m deep dried out. It was later reinhabited but never regained the economic position that it once had held. It was finally abandoned in the early 17th century and the ruins were rediscovered in 1884. The site was declared a national monument in 1948 and has been excavated since then. It has been well preserved.

There is a beautifully designed **museum** that includes a restaurant and library. Visitors are made to feel welcome, you can buy a guidebook and map of the site at the entrance gate and there are also informative guides.

The site was originally surrounded by an inner and outer wall (surprisingly thin). The most interesting buildings and features are concentrated around the entrance gate, although there are others. Most that remain are within the inner wall although there are some between the two walls. Coral rag and lime were used in all the buildings and some had decorations carved into the wall plaster. You can still see the remains of the bathrooms – complete with deep bath, basin and squat toilet. There are a large number of wells in the site, some exceptionally deep. The main buildings that remain are a sultan's palace, a mosque and a number of houses and tombs, a water system and a prison. Other finds include pieces of Chinese porcelain from the Ming Dynasty, beads from India and stoneware from Persia – some are displayed in the museum, others in Fort Jesus, Mombasa.

The **palace** can be entered through a rather grand arched doorway, which brings you into the reception court and then a hall. This is the most impressive building on the site. Off this hall there are a number of smaller rooms – including the bathrooms. You can also see the remains of the kitchen area that contains a small well.

The **Great Mosque** probably dates from the mid-15th century, and is the largest of the seven on this site. It is believed that substantial rebuilding was undertaken more recently. The *mihrab*, which indicates the direction of Mecca, was built of stone (rather than wood) and has survived well. As you leave, note the carved spearhead above the northeast doorway.

A great deal of trade seems to have been established here – silk and porcelain were exchanged for skins and, most importantly, ivory. China was keen to exploit this market and in 1414 a giraffe was given to the Chinese Emperor and shipped from Malindi. It apparently survived the trip. There was also trade with European countries and a Venetian glass bead has been found here too.

In all there are 14 houses on the complex that have so far been excavated. Each one is named after something that was found at its site – for example House of Scissors, House of Ivory Box. There is also one named after a picture of a *dhow* that is on the wall. In the houses you will again be able to see the old-style bathrooms. Deep pits were dug for sewage, capped when full and then used for fertilizer. Such techniques are still used in the Old Town district in Malindi.

The tombs are located to the right of the entrance gate and one of them is of particular interest to archaeologists as it actually has a date engraved on it – the Islamic year 802 which is equal to the year AD 1399. This is known as the Date Tomb and has enabled other parts of the site to be dated with more accuracy. There is also a tomb with a design that is common along the Swahili Coast – that of a fluted pillar. Pillar tombs are found all along the coast and were used for men with position and influence.

The site is in very pleasant surroundings – it is green and shady but can get very hot (cool drinks are available at the entrance). There are a spectacular variety of trees including combretum, tamarind, baobab, wild ficus and sterculia, a smooth-barked tree inhabited by palm nut vultures and monkeys because snakes cannot climb up the trunk. You may hear a buzzing noise. This is an insect that lives only for three or four days until it literally blows itself to pieces! There are usually monkeys in the trees above that are filled with the noise of many different types of birds.

It is in fact also a wildlife sanctuary and is home to the magnificent, and now sadly rare, black and white colobus monkey. This monkey has suffered at the hands of poachers for their splendid coats but a few remain and you may see some here. Also in the sanctuary are the golden-rumped elephant shrew (only seen at dawn and dusk) and various birds such as the harrier hawk and palm tree vulture.

Kipepeo Project

ⓘ *Just inside the entrance to the ruins, T042-32380, www.kipepeo.org, 0800-1700, US$1.50.*
This is a community-based butterfly farm established in 1994, which has trained local
farmers living on the edge of the Arabuko-Sokoke Forest Reserve, see page 85, to rear
butterfly pupae for export overseas. It also produces silk cloth and honey from other
insects. The project aims to link forest conservation with income generation for local
communities and at present is the only butterfly farm in Africa of this kind. The project has
led to a large increase in household incomes of those participating in the project and,
since butterflies are shortlived and hard to breed abroad, the market is quite reliable.
Kipepeo is Kiswahili for butterfly.

Malindi → *Phone code: 042. Population: 81,000.*

Malindi is the second largest coastal town in Kenya after Mombasa. It has a pleasant
laid-back atmosphere compared to Mombasa, and retains a village feel, especially along
the shore road. The streets are also cleaner and the people much friendlier. In the narrow
streets of the Old Town are bazaars and shops selling antique furniture and textiles. The
beach is excellent and popular and, although seaweed can be a problem (especially
before the Spring equinox), it is less so than on the beaches around Mombasa. A great
attraction is the Malindi Marine Park, with clear water and brilliantly coloured fish. It is also
one of the few places on the East African coast where the rollers come crashing into the
shore, there is a break in the reef, and it is possible to surf.

Ins and outs

Getting there Malindi Airport ⓘ *T042-31201, www.kenyaairports.com,* is 2.5 km from
the centre of town and is served by four airlines, as well as by chartered planes for safaris.
A taxi to the centre costs about US$7 and the resorts to the south will be about US$12.
There are also bus/*matatu* services from Mombasa daily. ▸▸ See Transport, page 110.

Getting around   You can either organize day trips through the hotels, or else try the public
transport in the way of *tuk-tuks* and *boda bodas*. Both these are surprisingly efficient, cheap
and easy to find in Malindi at any time of day or night. The main parts of town are relatively
safe, even at night, but exercise caution away from the main tourist areas, however, and
take a taxi if going further afield.

Tourist information ⓘ *Lamu Rd, T042-20747, malindi@tourism.go.ke, Mon-Fri 0800-1600.*
Although this tourist office closes out of season, it is relatively helpful and the staff friendly.

Background

The earliest known reference to Malindi is found in Chinese geography in a piece
published in 1060 written by a scholar who died in AD 863. The first accurate description
of the town is believed to have been written by **Prince Abu al-Fida**, who lived from 1273
to 1331. Archaeological evidence supports the theory that the town of Malindi was
founded by Arabs in the 13th century. In any event, locals claim that there was a big
Chinese trading influence. This belief is supported by the fact that many of the local
people still retain traces of Chinese features.

In 1498 **Vasco da Gama**, having rounded the Cape of Good Hope, stopped off at various ports along the coast. At Mombasa he was not made welcome – indeed attempts were made to sink his ships. At Malindi he found a much warmer reception. The good relations between Malindi and the Portuguese continued throughout the 16th century. The town was governed by Arabs, who were the wealthiest group. The wealth came from the trade with India and the supply of agricultural produce grown in the surrounding plantations.

The town went into a period of decline in the 16th century and in 1593 the Portuguese administration was transferred from Malindi to Mombasa. Although Malindi continued to

Malindi south

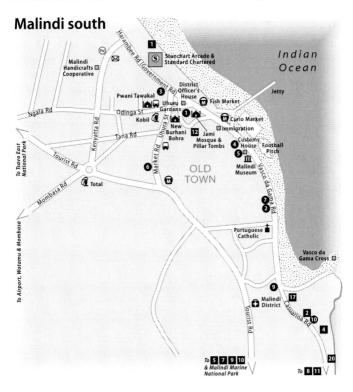

Sleeping 🛏
Coral Key Beach Resort **2**
Dream of Africa **11**
Driftwood Beach Club **4**
Kilili Baharini **5**
Lawfords **1**
Malindi Bandas &
 Campsite (KWS) **10**
Malindi Beach Club **8**
Ozi's B&B **12**

Polcino Oasis Village **9**
Scorpio Villas **17**
Stephanie Sea House **7**
Tropical Beach Resort **20**

Eating 🍴
Baby Marrow **9**
Bahari Fast Food **1**
Baobab Café **2**
I Love Pizza **4**

Malindi Sea Fishing Club **5**
Oasis Gelateria **10**
Old Man & the Sea **7**
Palantine **6**

A viewer's guide

Manta Place This dive site is one of the most distant and it takes about 45 minutes to reach by boat. The chances of seeing manta rays and whale sharks are high, and there are a very large number of moray eels. Depth varies between 15 and 24 m.

Black Coral This location is only suitable for experienced divers. At a depth of 30-40 m is the famous black coral. Its appearance is very unobtrusive and only a few divers recognize it. Another attraction is the blue and golden *cucumaia* or sea cucumber, which is very rare, plus huge basket sponges reaching up to 1.5 m in height. This whole reef is overgrown with whip wire corals.

Shakwe Wreck During a storm in 1990 the 25-m fishing trawler Shakwe capsized and sank. She lies at a depth of only 12 m, almost undamaged on her starboard side, but within a short period of time her hull has become overgrown with small coral heads in which there are many small crabs of different kinds. A shoal of batfish has established its home here, and there are large groupers, stingrays, and octopus. Only the wheelhouse of the wreck is accessible. The wreck is an ideal destination for beginners.

Soldierfish Place This dive site is only suitable for experienced divers due to its depths of 30-40 m. This spot is covered with many soft corals that provide shelter for hundreds of soldier fish, nudibranchs, groupers, stingrays and many other coral fish.

Canyon, Canyon North, Deep Place and Brain Coral These four dive areas are located on the northern reef and drop from 10 to about 27 m from where they turn into sandy bottom. In the Canyon the reef rises again after a 25-m-wide ditch. In this channel, where you sometimes experience a current, reef sharks or large stingrays can be spotted. The Brain Coral is a very old coral hill, now partly collapsing, which hosts a diversity of coral fish. All these dive locations are suitable for beginners.

South Reef, Canyon East, Dolphin Corner and Lion Fish These dive spots are also found on the outer reef and the descents are from 10 to 30 m and then end in sandy ground. As the name suggests, the Lion Fish is inhabited by a large number of various lionfish. At Dolphin Corner you may see dolphins with a bit of luck. On all these dive areas beginners can dive on the reef top.

suffer as Mombasa expanded and took more trade, the town's prosperity did improve during this period and the use of slaves was an important factor. In the first year of resettlement in 1861 there were 1000 slaves working for just 50 Arabs. Malindi had a bad reputation for its treatment of slaves.

The period under the **Imperial British East Africa Company** (IBEAC) began in 1887 when the Company acquired a 50-year lease from the Sultan of Zanzibar for territories in East Africa. The company administered the area, collected taxes and had rights over minerals found. Bell Smith was sent to the town as officer for the Company and he began to lobby for the abolition of the slave trade. From around 1890, slaves who wished and were able to, could buy their freedom. For those who could not, the company offered jobs, or found paid employment. Relatively few took up the opportunity and the process was a gradual one. With the Protectorate government abolishing the status of slavery in

1907, merchandise trade developed, and in the early 20th century the most important exports were rubber, grain, ivory, hides and horns.

During the second half of the British period the foundations were laid for what is now Malindi's most important industry – tourism. The first hotel, **Brady's Palm Beach Hotel**, opened in 1932, and famous visitors included Ernest Hemingway in 1934. In the 1960s, Malindi became a popular place to live for the European population, many of whom were retired farmers from the highlands. The first charter flight from Europe flew to the Kenyan coast in 1972, when there were just five hotels in Malindi, but by 1976 the hotel bed capacity in the town had tripled and hotels had been built at Watamu Beach. Malindi became very popular with Europeans, especially Germans and Italians and the latter are today estimated to own some 3000 properties and businesses in the area such as private villas, restaurants and nightclubs, which have not been altogether welcomed by the local people. As a result it is in Malindi that you will find some of the finest espresso coffee, Parmesan and hams to be found in Kenya, but the combination of these European trappings and the old Swahili town gives Malindi a somewhat Jekyll and Hyde character and may not be everybody's cup of tea. Indeed the Italian attachment to this town that baffles both visitors and locals is so strong that at the height of recent violence in the country over the 2007 elections, the Italians demanded that their government drop the adverse travel advisory against Kenya, and while most of the towns in Kenya were still reeling from the effects of this recent chaos, Malindi had almost fully recovered its tourist industry only three weeks after the skirmishes. On the downside, there are also rumours of a mafia presence in Malindi and in 2004, there was a high-profile drugs bust when Kenyan police seized a consignment of US$6 million worth of cocaine destined for Europe from a private villa and two Italians and five Kenyans were arrested. Additionally, sex tourism in Kenya is at its most acute and brazen in Malindi, which sits very uncomfortably on the traditional Muslim coast.

Sights

Although the history of the town dates back to the 12th century there are few remains of the ancient town. Two remains that are worth seeing, in the oldest part of the town, clustered around the jetty, are the **Jami Mosque** and two striking **Pillar Tombs**. These are thought to date from the 14th century. **Malindi Curios Dealers Associations** have a huge **market** here. Behind the Jami Mosque lies a maze of small streets that form the Old Town district. The oldest surviving buildings are the mosques of which there are nine (including the Jami Mosque) that date from before 1500. Contemporary accounts from the 14th century remark on two-storeyed houses with carved wooden balconies and flat roofs constructed from mangrove poles, coral and zinc mortar. None of these have survived. The smaller dwellings had timber and latticed walls covered with mud and mortar and woven palm frond roofs, called *makuti*. The density of the housing and the materials made old Malindi very venerable to fire, and periodic conflagrations (the most recent in 1965) destroyed all the older dwellings. The mosques survived by virtue of having walls of coral blocks and mortar.

The two buildings of note from the British period are the **District Officers' House** in front of Uhuru Gardens, and the **Customs House** behind the jetty. Both have verandas, and neither is in particularly good repair, but the District Officers' House is a handsome and imposing structure.

Fireworks at Malindi

In 1498 Vasco da Gama, sailing north up the East African coast had met with a hostile reception both in Sofala (now in Mozambique) and Mombasa. He needed to establish good relations with a town at the coast so that he could load fresh water and victuals and engage an experienced mariner to guide his fleet to the Indies. The bales of cotton cloth and strings of beads the fleet had brought with them to trade had proved useless – the coastal people had gold from Sofola, ivory from the interior, silk from the east.

Vasco da Gama decided to present some unusual items to the King of Malindi – a jar of marmalade, a set of decorated porcelain dishes and a candied peach in a silver bowl. He then invited the king and his people to witness a firework display on the shore. The king had a brass throne with a scarlet canopy brought down to the shore and with a court of horn players, flautists and drummers gazed out to the San Gabriel and da Gama's fleet. In quick succession the ship's canons fired shells into the air which burst over the King and his townsfolk on the shore. It was spectacular and exciting, the king was impressed and the Portuguese had an ally for their conquest of the mainland.

There are a couple of monuments that date from the Portuguese period, in particular the **Vasco da Gama Cross**, which is situated on the promontory at the southern end of the bay. It is one of the oldest remaining monuments in Africa and was built in 1498 by the great Portuguese explorer, Vasco da Gama, as a sign of appreciation for the welcome he was given by the Sultan of Malindi, and to assist in navigation. The actual cross is the original and is made of stone from Lisbon. You can reach it by turning down Mnarani Road. The small **Catholic church** close to the cross is also believed to date from the Portuguese period and is thought to be the same one that St Francis Xavier visited in 1542 when he stopped off at Malindi to bury two soldiers on his way to India. It is one of the oldest Catholic churches in Africa still in use today and the walls are original, although the thatched roof has been replaced many times.

Malindi Museum ① *close to the Customs House on Vasco Da Gama Rd, T042-31479, www.museums.or.ke, daily 0930-1800, US$7.50, children US$4.* This is one of Kenya's newest museums housed in an attractive 19th-century former house of an Indian trader. It was opened in 2004 and has a library on the top floor, where you can browse through local books of the region. The building was originally constructed in 1891, and in more recent years it has served as the office for Kenya Wildlife Service and is now a National Monument that was lovingly restored by National Museums of Kenya thanks to funding from the German Embassy. The house is on three floors with cool high rooms, intricate staircases and wooden shutters. There are several very interesting exhibits and everything is very clearly labelled. These include some sacred wooden carved grave posts of the gohu people, which are traditionally used as a link between the living and the dead. Sacrifices are made to them in preparation for harvesting and planting. There are a few boards about Vasco de Gama and his arrival on the coast in the 15th century, and a room of posters dedicated to 'Discover Islam' with information about how Muslim men and women live their lives. On the ground floor are some interesting early photographs of Mombasa, with corresponding modern photos on what the various areas look like today. Also on display is a strange-looking coelacanth, a prehistoric fish that was once thought to be long extinct, but in recent years a

Baobab trees

These huge trees have enormous girths, which enable them to survive during long dry patches. They live for up to 2000 years. You will see some extremely large ones – at Ukunda there is one with a girth of 22 m, which has been given 'presidential protection' to safeguard it. During droughts people open up the pods and grind the seeds to make what is known as 'hunger flour'.

The legend has it that when God first planted them they kept walking around and would not stay still. So He decided to replant them upside-down which is why they look as if they have the roots sticking up into the air.

few have been found around the coasts of east and southern Africa as well as Indonesia. The massive 1.7 m fish was caught at a depth of about 185 m off the coast of Malindi in 1991 and it has fleshy limb-like fins that move like our arms and legs. Scientists believe it could be a specimen that was part of a chain of creatures that evolved and moved to live on land some 360 million years ago. It was identified as an adult female coelacanth, and amazingly was found to be carrying 17 tennis-ball sized eggs, which would suggest that these rare fish are breeding along the Kenyan coast. There is a football pitch opposite the museum where you can watch teams of teenagers in respective coloured T-shirts play in the late afternoon.

Around Malindi

Malindi Marine National Park

ⓘ *Kenya Wildlife Service headquarters, Causuarina Point, T042-20845, www.kws.org, daily 0600-1800, US$20, children US$10.*

Situated within the Malindi Marine Biosphere Reserve is this small marine national park. Gazetted in 1968 this is an area of only 6 sq km that offers wonderful diving and snorkelling on the coral reefs off Casuarina Point. This park is popular and with good reason. The water is brilliantly clear, and the fish are a dazzling array of colours. There are two main reefs with a sandy section of sea bed dividing them. You can hire all the equipment that you will need and a boat here for around US$15, but it is advisable to check your mask and snorkel before accepting. The fish are very tame as they have been habituated by being fed on bread provided by the boatman. If you see any shells be sure to leave them there for the next visitor – the shell population has suffered very severely from the increase in tourism. Try and go at low tide as the calmer the sea, the better; also be sure to take some sort of footwear that you can wear in the water. You may also be taken to one of the sand bars just off the reef so take plenty of sun protection. Most of the resorts organize this excursion, many of which seem to have arrangements with local glass-bottomed boat owners, as does the Kenya Wildlife Services headquarters.

Tana River National Primate Reserve

ⓘ *T046-2035, www.kws.org, daily 0600-1800, US$20, children US$10.*

Situated 120 km north of Malindi on the Tana River between Hola and Garsen, the Tana River National Primate Reserve (TRNPR) is a highly diversified riverine forest that has at least seven different types of primate. It was gazetted in 1976 to protect the lower Tana

Swahili culture

The coastal region is the centre of this distinct and ancient civilization. The Swahili are not a tribe as such – they are joined together by culture and language – Kiswahili – which is the most widely spoken language in East Africa. It is one of the Bantu languages and was originally most important as a trading language. It contains words derived from Arabic and Indian as well as English and Portuguese.

The Swahili civilization emerged from the meeting of East Africa, Islam, the classical world and eastern civilizations. Traders, as well as immigrants, from Asia and Arabia have had a gradual influence on the coast, shaping society, religion, language as well as literature and architecture. These traders arrived at the ports of the east coast by the northeast monsoon winds, which occur in March and April (the Kaskazi wind) and left around September on the southerly wind (the Kusi wind). Inevitably some stayed or were left behind and there was intermarriage between the immigrants and the indigenous people.

Slavery was important to the coastal region and was not entirely an alien phenomenon. Long before slaves were being rounded up from the interior and shipped overseas, there was an important although rather different 'slave trade'. This involved a family 'lending' a member of the family (usually a child) to another richer family or trader in exchange for food and other goods. That child would then live with the family and work for them – essentially as a slave – until the debt had been paid off. However, as with bonded child labourers in India today, the rates of interest demanded often ensured that the debt could never be paid off and the person would remain effectively a slave. Later slavery became an important part of trade and commerce and the old system was replaced with something much more direct. Many slaves were rounded up from the interior (some of them 'sold' by tribal chiefs and village elders) and taken to the coast. Here they would either be sold overseas to Arabia via Zanzibar or put to work on the plantations that were found all along the coast. Successive measures by the British formally ended the slave trade by 1907 although it did continue underground for many years. When slaves were released they were gradually absorbed into the Swahili culture, but when their history was known it was almost impossible to be rid of the stigma associated with being a slave.

riverine forests and two highly endangered primates, the crested mangabey and the Tana River red colobus monkey and this is the sole habitat of these endangered primates. A number of other animals roam here including elephant, hippo, baboon, gazelle, duiker, lesser kudu, oryx, river hog, giraffe, lion, waterbuck, bush squirrel and crocodile. The TRNPR is located on the lower reaches of the meandering course of the Tana River, covering an area of 171 km of forest, dry woodland and savanna habitat on the east and west of the river. The forest here is of high diversity with nearly 300 tree species recorded. There is a research station for study of the primates. It is possible to go boating down the swirling Tana River. This reserve has been under threat by human demands for its resources. Clearing and cultivation have been problematic, along with the damage resulting from the pastoralists bringing their animals here for water.

The reserve is accessible via the Malindi–Garissa road. There are buses running between Lamu and Garissa, and some of them detour to Mnazini village just to the south of the reserve, from where it is possible to walk north along the river (there is a small boat ferry just before Baomo Village). However, most people visit as guests of the **Delta Dunes Camp**, the upmarket lodge on the Tana River, see Sleeping, page 104.

To the Lamu Archipelago

After leaving Malindi you cross the Sabaki River, and then the turning for the village of **Mambrui**. This village is believed to be about 600 years old and all that remains of the ancient Arab City is a mosque, a Koran school and a pillar tomb, which has insets of Ming porcelain. Further on you will eventually pass **Garsen**, a small town at the crossing of the Tana River where you can get petrol and drinks. Just south of Garsen on the Tana River there is a **Birdlife Sanctuary**, home to many herons. From here the road turns back towards the coast and Witu, another small old town. As you drive in this area you may see people of the Orma tribe as well as Somalis, for this is getting close to the border. Both groups are pastoralists, and you will see the cattle that represent their wealth. Finally, about five hours after leaving Malindi, you will get to **Mokowe** and you will see the Makanda channel, which separates Lamu from the mainland. Here there is a small café and if you are in your own vehicle you can park it up here and arrange and pay for an *askari* to look after your car whilst you visit Lamu. This is also where the buses stop.

North coast listings

For Sleeping and Eating price codes and other relevant information, see pages 11-16.

Sleeping

Excluding Easter, low season on the coast is usually 1 Apr-30 Jun, when many of the hotels discount their rates considerably. If you are staying in one of the big hotels then the chances are that you will eat there. If you wish to try other places, you will usually need to have your own transport or else take a taxi.

Nyali, Kenyatta and Bamburi beaches *p82*

There are more than 30 almost back-to-back beach resorts along the 6 km or so strip of coast immediately north of Mombasa. None of them are cheap and budget travellers have a better choice of accommodation south of Mombasa on Diani Beach.

$$$$ Voyager Beach Resort, Nyali Beach, reservations through **Heritage Hotels**, Nairobi, T020-444 6651, www.heritage-east africa.com. Completely renovated in 2007, this is a large resort with over 200 a/c comfortable rooms, some with sea views, set in spacious grounds, although the beach here is at its narrowest at Nyali. **Barakuda Diving** has a base here, and a full range of watersports is on offer including daily *dhow* and glass-bottom boat trips and they have a fully equipped boat for fishing, plus 3 swimming pools, several restaurants and bars and a kids' club. Good all round family resort.

$$$ Bahari Beach Hotel, Nyali Beach, T041-547 2822, www.baharibeach.net. Set in gardens, the 100 rooms are in whitewashed thatched blocks with a/c, balconies or terraces, there's a large pool, but only a narrow beach that is covered at high tide. Fairly good-value rates are all inclusive of buffet meals, sodas and beer, and facilities include watersports, a PADI dive centre and tennis courts.

$$$ Mombasa Beach Hotel, Nyali Beach, reservations, Nairobi T020-244 173, www.safari-hotels.com. Although in a block built in 1969, this is a pleasant hotel, up on a cliff looking over the beach and the sea, fully renovated in 2006. The 152 rooms have a/c and balconies, and it's very well managed with business facilities, tennis courts, 2 swimming pools, 1 of which is down at the beach, watersports, bars and restaurants.

$$$ Neptune Beach Resort, Bamburi Beach, T041-548 5701, www.neptunehotels.com. Newly refurbished in not very classy cane and floral decor this is the sister resort to the Neptune resorts to the south of Mombasa and is a very similar set up with the usual resort facilities such as pool, shops, beauty treatments, hairdresser, kids' club and TV room. Most of the 78 a/c rooms have ocean views. Has a nice informal atmosphere and good value rates are all-inclusive of buffet meals and some drinks.

$$$ Nyali Beach Hotel, Nyali Beach, T041-471 551, www.nyalibeach.co.ke. This opened in 1946 and was the first hotel to be built on the mainland outside of Mombasa though obviously it has been refurbished and extended many times since then. It now has 170 rooms with a/c, minibar, satellite TV and balconies or terraces set in 8 ha of gardens. Facilities include 6 restaurants, 5 bars, nightclub, tennis courts, 2 swimming pools and evening entertainment. A kitesurfing centre is based here and 2 free beginners' scuba lessons are included in the room rates.

$$$ Reef Hotel Kenya, Nyali Beach, T041-471 771, www.reefhotelkenya.com. Recently renovated, the 160 rooms all have a/c, TV and balconies. Facilities include 3 swimming pools, tennis court, jacuzzi, and 3 restaurants serving mediocre buffet meals. There is a lively nightlife here with several bars, a disco and shows and there's a dive centre and they rent out sea kayaks and windsurfers. Fairly ordinary, but

reasonably priced from US$145 for a double including all meals.

$$$ Severin Sea Lodge, Bamburi Beach, T041-548 5001/2, www.severin-kenya.com. This consists of about 180 imaginatively designed *makuti* thatched rondavels all of which are a/c and very comfortable. Facilities include 2 swimming pools, tennis courts, watersports and massages are available. There is a choice of international restaurants including the **Imani Dhow**, which as the name suggests is set in a *dhow* but it's not in the water.

$$$ Traveller's Beach Hotel & Club, Bamburi Beach, T041-548 5121, www.travellers beach.com. A consistently popular resort with lots of fun activities, friendly professional staff and a relaxed holiday atmosphere, although the 128 rooms could do with a refurb. Facilities include a gym, spa, indoor and outdoor games, 4 swimming pools, 1 of which you can swim in to reception, watersports, the excellent **Sher-e-Punjab** Indian restaurant (see under Eating), plus an Italian and buffet restaurants. It also runs the tented camp in the **Mwaluganje Elephant Sanctuary** (see page 66).

$$ Fisherman's Leisure Inn, Nyali Beach, T041-547 1274, www.fishermans.visit-kenya.com. Very clean and great value, 5 mins from the beach by walking through the **Nyali Reef Hotel**, choice of double hotel rooms or 2-bedroom apartments with kitchenette, all with a/c and TV. Also has a decent restaurant,a bar with billiards table, swimming pool and a jacuzzi. Rates start at US$60.

$$ Indiana Beach Apartment Hotel, Bamburi Beach, T041-548 5895, www.indianabeach kenya.com. Unremarkable and simply furnished, the 39 rooms are in a boring white concrete block with balconies, and have a/c, minibar and TV, and some have kitchenettes. But on the plus side there's a pleasant thatched restaurant and bar almost on the beach, a good Indian restaurant, 3 swimming pools, a PADI dive school and a gym.

$$ Kenya Bay Hotel, Bamburi Beach, T041-548 7600, www.kenyabay.com. A friendly, laid back and traditionally built hotel with reception under *makuti* thatch, popular with a number of nationalities, the 106 comfortable a/c rooms are in 3-storey blocks with balconies or terraces, and there are some spacious communal areas with stone floors and Swahili-style furnishings. PADI dive school, jet-skis can be hired, pool, 3 restaurants, 2 bars and a disco, and Masai dancing and acrobats in the evening.

Mtwapa and Shanzu Beach *p83*
Shanzu Beach

With the exception of the **Serena**, the hotels at Shanzu Beach are managed by the UK-based **African Safari Club**, T+44(0)845-345 0014, www.africansafariclub.com, are very similar and are only available for package holidaymakers from the UK. These are the **Coral Beach**, **Vasco de Gama**, **Shanzu** and **Paradise Beach**, and **Flamingo Beach**. They are all in a long line next to each other, guests are free to use facilities at all of them regardless of which one they are staying at and there is a central watersports centre. Rates are all-inclusive and include flights from Gatwick with 2nd and 3rd weeks coming down in price considerably. They also have hotels in Kilifi and Watamu.

$$$$ Serena Beach Hotel & Spa, reservations Nairobi, T020-354 8771, www.serena hotels.com. A very pleasant luxury hotel carefully designed to resemble Swahili architecture with about 120 rooms in double-storey cottages with carved balconies arranged in winding lanes full of lush vegetation. There's a nice Persian water garden with restaurant, ice cream shop and a number of boutiques, a decent-sized pool with swim-up bar, and a wide beach frontage. It's superior to some of the other resorts and popular with a broad range of nationalities.

Kikambala Beach *p84*

These are the last stretch of resorts before you reach Kilifi.

$$$ Sun 'n' Sand Beach Resort, T041-32408, www.sunnsand.info. This is an expansive resort set on 7 ha with 200 m of beach frontage and popular with European package holidaymakers, although the 300 rooms set in 4-storey blocks are well overdue for refurbishment. It has a good range of facilities including 5 restaurants, many bars, nightly entertainment, a business centre and conference facilities, 3 swimming pools, 1 of which has a 100-m slide. Rates are all-inclusive and include 1 pool scuba lesson.

$$$ Le Soleil Beach Club, reservations, Nairobi, T020-203 7784, www.lesoleilkenya.co.ke. The 82 standard and 29 family rooms here are pleasantly furnished and have a/c and TV. Rates are half board, but you can upgrade to all-inclusive from a not unreasonable US$14 per person per day. There's a large pool with swim-up bar, a roof-top sundeck, several restaurants and bars, 1 of which sells seafood by weight and is cooked over a wood-burning grill. Plenty of activities and entertainment.

$$ Boko Boko, off the main road before the village of Kikambala, about 7 km north of the Mtwapa Bridge, www.bokoboko-kenya.de. This is a German/Kenyan enterprise with 3 simple but spacious cottages set in a peaceful verdant patch of jungle that is full of small mammals, butterflies and birds, surrounded by the *shambas* of the local Giriama people. The beach is about a 2.5-km walk or bike ride away, there's a swimming pool, fish pond with some interesting aquatic life, and it's home to 4 giant tortoises. It's also home to the excellent **Porini Seychellois Restaurant**, see under Eating.

Kilifi *p85*

$$$$ Kenya Holiday Villas, reservations UK, T+44 (0)1256-881909, www.kenyaholiday villas.com, has a number of luxury private villas in the Kilifi area, each of a very high standard with Moorish architecture and have staff to cook and clean and their own pool and they can sleep 4-8 people. For families or groups these make a pleasant alternative to the resorts.

$$$$ Kilifi Bay Beach Resort, Coast Rd, about 6 km out of Kilifi, T041-522 511, www.mada hotels.com. Well designed by an Italian and the best place to stay in Kilifi, the complex accommodates guests in 50 thatched cottages with private balconies. Activities include windsurfing, canoes, snorkelling and diving, bicycles can be hired and free massages are on offer. It has well-tended surroundings, located on cliffs with path down to beach, and there are 2 swimming pools, restaurants and bars.

$$$ Baobab Lodge Resort, Coast Rd, about 3 km out of Kilifi, T041-522 570, www.mada hotels.com. Also managed by **Mada Hotels** and much cheaper than the Kilifi Bay (above), located on a bluff with good ocean views but not much of a beach, although there's a large shaded swimming pool with swim-up bar and pleasant tree-filled gardens. The 30 a/c rooms are either in a double-storey block or spacious rondavels, and there are 2 bars and a restaurant, evening entertainment and again bicycles can be hired and free massages are on offer.

$$$ Mnarani Beach Club, south side of Kilifi Creek, reservations South Africa, T+27 (0)12-4251000, www.mddm.co.uk/mnarani. Overlooking Kilifi Creek, this hotel is among the oldest in the country. It has been beautifully restored, with 84 guest bedrooms in natural wood finishes and smaller creek cottages. All rooms have a/c, mosquito nets and phones. It is set in marvellous gardens and has wonderful views, facilities include watersports (sailing, windsurfing and waterskiing), a bar, and restaurant overlooking the creek, a swimming pool, a beauty therapist and evening entertainment. Children are not permitted. The restaurant is open to non guests and is of a very high standard, with superb seafood, excellent atmosphere and speciality nights.

$ Dhows Inn, south side of the creek on the new road leading to the bridge, T041-522 028. Small hotel with rooms set in thatched blocks in the pleasant garden, with bathrooms and mosquito nets, clean and fairly basic but good value, and there is a popular bar and restaurant. However, theft has been a problem here in the past.

Watamu p86

There are a number of resort hotels and unlike further south, a few options for budget accommodation. Again, as an alternative to the resorts, families or groups of friends may want to consider renting a house or cottage, many of which are very nice near the beach and sometimes have a pool. Visit www.discoverwatamu.com under holiday lets. You can eat at all the big hotels, which do various set menus and buffets.

$$$$ Kilulu Island, 3 km south of Watamu, reservations, Germany T+49 (0)40-330 000, www.vladi-private-islands.de. A super luxury villa with 3 elegant bedrooms, a large lounge with satellite TV, private bar, separate dining room, guest bath, covered sun terrace and a private swimming pool with marvellous views of the ocean and private beach. You can arrange all meals with the cook, or dine at one of the nearby hotels. US$2477 per day for 6-8 people all-inclusive, with staff.

$$$$ Hemmingways, about 1 km south of Watamu, T042-32624, www.heming ways.co.ke. A member of the **Small Luxury Hotels of the World** group, this is Watamu's famous fishing club and there's an enormous stuffed marlin over the reception desk. Very stylish a/c rooms, the ones in the new block are exceptionally spacious and have great sea views, while the individually designed suites have additional lounges and dining rooms. The food is very good and overseen by an internationally acclaimed head chef and fishermen can get their catch prepared to their liking. As well as fishing, other water-sports can be arranged and there's a pool and spa, but not much for children to do.

$$$ Aquarius Beach Resort, T042-32069, www.aquariuswatamu.com. Despite the name, not on the beach but a fairly pleasant Italian-run resort with 54 a/c rooms in thatched buildings set around a large swimming pool and tropical gardens and it has an additional restaurant and bar actually on the beach. Italian food, rents out bikes and can arrange deep-sea fishing. Out of high season rates are good value.

$$$ Ocean Sports, next door to Hemmingways, T042-322 88, www.ocean sports.net. This has recently had a complete refurbishment and has a series of thatched cottages set in gardens with sunny blue and white decor, plus a 3-bed self-catering unit sleeping 8, and a very attractive campsite (**$**) with good shared ablutions, a BBQ and tents for hire. There is a large bar and restaurant and all the other usual facilities and an especially nice large wooden deck overlooking the beach, where Sun lunch is a huge buffet, popular with expatriates and particularly good value. Activities include big-game fishing, diving, snorkelling, tennis and squash. Friendly atmosphere and well recommended.

$$$ Turtle Bay Beach Club, just to the south of Ocean Sports, T042-32003, www.turtle bay.co.ke. A good value and fun all-round family all-inclusive resort popular with British guests, with 145 rooms in 4 ha of grounds, plenty of food and drink on offer as well as lots of activities and entertainment, and it looks after guests very well. Facilities include bike rental, tennis, diving, kids' club, Kiswahili lessons, tuition for windsurfing and sailing, and an enormous swimming pool.

$$ Ascot Residence Hotel, T042-32326, www.ascotresidence.com. Not on the beach, but good central location in the village, with comfortable and spacious rooms in white-washed blocks with *makuti* thatched roofs, a bar, tennis courts, pizzeria, grill, and boutique. Civilized and friendly Italian management, and clientele include many retired Italians. The highlight here is the dolphin-shaped swimming pool. Excellent value.

$ Bustani Ya Eden, to the east of Turtle Bay Rd, T042-32262. Just 6 small, very pleasant chalets available at a very good rate for 2 sharing a room, s/c, hot and cold water, fans, 300 m to beach, speciality African and seafood restaurant, a friendly Dutch/Kenyan couple run the place.

$ Marijani Holiday Resort, to the north of the village, T042-32448, www.marijani-holiday-resort.com. An exceptionally friendly Kenyan/German enterprise 100 m from the beach offering spacious rooms with nets, fans, hot water and large 4-poster beds. Some cottages have a kitchen so you can choose bed and breakfast, or self catering, and dinner can be arranged with notice. It's set in lovely well-established gardens, which are home to parrots, tortoises, cats and dogs. Bicycles and surfboards can be rented.

$ Villa Veronica, T042-32083. Among the better of the basic board and lodgings in Watamu, with clean rooms arranged around a shady courtyard, with en suite bathrooms and mosquito nets. It's a friendly family-run place, and the price includes breakfast, but thanks to the bar around the corner, can be noisy and sometimes has power problems.

Malindi *p90, map p91*

Tourism in Malindi is very seasonal, being packed into the periods of European holiday: Jun-Aug, Christmas and New Year and, to a certain extent, Easter. Outside these months you should bargain and can often pay as little as a third of the high-season rate.

There are a clutch of basic local lodgings in the town centre near the bus stand. Most charge little more than US$5 for a bed with or without bathroom but are mostly run-down and pretty grim. They often suffer from having more mosquitoes and being hotter as they do not get the sea breezes. They can also be noisy. Far better to stay near the beach. Most of the large resorts permit day visitors for a fee to use the pool and beach.

$$$$ Dream of Africa, Silversands Beach, 3 km south of Malindi, T042-20444, www.plan hotel.com. On the same property as the **Malindi Beach Club** (below), this super luxury and stylish lodge opened in 2005 and has consistently had good reports, with 35 spacious rooms with a/c, internet, satellite TV and jacuzzis in striking terracotta and white low-rise buildings within an easy stroll to the beach. There's a restaurant, 2 bars, pool, and watersports are available to guests at the **Tropical Beach Resort** (below), which is under the same management.

$$$$ Kilili Baharini, 4 km south of Malindi, T042-20169, www.kililibaharini.com. Exclusive luxury hotel in thatched *banda* style, 27 vast and exquisitely decorated rooms, almost entirely white with some antique furniture, several swimming pools, restaurants, bars, a/c, Italian-run Wellness Centre using expensive Italian products, the food is Italian too. Very stylish.

$$$$ Lawfords, Harambee Rd, T042-21265, www.lawfordsmalindi.com. This was for many years Malindi's most popular hotel that opened in 1936 and closed in 2003, and Ernest Hemmingway was once a guest. In 2006, it reopened as a luxury resort, and now has 60 suites and 10 3-storey villas with very elegant furnishings and works of art on the wall, a/c, Wi-Fi, TV and DVD player and minibars, all set in magnificent gardens full of flowering shrubs and baobab trees. There are 2 superb restaurants serving Mediterranean cuisine, several bars including a whiskey and cigar bar with leather furniture and books, 2 vast swimming pools, 1 in the shape of Africa, and a luxury spa.

$$$$ Malindi Beach Club, Silversands Beach, 3 km south of Malindi, T042-20444,
www.planhotel.com. A very exclusive boutique hotel with 23 beautifully decorated rooms spread across 8 Arab/African style 2-level villas set in marvellous colourful gardens on a private beach. Each has a wide balcony or terrace with day beds, a/c, satellite TV and minibar. There's a romantic restaurant with Moorish arches, 2 bars, 2 swimming pools and again watersports are available at the **Tropical Beach Resort**.

$$$ Coral Key Beach Resort, Casuarina Rd, 2 km south of town, T042-30717, www.coral keymalindi.com. Very attractive layout; the 150 a/c rooms have wide verandas with comfortable furniture. Facilities include 5 swimming pools, tennis, beach bar, restaurant and pizzeria, boutique, and there's a popular disco on Fri night open to all. Italian managed, rates drop significantly in low season.

$$$ Driftwood Beach Club, Casuarina Rd, 3 km south of town, T042-20155, www.drift woodclub.com. 1 of the older hotels in Malindi, this has managed to retain a clubby but informal character. It has a range of a/c rooms, and 2 2-bed cottages that share their own pool and are ideal for 2 families, breakfast is included in the price. Facilities include what is probably the best restaurant in Malindi (the seafood in particular is spectacular), watersports including fishing, diving and windsurfing, and a squash court. Temporary membership is very cheap, so a lot of people drop in to use the facilities and the atmosphere in the pub is friendly, often boozy, and ex-pat orientated.

$$$ Eden Roc, Lamu Rd, T042-20480, www.edenrockenya.com. On a clifftop overlooking the bay in 9 ha of generous grounds containing lily ponds, this is a large hotel that was opened in 1957 by German big-game hunters, although it has been renovated and extended many times since then, and still tends to cater to German package tours. The 150 en suite rooms vary in price depending on whether they have a/c or fans, and if rates are bed and breakfast or half board, but they start at an affordable US$70. It has its own beach, although it's a long walk through the gardens and the sea is 100 m away, plus 4 swimming pools, tennis courts, watersports, open-air disco and business centre.

$$$ Scorpio Villas, Casuarina Rd, 2 km from town, T042-20194, www.scorpiovillas.co.ke. An excellently Italian-managed complex with friendly service, the 25 villas are set in magnificent gardens, 3 swimming pools, a restaurant and bar and the beach is very close. The cottages are furnished with enormous Zanzibar beds and day couches on the terraces and balconies. Rates are bed and breakfast, full board or half board, and drop significantly during low season.

$$$ Stephanie Sea House, Casuarina Point, close to the Kenya Wildlife Service HQ, 6 km south from Malindi, T042-20720, www.stephanieseahouse.com. Run by Italians, with mostly Italian guests, the 50 thatched simply furnished cottages are set in tropical gardens with Lamu-style furnishings, a swimming pool and restaurant, mostly Italian food but once a week a Swahili dinner is held next to the pool, watersports can be arranged.

$$$ Tropical Beach Resort, Casuarina Rd, 3 km south of Malindi, T042-20442, www.plan hotel.com. Originally 2 resorts, now joined as 1 all-inclusive place catering largely for package tours, set in established gardens with lots of *makuti* thatched buildings with over 140 rooms with high standard furnishings in either Swahili-style or with a colonial feel. The good facilities include swimming pool, dive school, watersports centre, bars, buffet restaurant, and a disco on the beach.

$$ Polcino Oasis Village, on Silver Sands Beach, 3 km south of town, T042-31995, www.holidays-kenya.com. Constructed in a 'U' shape with white walls and *makuti* roofs, this has a disco, a large 25-m swimming pool,

60 1- to 3-bed apartments with kitchenettes, plus 24 en suite hotel rooms, an internet café, bar, and restaurant serving seafood, Italian and Indian dishes. Good value for groups or families of 4 when rates work out at about US$20 per person.

$ Lutheran Guest House, north of the town off the Lamu Rd, behind Sabaki Centre, T042-30098. Good value and popular, a range of rooms here including singles and doubles with or without bathroom, and 2 clean self-contained cottages, which have ceiling fans and mosquito nets, and are set in a pretty patch of garden. No alcohol is allowed on the premises.

$ Malindi Bandas and Campsite (KWS), Casuaria Point, adjacent to Malindi Marine Park, the *bandas* must be booked in advance with the warden T042-20845, or **Kenya Wildlife Service**, Nairobi, T020-600 800, www.kws.org. Run by the Kenya Wildlife Service, there are 4 simple *bandas* sleeping 2 with linen, towels and mosquito nets, a camping area with washing block, and a communal cooking area under thatch, which has a stove, fridge, electric kettle, utensils and crockery but you must bring all food. *Bandas* are US$35, while camping is US$5 per person.

$ Ozi's B&B, T042-20218, ozi@swiftmalindi. com. Situated overlooking the beach very close to the jetty, this hotel has a range of 16 rooms with nets and ceiling fans and mostly with shared bathrooms, ask for a front-facing room for ocean views. It is simple, but clean and good value and is one of the most popular of the budget hotels; the price includes a very good breakfast. Downside is you maybe woken during the night by the calls to prayer from the nearby mosque. Special offer is washing 5 items of clothing per day for free!

$ Sabaki River Camp & Cottage, about 8 km north of Malindi, T0722-861 072, www.sabakirivercampandcottage.com. Head north from Malindi, cross the bridge over the river, then immediately turn right to go through the village. Ask here for directions to the home of Rodgers Karabu, which is about 1 km further on. The cottage is on a hill overlooking the mouth of Sabaki River, where thousands of birds, including flamingos, gather, and this region has been earmarked as an important bird site for Kenya. Only 2 rooms, they are large and have en suite bathrooms, no electricity and lanterns are used, basic meals can be arranged for US$12 a day. The campsite is located on a breezy dune under cashew nut trees 150 m from the cottage, washing and drinking water is provided in tanks, shower, flush toilet, fireplace and cooking grill. Rooms cost US$30 and camping costs US$7. Good value in scenic location and very different to the huge resorts.

Tana River National Primate Reserve p95

$$$$ Delta Dunes, reservations T0727-464 763, www.tanadelta.org. This is a small and remote exclusive camp with just 6 large airy cottages built of mangroves, thatch and driftwood situated in groves of indigenous trees on top of dunes with good ocean views. Situated on the estuary of the Tana River it is a 3-hr drive from Malindi. Meals are enjoyed in a mess tent, which is home to a resident family of genet cats. Expeditions down the river to the local villages may be arranged, or a 3-hr excursion to the **Tana River Primate Reserve**. It is expensive but you will be very well looked after and the food is excellent. You can be picked up from the nearby airstrip or from Malindi, and will be taken there by 4WD.

🍴 Eating

You are not restricted to eating at your hotel and there are a number of other places to try, though you will need a car or taxi in the evening. There are also a number of good restaurants in the resorts where non-staying guests are welcome.

Nyali, Kenyatta and Bamburi beaches p82

$$$ Il Covo, between **Traveller's Beach Hotel & Club** and **Kenya Bay Hotel**, Bamburi Beach, T041-548 7481, www.ilcovo.net. Daily 1100-2400. Open until late when it turns into a very popular disco, this is set on 2 storeys with broad wooden decks and good ocean views. There's a variety of cuisine such as the Italian restaurant and pizzeria, a sushi and tepanyaki bar, and it also does seafood and grills and a good choice of cocktails. Offers free transport from/to the local hotels.

$$$ Mvita Grill, Nyali Beach Hotel, Nyali Beach, T041-471 987. Tue-Sun 1900-2400. An established and atmospheric award-winning gourmet restaurant overlooking the beach, with chandeliers and candle-lit tables, and excellent professional service. With a leaning towards seafood, the dishes are delicately presented, sorbet is offered between courses and there's a good wine list.

$$$ Sher-e-Punjab, Traveller's Beach Hotel & Club, Bamburi Beach, T041-493 283. Tue-Sun 1200-1430, 1900-2230. An excellent Indian with an established reputation and relaxed atmosphere, with a long menu of jalfrezi, korma, tikka and biryani dishes and plenty of choices for vegetarians. At Sun lunchtime there's a good-value buffet.

$$ Gold Chopsticks, on the main road close to the entrance of **Haller Wildlife Park**, T041-548 5496. Daily 1100-1430, 1800-2300. Very popular Chinese restaurant with an impressive fountain in the middle of it with especially good seafood dishes including excellent ginger crab and a good range of 'sizzling' dishes. Good service, and refreshing a/c. This is the north-coast branch of the Galaxy Chinese restaurant, which also has branches in Mombasa and on Diani Beach.

$$ Yul's, next to the **Bamburi Beach Hotel**, T041-203 9284. Daily 0900-2300. Popular thatched bar/restaurant under the palms right on the beach with an excellent variety of good food including seafood grilled over charcoal – try the seafood platter or red snapper in garlic butter – plus pizza, giant burgers, salad, steak, Indian curry and imported Italian coffee. They also make their own ice cream, which is drizzled with flavoured sauces and decorated with fresh fruit. Finally, they also offer watersports such as windsurfing and jet skis, so this is a pleasant place to spend an afternoon.

Mtwapa and Shanzu Beach *p83*
$$$ The Moorings Floating Seafood Restaurant, on the north side of Mtwapa Creek to the left of the bridge, T041-548 5045, www.themoorings.co.ke. Tue-Sun 1000-2400. A magical floating wooden deck and a marvellous spot to watch the sun sink over the mangroves and baobab trees along Mtwapa Creek and the tables are atmospherically candlelit after dark. It has a fairly short menu but offers excellently prepared seafood, plus steak, chicken and pasta, and has a well-stocked bar with long cocktail list, and a boutique selling *kikoy* items, accessories, shoes and beachwear.
$$ Trekkers, next to the **Ngomongo Villages**, Shanzu Beach, T041-206 8504. This is an outdoor entertainment complex and restaurant that offers a range of international cuisine and seafood, as well as *nyama choma* that you can watch being grilled, plus a sports bar with an enormous TV screen, and in the evening it turns into an open-air disco with a stage and good lighting. Sun is family day with kids' entertainment like face-painting, popcorn and ice cream.

Kikambala Beach *p84*
$$ Porini Seychellois Restaurant, off the main road before the village of Kikambala, about 7 km north of the Mtwapa Bridge, T0733-728 435, www.porini-kenya.com. Daily 1200-2230. Set in an open-plan thatched building surrounded by a stunning tropical garden (porini means 'bush' in Kiswahili) where giant tortoises roam, this is

a unique restaurant specializing in Seychellois cuisine. The staff wear Seychelles traditional dress and assist diners with washing their hands in clay pots of warm lime water before a feast of spicy grilled meat and chicken, whole fish baked in coconut milk and Creole jumbo prawns, served with fragrant rice and cassava. You can also stay here at the **Boko Boko** cottages (see page 99).

Malindi *p90, map p91*
Most of the restaurants in the hotels are open to non-residents; their set menus and buffets can be good value.
$$$ Baby Marrow, south of town near the hotels. Daily 1100-1400, 1800-2300. Located under the arms of an enormous tree and under a thatched roof, this is very intimate with huge lampshades, terrace and lovely atmosphere, rustic decor with chunky wooden furniture, all lit up at night by delicate lights in the garden out front, very good continental food and service. Recommended.
$$$ La Griglia, at the **Malindi Casino**, Lamu Rd, T042-30878. Upmarket restaurant and cocktail bar at the back of the casino with an attractive gold and maroon decor, outdoor tables under palm trees and Lamu-style furniture. It specializes in Italian food, grills and seafood and there's a good range of gooey chocolate desserts.
$$$ Lorenzo's Restaurant, at the **Mwembe Resort**, west of town, 900 m off the main road, T042-30573. Daily 1900-2230. Set in the grounds of an upmarket Italian timeshare resort, this offers superb Italian cuisine and seafood. The nicely dressed tables with flowers and candles are set under a terracotta roof with open walls overlooking the swimming pool and manmade waterfalls in tropical gardens.
$$$ The Old Man and the Sea, beachfront, north of the Portuguese chapel, T042-31106. Daily 1200-1430, 1900-2300. Very stylish and the best place to eat in town, named after

the Hemmingway book, romantic, set in a lovingly restored low Arabic house with stone seats and arches, only a few tables so reservations are essential, impeccable service and gourmet food. Starters include lobster pâté and smoked sailfish, followed by whole crab, or the recommended Indian Ocean seafood platter.

$$ Baobab Café, T042-31699. Daily 0800-2300. On the sea front with good views, close to the Portuguese church, this has red and white checked tablecloths and friendly staff and a wide ranging menu. You can have breakfast here, snacks and a beer or fruit juice, as well as full meals such as chicken or fish curry, though the quality of the main dishes is inconsistent.

$$ Driftwood Beach Club, Casuarina Rd, 3 km south of town, T042-20155, www.drift woodclub.com. Daily 1230-1430, 1930-2200. This is a nice way to spend a lazy day, you can eat here and for a small fee use the pool and sun loungers. The excellent restaurant has a set menu, an à la carte menu, a Fri night BBQ next to the pool and a great curry buffet at Sun lunchtime and serves snacks at the bar.

$$ I Love Pizza, Vasco da Gama Rd, T042-20672. Daily 1200-1500, 1830-2330. A good-value and established Italian restaurant that has been going since 1982, serving pizza, pasta, seafood dishes and other food. Located in an atmospheric Arab house, lobsters, crabs, giant prawns combine themselves very well with *pappardelle* or spaghetti, rice or *trenette*.

$$ Malindi Sea Fishing Club, beachfront, near the Malindi Museum, T042-30550. Daily 1200-2030. Comfortable club decor including giant stuffed fish on the wall, bar, and excellent views out over the ocean. Serves grills, seafood including a very good prawn curry, plus cheaper burgers and chicken and chips. Members congregate here for lunch and sundowners.

$ Bahari Fast Food Restaurant, close to the Juma Mosque. Popular local café with excellent chapattis, beef stew, good

value, very busy at breakfast and lunch, closed in the evenings.

$ Beer Garden, opposite Galana Centre, north of the shopping centre. Daily 0900-late. Good for snacks like burgers or chicken and chips and plenty of cold beer, this open-air bar is popular in the evenings with a mainly German clientele.

$ Karen Blixen Café, Galana Centre, Lamu Rd. Daily 0800-1800. Imaginatively designed with photos of Karen Blixen and Denys Finch-Hatton on the walls and tables under umbrellas in the courtyard, this popular café sells sandwiches, juices, good Italian coffees, and some light meals at lunchtime.

$ Oasis Gelateria, next door to the **Coral Key Beach Resort**, Silversands Beach. Daily 0800-2300, shorter hours in low season. Snack bar serving sandwiches and basic meals like omelette and chips, good coffee and delicious fresh mango juice, but it's best known for its 40+ flavours of ice cream and is popular with Kenyan families.

$ Palantine, opposite the main market. Local basic canteen open 24 hrs selling Swahili food and chai (tea), and here you can get the likes of *ugali*, omelette and chips, pilau rice, or filling chapattis with *maharagwe* (beans) or *na machicha* (a kind of spinach).

🎝 Bars and clubs

Mombasa to Kilifi *p77*
There are a string of large nightclubs along the north coast, popular with both holidaymakers and locals. These can be fun but men must be prepared to be hounded by prostitutes. Some may close during the week in low season.

Nyali, Kenyatta and Bamburi beaches *p82*
Castaways, next to the **Bamburi Beach Hotel**, Bamburi Beach. Daily 1000-late. A popular laid-back expat-run bar overlooking the beach with pool tables and giant TV screens for crucial sports events, plays

European pop music, and has karaoke every Sat night. The restaurant serves Western dishes and seafood and has good ocean views.

Mamba International Night Club, at the **Mamba Village** behind Nyali Beach, T041-547 5180. Daily 1700-late. This has a rather staggering 13 bars and can hold thousands of people under an enormous conical shaped *makuti* thatched roof. There's a laser show on weekend nights and music is a mixture of rap, reggae, commercial disco and African music and live bands or DJ 'spin-offs' feature on Fri nights.

Pirates Beach Bar, just to the south of **Traveller's Beach Hotel & Club**, Bamburi Beach, T041-548 7119. Daily 1900-late. This is another large venue with 5 bars, dance floor on the beach, pool tables, giant TV screens, and a restaurant serving basic grills and seafood, which offers snacks like burgers and kebabs late at night. There are also some swimming pools and curly water slides here open 0900-1700.

Tembo Disco, on the Mombasa–Malindi road near the entrance of the **Haller Wildlife Park**, T041-548 5074, www.tembo.net. This is another large establishment set in a series of *makuti* thatched buildings with a 24-hr beer garden and *nyama choma* and seafood restaurant and a disco from 2100 to about 0500 if the demand is there, which certainly is in high season. There are 7 bars in total and a pool lounge where regular competitions are held. The newest additions to the complex are a pole-dancing club called **Lollipop** and some 'guest rooms' – use your imagination.

Mtwapa and Shanzu Beach *p83*
Casaurina Nomad, on the Mombasa–Malindi road, 500 m on the right after crossing the Mtwapa bridge, T041-548 7515, www.casaurina.com. This is open 24 hrs and the restaurant serves up English fry-ups from early morning and burgers, steaks, fried chicken, *nyama choma* and snacks later in the

day and night. There's a large open air dance floor with good lighting and mixed music, several bars, pool tables and entertainment such as acrobats or traditional dancing, and it's a popular local venue for events such as talent shows and beauty contests.

Malindi *p90, map p91*
Most of the large resorts have discos and there is also occasionally live music – ask around. There is a particularly dense crop of bars and discos in the northern part of town around the **Galana Shopping Centre** where it's easy enough to walk from one to the next until you find one that suits. They make for a lively night out in high season. See also Eating.

Casino Malindi, Lamu Rd, T042-30878, www.casinomalindi.com. Daily 0900-0500. Fairly upmarket Italian-owned casino with a/c, pleasant cocktail bar and restaurant, with slot machines and gaming tables. Open until 0500 in season. Casino chips can be bought in euro and US$, and it accepts credit cards.

Club 28, near **Eden Roc Hotel**, T042-20480. Daily in season 2200-late. Not for the timid, this small, hot and sweaty club heaves with prostitutes so expect a lot of unwanted attention and has indoor and outdoor bars and a grill for fried chicken and *nyama choma*.

Fermento Disco Bar, Galana Centre, T042-31780. Wed, Fri, Sat out of season, more nights in season if there is the demand. Serves Italian food and grills, and has a very large disco with karaoke and occasional live music, opens at 2200 and things gets underway at about 2300. The rather steep entry fee of US$15 includes the first drink.

Palm Garden, Lamu Rd, T042-20115. Daily 1200-late. You can sit in the shade of thatched *bandas* and the food is adequate – curries, chicken, seafood and so on – and it is very good value. There is also a lively bar, with pool tables that has live music at the weekends but again is notorious as a hangout for prostitutes.

Stardust Club, Lamu Rd, T042-20388. Daily 2100-late. In a big white building opposite the Galana Centre, this starts fairly late in the evenings but is nevertheless very popular and is open until at least 0400 in season, and Sat is the big night. There are 2 dance floors, the outside one has some palm trees in the middle of it and some elevated comfortable lounge areas.

Stars and Garters, opposite Kenya Commercial Bank. Daily 1800-late. Grills, seafood, good coffee and ice cream, thatched informal bar, big screen TV for watching sport, especially English football and gets busy when there is an important match on. Turns into a disco on weekend nights.

⊙ Shopping

Watamu p86
There's a clutch of curio stalls in the village near the mosque and a supermarket called **Mama Lucy's**.

Malindi p90, map p91
Handicrafts
There are numerous craft stalls at the Malindi curio market near the jetty. In general the quality is reasonably good as are the prices – although you must expect to haggle. During the low season when there are not many tourists about, you may pick up some good bargains. There are also a number of quality shops on the roads lining the Uhuru Gardens, and the back streets around here selling very good cloths and items such as bags, clothes and cushions made from *kikoys*. Many of these also sell Swahili antiques, presumably to decorate the Italian villas in the area.

Malindi Handicrafts Cooperative off Kenyatta Rd, T042-30248, www.malindi handicrafts.org. Daily 0830-1800. This was established in 1986 and currently represents over 1500 artists in the region and is now among the largest producers of crafts in Kenya. You can visit a number of workshops behind the shop. There is an excellent selection of crafts here, though there is no bargaining in the shop itself, but you can talk to the carvers themselves and have something custom-made. The cooperative has sponsorship from the EU among other interested parties. They are currently involved in a program that encourages not using rare traditional hardwoods such as ebony for carvings but to instead use fast growing wood from trees such as acacia, palm and mango, and the World Wildlife Federation (WWF) has recently installed an experimental solar-powered kiln at the site to be used to harden these woods, which have a high water content; hence their ability to grow fast.

Shopping centres
Galana Centre has the **Karen Blixen Café**, the **Fremento** nightclub, a bureau de change and a supermarket.

▲ Activities and tours

Nyali, Kenyatta and Bamburi beaches p82
Bike the Coast, based at Mombasa Go-Kart (see below), T041-222 4055, www.bikethe coast.com. This is offers enjoyable off-road scenic guided mountain bike tours around the north coast through local villages and plantations over distances from 20 to 30 km and taking 1½-2½ hrs. Bikes, helmets, gloves and drinking water are provided.

Mombasa Go-Kart, on the Mombasa–Malindi Rd, 12 km north of Mombasa, www.mombasa-gokart.com. Tue-Sun 1600-2200. This is a 500-m bendy floodlit go-kart track. 10 mins cost around US$15.

Nyali Golf and Country Club, across the road from Mamba Village, T041-472 613, www.nyaligolf.co.ke. Some 64 ha of land were set aside for this golf clubs construction, and in 1956 the first 9 holes were completed, with the 2nd 9 completed in 1980. Playing golf here is said to be challenging as the winds influence playing conditions. Green fees are about US$40.

Peponi Divers, Bahari Beach Hotel, Nyali Beach, T0722-412 302, www.peponidivers.ch. Single dives, half- or full-day trips and PADI courses and picks up from all the nearby hotels. English, French and German speaking.
Prosurf Kenya, at Nyali Beach Hotel, Nyali Beach, the **Severin Sea Lodge**, Bamburi Beach and also at the **Serena Beach Hotel & Spa** on Shanzu Beach, T0733-622 882, www.prosurfkenya.com. These are watersports centres with a good range of equipment including canoes and catamarans and can organize diving. The one at Nyali beach has instructors and equipment for both kite and windsurfing, while the others just have windsurfing.

Mtwapa and Shanzu Beach *p83*
Kenya Marineland, about 500 m north of the bridge over Mtwapa Creek, turn right along a dirt track for 1.5 km, T041-548 5248. Here there is a small snake and reptile park, an aquarium and a souvenir shop but most people come here for the daily excursion by *dhow* up the Mtwapa Creek. This is usually booked through the beach resorts and it's touristy, but affords excellent views of the mangrove-lined creek and includes a BBQ lunch and the opportunity for snorkelling. The crew entertain on board with acrobatics and rope climbing and there are some friendly women who do henna tattoos and hair braiding. The *dhow* usually departs about 0930 and is back by about 1600 and costs in the region of US$90 per person. There are also occasional 3-hr sunset cruises.
Vipingo Ridge Golf Club At the time of writing 2 new 18-hole, 72-par golf courses were being built on the north coast on a 162-ha plot near Vipingo, north of the Mtwapa Creek. For progress visit www.vipingoridge.com.

Watamu *p86*
If you happen to be in Watamu in Oct, look out for the Wildman Kenya Triathlon based at the **Turtle Bay Beach Club**. This attracts some

200 participants and is open to amateurs and involves a 1.8-km swim in the ocean, a 68-km bike ride, and a 12-km run with the last 1.5 km along the beach. For more information visit www.wildflowerkenya.com.
Aqua Ventures, at Ocean Sports, T042-32420, www.diveinkenya.com. A PADI Resort centre; single dives start from US$40.
Blue Fin Diving, next to the **Blue Bay Village**, timeshare resort, T042-32099, www.bluefin diving.com. An established operator with 6 diving boats, 3 Bauer air compressors and 100 diving tanks (INT and DIN), which is represented in 21 resorts in Watamu and Malindi. A 4-day PADI Open Water course is US$425, while 2 dives for experienced divers costs US$100.
Hemingways Fishing Centre, Hemingway's Hotel, T042-32624, www.hemingways.co.ke. Organizes deep-sea fishing for big game fish in season, which is usually the beginning of Jul to mid-Apr with Aug being especially good for black marlin. Fully equipped boats cater for 4-6 people.

Malindi *p90, map p91*
Deep-sea fishing
Kingfisher, T042-20123, www.kenyasport fishing.net. Offers 7-hr or 10-hr day deep-sea fishing trips for 2-4 people in one of their 6 fully equipped boats and operates out of the **Malindi Sea Fishing Club**, south of the jetty, which also has a notice board for fishermen.

Golf
Malindi Golf and Country Club, north end of town, right fork off Lamu Rd, T042-20404. Very unusual 11-hole and 15-tee course spread out on 54 ha. Inexpensive daily membership is available, as well as club hire and caddies. Facilities include tennis and squash.

Scuba-diving
Most of the resorts can organize watersports, and **Blue Fin Diving**, is represented at many of them (see Watamu, above).

You can organize shuttles from Mombasa's Moi International Airport to all the North Coast resorts through the resorts themselves or with the taxi companies in the arrivals hall (see page 59).

Kilifi p80

Kilifi is about 50 km from **Mombasa**, and 45 km from **Malindi**. The buses that go between the 2 towns do pick people up here although only if there is space as they may be full. It might be easier to get a *matatu*. **Tana Express** and **Tawfiq** have booking offices near the bus station.

Watamu p86

Watamu is about 50 km north of **Kilifi**, and 3 km off the main road. From Watamu to **Malindi**, the 15 km, takes about 30 mins, there are plenty of *matatus* and it costs about US$1.

Malindi p90, map p91
Air

Malindi Airport is 2.5 km from the centre of town, T042-31201, www.kenyaairports.com, and is served by 4 airlines, and by chartered planes for safaris.

Air Kenya, has 1 daily flight between Malindi and **Nairobi** that departs Nairobi at 1530, arrives in Malindi at 1730, departs at 1745 and arrives in Nairobi at 1855.

Fly 540, has 1-2 daily flights between Malindi and **Nairobi** (1 hr 15 mins) from US$79 1 way, and at least 2 daily flights between Mombasa and Malindi (15 mins) from US$30 1 way.

Kenya Airways, has daily flights between Malindi, Nairobi and Lamu. The flight departs **Nairobi** at 1100, arrives in Malindi at 1215, departs at 1240 and arrives in **Lamu** at 1315. It then departs Lamu at 1340, arrives at Malindi at 1410, and departs for Nairobi at 1440, where it arrives at 1555. It is a popular route so be sure to book well ahead and confirm your seat.

Mombasa Air Safari, has daily flights between Malindi, **Mombasa** and **Lamu**. The flight departs Mombasa at 0800, arrives at Malindi at 0845, departs at 0845 and arrives in Lamu at 0915. On the return leg it departs Lamu at 1700, arrives in Malindi at 1730, departs at 1750, and arrives in Mombasa at 1810.

Airline offices **Air Kenya**, Wilson Airport, Nairobi, T020-605 745, www.airkenya.com. **Fly 540**, Mombasa, T041-343 4822, www.fly540.com. **Kenya Airways**, on Lamu Rd opposite Barclays Bank, T042-20237, at the airport, T042-20192, www.kenya-airways.com. **Mombasa Air Safari**, Moi International Airport, T041-343 3061, www.mombasa airsafari.com.

Bus

There are plenty of buses between Malindi and **Mombasa**. The bus companies all have offices in Malindi around the bus station, but booking is not usually necessary. They mostly leave early in the morning and take about 2½-3 hrs. Non-stop *matatus* are faster, and take under 2 hrs. They leave when full throughout the day.

The bus to **Lamu** takes about 5 hrs and costs about US$8. They leave in the morning between 0800 and 1000. These buses will usually have come from Mombasa. **Pwani Tawakal Bus Company**, T042-31832, http://pwanitawakal.com, is recommended for the **Lamu** service and they have 3 services a day in both directions; the office is opposite the Kobil petrol station near the market. Try and buy the ticket the day before you want to travel to guarantee a seat. The bus will take you to the jetty on the mainland from where you get a ferry across to Lamu (see page 116).

Safety In the 1990s, there were security problems, including fatalities, with armed bandits known locally as *shifta* hijacking and robbing vehicles on the road to Lamu. However there hasn't been an incident for a number of years and these days it is considered safe to travel by bus from Malindi to Lamu, though on the last stretch of road towards Lamu, armed guards hop on the buses.

Tuk-tuks and boda bodas

All over Malindi are cheap *tuk-tuks* that cost no more than US$2 from 1 end of town to the other. There are also plenty of bicycle taxis known as *boda bodas* with a single seat on the back that will cost no more than US$1. There used to be car-hire companies in Malindi, and indeed bicycle hire, but with the introduction of what is excellent public transport, they have become defunct.

❶ Directory

Nyali, Kenyatta and Bamburi beaches *p82*

Banks There are a few shopping centres along the Mombasa–Malindi road between Nyali and Shanzu beaches and each have banks with ATMs. These include the **Planet Centre** and **Nova Centre** near the entrance to Haller Park, the **Ocean View Plaza** just to the north of **Pirates Beach Bar** and there's a **Barclays Bank** close to the entrance of **Traveller's Beach Hotel & Club**.

Kilifi *p85*

Banks There are 2 banks in Kilifi, which are open Mon-Fri 0830-1300 and Sat 0830-1130. The Kenya Commercial Bank has an ATM. Post office Next to the market.

Watamu *p86*

Banks There are no banks in Watamu but the big resorts will change money, although the rate will not be very good. The nearest ATMs are in Malindi.

Malindi *p90, map p91*

Banks There are a number of banks in Malindi. **Barclays** is on the main coastal road (the Lamu road) opposite the (closed) **Blue Marlin Hotel** and is open Mon-Fri 9000-1500, and Sat 0900-1100. It has an ATM. There is also a **Standard Chartered Bank**, just to the south of here. **Kenya Commercial Bank** is also on Lamu Rd on the opposite side to Barclays. There are several forex bureaus in town including one in the **Galana Centre** and **Dollar**, next to the **Standard Chartered Bank**. Immigration Opposite the curio market T042-20149. Internet **Intercommunications**, and **YNet**, both on Lamu Rd, offer email access, as does the post office, but the fastest connection is at the **Book Cafe**, in the FN Centre on Lamu Rd, which also sells a good range of books and serves cold drinks and ice cream. Medical services **Malindi District Hospital**, Tourist St, T042-20490. **Buhani Pharmacy**, Uhuru St, near Uhuru Gardens. Post office Opposite the police station on Kenyatta Rd and is open Mon-Fri 0800-1700, Sat 0900-1200. Tidal information Posted at Customs and Excise, near the jetty.

Contents

Footprint features

Lamu Archipelago

Ins and outs

Getting there

Air Kenya, Fly 540, Kenya Airways, and Mombasa Air Safaris have flights to the **Manda Island airstrip** ⓘ *T042-632 018, www.kenyaairports.com*. Flying to Lamu is a fantastic way to get a handle on the geography of Kenya's coast: tarmacked roads become dirt tracks criss-crossing each other and leading to tiny rural settlements shrouded in palmy forest, sand spits stretch tentacles out into the blue Indian Ocean, and after less than an hour the island of Lamu comes into view. Planes lands on the airstrip on Manda Island, just to the north. This is a delightfully simple airport with just a few benches set under *makuti* thatch for waiting passengers and a hand-drawn luggage trolley that takes bags down to the waiting boats to take you across the Lamu Channel. Some of the more expensive hotels will ferry you and your luggage over from the airstrip, otherwise there is always the motorized ferry and *dhows* to meet the planes at the jetty that will take you across for a few shillings.

The road to Lamu is tarmac to Malindi, a rough track to Garsen then a further 20 km of tarmac after which there is a good graded coral and sand section to Mokowe. Buses to Lamu go fairly regularly but the route is popular so you should book in advance. The trip takes about four to five hours from Malindi and costs US$8. They leave in the morning at between 0800 and 1000, and will have come from Mombasa first with departures approximately two hours earlier, which cost US$10. If possible sit on the left side of the bus (in the shade) and keep your eyes open for wildlife. In previous years, these buses have been targeted by armed robbers, and consequently armed guards ride on the bus for the last few kilometres to Lamu. However, there hasn't been an incident for a number of years and the buses are regarded as safe these days. The bus will take you as far as the jetty at Mokowe on the mainland from where you get a ferry, about 7 km, taking about 40 minutes, across to Lamu. All the bus companies put their passengers on the same boat and there's plenty of help with your luggage. The bus trip to and from Lamu is long, so ensure you have enough water, although every time the buses stop in the tiny settlements along the way, hawkers are waiting to throw hands through the windows with drinks, bananas and other snacks. If you are in your own vehicle it is also possible to park it up at the Mokowe jetty, which is effectively Lamu's nearest car park, but you will have to pay an *askari* to look after your car. ▸▸ See Transport, page 134.

Getting around

There are no vehicles on the island except for the District Commissioner's Land Rover, a tractor owned by the town council and an ambulance at the hospital, and on Manda Island there's a fire engine at the airstrip. Donkeys, *dhows* and bicycles dominate and everywhere is walkable. The two main thoroughfares in Lamu town are the waterfront, also known as Kenyatta Road, and the Main Street, which is one block back from the waterfront, also known as Harambee Avenue. The maze of streets mean that it is easy to get lost; just bear in mind that Harambee Avenue runs parallel to the waterfront and the all the streets leading into town from the shore slope uphill slightly.

Safety

Safety is not a major problem in Lamu, however, there have been a number of incidents over the last few years. Avoid walking around alone after dark in secluded areas of town and don't go to remote parts of the island unless you are with a group. On the beach, stay within shouting distance of other people. The increase in tourism has led to an inevitable rise in the number of touts or 'beach boys'. If they accompany you to your hotel, a substantial 'commission' (30%) will be added to your daily rate. To avoid using their services, try and be firm with them that you don't want their services or carry your own bags to a waterfront restaurant first, have a drink and look for accommodation later. You will have no problem finding a room. Also be aware that while the presence of touts can be annoying and they can be pretty persistent, they also elicit some aggressive attitudes in some visitors, which does not always bode so well among the local people. In short, some travellers complain bitterly about them, while others actually make firm friends and enjoy their additional helpful local knowledge and services (*dhow* trips for example). It's just a case of your personal attitude and patience on how to deal with the touts.

Tourist office
Lamu Tourist Information Centre ① *on the harbour front to the north of the landing jetty, north of the Donkey Sanctuary, T042-633 132, lamu@tourism.go.ke*, and next door the **Lamu Tour Guides Association**. Both have friendly staff, and can organize walking tours of the town and *dhow* trips to islands. Both are closed on Sundays and public holidays. A three-hour walking tour of the town costs in the region of US$20 for one to three people.

Background

The town of Lamu was founded in the 14th century, although there were people living on the island long before this. Throughout the years, and as recently as the 1960s, the island has been a popular hide-out for refugees fleeing the mainland.

The original settlement of Lamu was located to the south of the town, and is said to be marked by Hidabu hill. There was also another settlement between the 13th and 15th centuries to the north of the present town. By the 15th century it was a thriving port, one of the many that dotted the coast of East Africa. However, in 1505 it surrendered to the Portuguese, began paying tributes, and for the next 150 years was subservient to them and to the sultanate of the town of Pate on the nearby island, part of the Omani Dynasty that ruled much of the East African coast.

By the end of the 17th century, Lamu had become a republic ruled by a council of elders called the Yumbe, who were in principle responsible to Oman. In fact the Yumbe were largely able to determine their own affairs, and this period has been called Lamu's Golden Age. It was the period when many of the buildings were constructed and Lamu's celebrated architectural style evolved. The town became a thriving centre of literature and scholarly study and there were a number of poets who lived here. Arts and crafts flourished and trade expanded. The main products exported through Lamu were mangrove poles, ivory, rhino horn, hippo teeth, shark fins, cowrie shells, coconuts, cotton, mangoes, tamarind, *sim sim* (oil), charcoal and cashews. Rivalries between the various trading settlements in the region came to a head when Lamu finally defeated Pate in the battle of Shela in 1813. However, after 1840 Lamu found itself dominated by Zanzibar, which had been developed to become the dominant power along the East African coast. At a local level there were factions and splits within the town's population – in particular rivalries between different clans and other interest groups.

New products were developed for export including *bêche de mer* (a seafood), mats, bags, turtle shell, leather, rubber and sorghum. Despite this, toward the end of the 19th century Lamu began a slow economic decline as Mombasa and Zanzibar took over in importance as trading centres. The end of the slave trade dealt a blow to Lamu as the production of mangrove poles and grains for export depended on slave labour. Additionally, communications between the interior and Mombasa were infinitely better than those with Lamu, especially after the building of the Uganda Railway.

The airstrip on Manda Island was established in the early 1960s and the first visitors as such were white settlers on day tours who reputedly flew in for the day with packed lunches as there were no hotels. Then, as places to stay started to open their doors in the early 1970s, it became known as an exotic, remote and self-contained destination and began to attract hippies and other non-conformists drawn by its undisturbed traditional culture. Since then budget hotels have become popular with backpackers, and today there are also numerous top-end places to stay and some luxury villas to rent. Some people argue that Lamu's popularity and increased tourism will ultimately undermine the unique value system and culture of this Swahili settlement. Indeed there is a sign posted for the benefit of tourists at the airport: "Please remember that Lamu is a conservative Muslim town with a heritage of peace and goodwill. This is our home. Please tread gently here for our children are watching. Please respect this, and enjoy the unique atmosphere of our enduring yet fragile culture". Nevertheless, it cannot be argued that in recent decades the tourist trade has helped improve Lamu's economic prospects greatly.

Lamu Island → *Phone code: 042.*

Lamu Island is 16 km by 7 km, with a third covered by sand dunes. The best beach on the island stretches for 12 km at Shela. Elsewhere, the coast of the island is covered with crawling mangroves attracting a number of birds. It is possible to walk all over the island, and there are many tracks into the interior. Alternatively, *dhows* make the short hop between Lamu Town and Shela and Mantondoni.

Lamu Town

The town dates back to the 14th century although most of the buildings are actually 18th century, built in Lamu's Golden Age. The streets are very narrow, and the buildings on each side are two or three storeys high and as the houses face inwards, privacy is carefully guarded. The streets are set in a rough grid pattern running off the main street called **Harambee Avenue**, which runs parallel to the waterfront and used to open out to the sea, although building from the mid-1800s onwards has cut it off from the quayside. The narrow waterfront stretches the length of the town where cannons still point seaward. Touts offer *dhow* rides and white billowing sails occupy every inch of shoreline. The smaller ones serve as local taxis for Manda or the nearby Shela Beach, and the large ocean-going vessels are stacked high with mangrove poles and sand. Muscled sailors with *kikois* hoisted around their waists heave wooden carts from the docks or slumber on deck amongst charcoal burners and grain sacks.

Carved doors are one of the attractions for which Lamu has become known. This artesanal skill continues to be taught, and at the north end of the harbour you can see them being made in workshops by craftsmen and apprentices. There are over

Lamu's houses

Most of Lamu's houses were built in the 18th century and were constructed out of local materials, with cut coral-rag blocks for the walls, wooden floors supported by mangrove poles and intricately carved shutters for windows. They were traditionally built in an oblong shape around a small open courtyard with two to three storeys and flat roofs covered with *makuti* thatch. It was required that a father give his daughters their own living quarters when they married, so he would add another storey to the house or build an adjoining house. When this was across a street, a bridge would be built between the two houses to allow the women to move between them without being seen from the street. In some of the grander houses the ground floor was occupied by slaves or used as warehouses or workshops, and the family members lived above. To keep them private, the outer walls only had slits for ventilation and all the light came in through the inner courtyard. The main entrance was through a porch with stone seats, a *baraza*, on either side and a wooden carved door, which led into an inner porch and the courtyard. The men of the family would also handle business matters in this area, keeping such things away from the women who resided in the deeper areas of the home. Staircases started at the front door but because of the narrowness of the houses they twisted and turned in many directions before reaching their final destination within the house. Slaves would sleep under the staircases. A *sabule* (guest room) was typically at the top of a staircase, separate from the main family staircase, and had its own bathroom.

In the absence of guests (usually visiting kin or trading partners), the head of the family would often sleep in the *sabule*, particularly when his wife had close female kin staying with her. The living rooms on the main family floor traditionally faced north and towards Mecca and there were no separate rooms as such for sleeping, with beds simply put in curtained alcoves. However, one room was put aside for the husband and wife and the very young children to sleep, and was usually set up a step higher than the rest of the rooms; in some of the grander houses they were very cool and spacious with wall niches to display pieces of pottery. The kitchen was usually on one of the upper floors, firstly so the smoke wouldn't blow into the sleeping or living areas, and secondly so women could prepare food away from visitors. There was also a room that was specifically set aside for childbirth, and was additionally used for the laying out of corpses, and for the seclusion of widows.

20 mosques on the island, but they don't have minarets and mostly they are usually not very grand affairs and some are little different from other buildings. You can usually pick them out by the pile of sandals outside the doors during prayer time. You will need to seek permission before entering to look around.

The oldest mosque in Lamu is believed to be the **Pwani Mosque**, near the fort, which dates back to 1370, and today is just a crumbling ruin though an Arabic inscription can still be seen on one of the walls. The **Jumaa** (or Friday) **Mosque** is at the north end of town and is the second oldest in Lamu, dating from 1511. Then comes the **M'na Lalo Mosque**

(1753), more or less in the centre of town, just a little to the north of the museum and set back from Harambee Avenue. This mosque was built in Lamu's Golden Age, and it was followed by **Muru Mosque** (1821) on Harambee Avenue, **Utukuni Mosque** (1823), well into the interior part of the town, and **Mpya Mosque** (1845), in the town centre. **Mwana Mshamu Mosque** (1855) is in the northwest area of the town; **Sheikh Mohamed bin Ali Mosque** (1875), in the town centre, and the **N'nayaye Mosque** (1880) on the northwest fringe of town. Two mosques have been built in the 20th century, the **Riyadha Mosque** (1901), to the south of the town, which is the main centre for the Maulidi Festival (see box page 123), and the **Bohora Mosque** (1920), which is fairly central, just inland of Harambee Avenue. The **Mwenye Alawi Mosque** (1850) at the north end of Main Street was originally for women, but it has since been taken over by the men. The small Ismaili community did have their own **Ismaili Mosque**, on the Kenyatta Road at the south end of town, but this is now in ruins. Adjacent to the Riyadha Mosque is the **Muslim Academy**, funded by Saudi Arabia, and which attracts students from all over the world.

The excellent **Lamu Museum** ① *Kenyatta Rd, www.museums.or.ke, daily 0930-1800, US$7.50, children (under 18) US$3.60*, is run by the National Museums of Kenya and plays an important role in the conservation of old Lamu. It's set in a beautiful whitewashed house built in 1891, which was where the British colonial administrators lived before Independence. Before that, it had housed Queen Victoria's consul – one Captain Jack Haggard, brother of the more celebrated author of King Solomon's Mines. It has a fine carved wooden door inlaid with brass studs, the ground floor has a good bookshop and the entrance has some photographs of Lamu taken by French photographer Guillain in the period 1846-1849, as well as a large aerial photo of Lamu Town. In a lobby to the right is a Swahili kitchen with pestles and mortars and vermicelli presses. Also on the ground floor are examples of decorative 18th-century *Kidaka* plasterwork, carved Lamu throne chairs with wicker seats and elaborately carved Lamu headboards. To the rear are displays on the archaeological excavations of the Takwa Ruins (see page 132) on Manda Island, and at Siya and Shanga on Pate Island (see page 122). On the first floor, the balcony has a display of large earthenware pottery. The balcony room has photographs and models of seagoing vessels, mostly *dhows*, and the various types and styles in use. Just behind the balcony room is a display of musical instruments used in festivals and celebrations, including drums, cymbals, rattles and leg rattles. The most celebrated exhibits are the two **Siwa horns**. These are in the shape of elephant tusks, with the mouthpiece on the side. The Lamu horn is made of brass, the horn from nearby Pate is of ivory. They date from the 17th century, are elaborately decorated, and were blown on special occasions such as enthronements or weddings. Local tribes are featured in a side room, and there are displays on the **Oroma** from around Witu, Garsen and southwest of Lamu; the **Pokot** from west of the Tana River, and the **Boni** from the north of Lamu. The jewellery includes nose rings, earrings, anklets and necklaces in bead designs and in silver. There are some illustrations of hand and feet painting, in henna, in black and red. The two end rooms are examples of typical Swahili bridal rooms with furniture and dresses on display.

Swahili House Museum ① *inland from the museum, www.museums.or.ke, daily 0930-1800, US$7.50, children (under 18) US$3.60*. This is a traditional and fully restored 18th-century Swahili house with period furniture and, although it's quite small, it is interesting and the guides are great. There are three areas on the main floor, and a centre aisle has beds off to the left and right. The beds are wooden with rope and raffia forming

Alley cat

With their long necks and saucer like eyes, narrow bodies and straight legs, the cats of Lamu are the only cats on earth to bear the same physiques as the cats depicted in Egyptian hieroglyphics. One popular theory suggests that these cats may be the only remaining descendant of a breed of cats that were once found in ancient Egypt and now extinct in North Africa.

Traders may have carried the cats to Lamu on *dhows* hundreds of years ago. Other breeds of cat have since been brought to the island, and as a result the local gene pool has been distilled, yet the distinctive-looking Lamu cats still survive among the winding streets. There is a cat clinic to the north of the Donkey Sanctuary where a resident vet treats injured animals.

the base. The main room has a particularly fine **kikanda** plaster screen on the wall; at one time, all of Lamu's houses were plastered white with this limestone wash as it represented purity. Although historically, when people had slaves in the homes, the areas where the slaves slept weren't plastered. Furnishings include a clock with an octagonal frame and a pointed pendulum case, a style found all along the East African coast. In the kitchen is an *mbuzi* (coconut grinder) and a *fumbu*, a straw implement resembling a large sock, which is used for squeezing the coconut juice from the shredded fruit. There is also a large wooden pestle and mortar, a pasta maker, a water boiler and a flour-grinding stone, as well as other pots and pans. Outside are a well and a garden with frangipani.

The construction of the **Lamu Fort** ① *Harambee Av, www.museums.or.ke, daily 0930-1800, US$7.50, children (under 18) US$3.60*, began in 1813 shortly after Lamu's victory at the Battle of Shela and was completed in 1821. The battle was an attempt by the people of Pate, allied with the Mazrui clan from Oman in Mombasa, to subjugate Lamu, but the attempt failed totally, and victory at Shela signaled the rise of Lamu as the leading power in the archipelago. The fort used to sit on the water's edge, as did Harambee Avenue, but over time another row of houses was built on discarded rubbish, which put the fort 70 m back from the water and the waterfront at where it is today. The construction is of coral blocks, covered with mortar that has a yellowy-orange hue marked by black patches and inside is a central courtyard surrounded by internal walkways and awnings. It is possible to walk round the battlements, and they afford a good view of the nearby area. It initially served as a barracks for a garrison of soldiers sent by the Sultan of Oman to protect Lamu. Their presence must have been protective as merchants built houses nearby that date from the same period. Between 1910 and 1984 it served as a prison both under the colonial and Kenyan governments. Now it has a not very good exhibition on the environment, a shop and a library, plus a pleasant café overlooking the busy square at the entrance, which is the best vantage point to look at the fort given the hefty entrance fee for non-residents. It's generally used as a community hall for the local people.

In the southwest part of town is a fluted **Pillar Tomb**, thought to date from the 14th century, though it's in danger of collapse. It can be reached by going south, turning inland just after the Halwa Shop, towards the Riyadha Mosque, and continuing on.

Another tomb is the **Mwana Hadie Famau Tomb**, a local woman believed to have lived here in the 15th or 16th century. This is situated a little inland from the museum. The tomb had four pillars at the corners with inset porcelain bowls and probably a central pillar as well. Legend has it a hermit took up residence in the hollow interior of the tomb, and became a nuisance by grabbing the ankles of passing women at night-time. The solution was to wall up the tomb while the hermit was not at home.

Behind the fort is the **House of Liwali Sud bin Hamad**, a fine example of Swahili architecture. A Liwali was a governor appointed by the Sultan of Zanzibar. It is still possible to appreciate how it looked when it was a single dwelling, though it is subdivided now.

On Main Street, just next to the **New Star** restaurant, is the site of the offices of the German East Africa Company. Originally the Germans thought that Lamu would make a suitable secure base for their expansion into the interior (much in the same way as the British used Zanzibar). The agreement regarding British and German 'spheres of influence' in 1886 caused the Germans to turn their attention to Bagamoya, although they opened a post office in Lamu in 1888, which closed three years later. The site is now the missable **German Post Office Museum** ⓘ *Harambee Av, daily 0930-1800, small entrance fee*, which has a few faded photographs from the era and not much else. Towards the rear of the town is the **whetstone** for sharpening knives, said to have been imported from Oman as local stone was not suitable.

Donkey Sanctuary, in the northern part of the town close to the waterfront. This is run by the International Donkey Sanctuary ⓘ *based in the UK, http://drupal.thedonkeysanctuary. org.uk*, a charity concerned with the welfare of donkeys worldwide. In 2008 it celebrated its 21st anniversary in Lamu on 4 July – dubbed by one employee as Independence Day for the donkeys of Lamu. There are an estimated 2200 donkeys on the island, which are used in agriculture but also in carrying household provisions and building materials. They generally plod around town on their own and in theory each is owned by someone, although how donkey and owner stay connected is somewhat mystifying. The founder of the trust, Dr Elizabeth Svendsen, first visited Lamu in 1985 while on holiday, and after seeing the poor condition of the working donkeys, established the sanctuary and clinic here in 1987. There is a small enclosure that anyone can visit where sick donkeys receive free care, and the donkeys that roam the town can find fodder and water. It's rather endearing here to see a donkey with a cartoon-like criss-cross bandage somewhere on it covering a minor wound. The twice-yearly de-worming programme on Lamu and the surrounding islands has contributed hugely to the better health of the donkeys, and primitive practices of bleeding a donkey or burning them with hot irons to treat illness is thankfully much reduced. The donkey awards in March/April are organized by the Lamu Donkey Sanctuary in conjunction with the Kenya Society for the Protection and Care of Animals (KSPCA) to promote animal welfare. Prizes are given for the best-cared-for donkey, and a surprising number of local people turn out to proudly parade their well-groomed beasts of burden.

Matondoni Village

This is a village of mud and thatched huts of a few hundred people on the western side of the island, about 8 km from town, where you can see *dhows* being built and repaired on the beach. The easiest way to get there is to hire a *dhow* between a group – you will have to negotiate the price and can expect to pay around US$30-40 for the boat. Alternatively you can hire a donkey – ask at your hotel. A third option is to walk, although you should leave early as it gets very hot. The walk will take a couple of hours and is quite complicated. You want to turn-off the main street roughly opposite **Petley's** and keep walking west inland. Ask for directions from there; you want to keep going in the same direction of the telephone wires which go to Matondoni – if you follow these you should get there eventually.

Shela

Sticking out on the southeastern tip of Lamu, this village is a smaller duplicate of Lamu town and is the upmarket end of the island. It is a tangle of narrow, sandy lanes, tall stone houses, some smaller thatched dwellings, and a spacious square ringed with a few market stalls and small shops. Here in the cool of the evenings the elders gather to talk and women come out to shop. Also look out for boys washing donkeys on the beach at low tide. In the town are a number of old buildings including several wonderfully restored houses that you can rent (at a price). The people of Shela were originally from the island of Manda and speak a dialect of Swahili that is quite different to that spoken in Lamu. The **Friday Mosque** was built in 1829 and is noted for its slender, conical minaret. The 12-km Shela Beach starts a five-minute walk from the village. Shela is just 3 km or a 40-minute walk from Lamu, go down to the end of the harbour and then along the beach. If you don't want to walk you can catch a *dhow* taxi.

Southern shores

The southern shores have the best beach, which begins just to the south of Shela – 12 km of almost deserted white sand that backs onto the sand dunes. As there is no reef the waves get fairly big. Here you can stroll for miles along the deserted shoreline littered with pansy shells, otherwise known as sand dollars, where foamy waves sweep bare feet and cormorants attempt balancing acts on the sea breeze.

Manda Island

This island is just to the north of Lamu and has the airstrip on it. It is very easy to get to and is a popular day trip to see the ruins at Takwa. The island is about the size of Lamu but has only a small permanent population – partly because of a shortage of fresh water and thus cultivable land. About a fifth of the island is made up of sand dunes and sandy flat land with just thorn bushes and palms. Another three fifths of the island are mangrove swamps and muddy creeks. The island is separated from the mainland by the narrow Mkanda Channel and the main port is **Ras Kilimdini**, which is located on the northern side of the island.

Ins and outs

Access to Manda Island and the towns is by way of motorized ferry to the airstrip as well as by *dhow*. However *dhow* is the easiest as it will take you closer to the ruins, otherwise you will have to walk across the island. The *dhow* will cost about US$30-40 for a group of four to five people. See page 134 about organizing a *dhow* from Lamu. It takes about 1½ hours and is dependent on the tides. You may have to wade ashore through the mangrove swamp.

Sights

The **Takwa Ruins** ⓘ *www.museums.or.ke, daily 0930-1800, US$7.50, children (under 18) US$3.60,* are ruins of another ancient Swahili town that is believed to have prospered from the 15th to the 17th centuries, with a population of 2000 to 3000 people. It was abandoned in favour of the town of Shela on Lamu, probably because salt water contaminated most of the town's supplies of fresh water. The ruins consist of the remains of a wall that surrounded the town, about 100 houses, a mosque and a tomb dated from 1683. As with many of the other sites on the coast, the remains include ablution facilities. The houses face north towards Mecca as does the main street. There is a mosque at the end of the street that is thought to have been built on the site of an old tomb. The other feature of the ruins is the pillar tomb, which is situated just outside the town walls. The ruins have been cleared but little excavation has been done here. The creek that Takwa is located on almost cuts the island in half during high tide.

Pate Island

Pate Island is about three times the size of Lamu and located about 20 km to the northeast. Unlike both Lamu and Manda, it does not have a large area taken up by dunes. The island is divided into two parts – indeed it may have once been two islands, but the channel dividing them is so shallow that only the smallest boats can go down it. The land is very low lying and the towns are situated on shallow inlets that can only be reached at high tide. The only deep-water landing point is at **Ras Mtangawanda** in the west of the island, but as it is not a sheltered harbour it has never had a major settlement. Although it is fairly easily accessible it does not receive many visitors.

Ins and outs

To get Pate Island, there's a motorized public ferry that departs usually daily from the Lamu jetty about one hour before high tide – you'll need to check locally when this is. The reason for this is the Mkanda Channel is only accessible by boat at high tide. The ferry not only carries passengers but goods from Lamu to Pate, so it's a long and uncomfortable ride and you may find yourself wedged between boxes and many other people. You will also need plenty of food and water. However they do pull a blue tarpaulin over the boat to protect against the sun. After two to three hours, it stops at the near on deserted Mtangwanda on Pate Island, which is the nearest point to Pate Town. It takes about an hour to walk to Pate Town from here. After a further four to five hours the ferry stops at Faza, and then goes on to Kizingitini, which takes about another hour. Again you'll have to check locally when the ferry returns from these places on its run back to Lamu as times are determined by when it is high tide in the Mkanda Channel. Sometimes much smaller *dhows* link the points on Pate Island but again are dependent on the tides. Generally, when visiting Pate Island the best thing to do is to get off the ferry at Mtangwanda, walk to Pate Town, and then walk through Siyu to Faza from where you will be able to get the ferry back to Lamu. Alternatively a group can organize a *dhow* in Lamu to explore for a few days, but there is nowhere to stay as such though camping is possible if you have a tent.

Pate Town

The town of Pate is only accessible from the sea at the right tide – and you will have to walk from the ferry's landing place at Mtangwanda. It is in the southwest corner of the island and is one of the old Swahili towns that dot the coast. The town shows strong Arabic and Indian influences, and was once most famous for the silk that was produced here. The old stone houses are crumbling and tobacco has been planted amongst the ruins. The main ruins are those of **Nabahani**, which are found just outside the town.

Maulidi

Maulidi is the prophet Mohammed's birthday, and this religious festival has its origins in Egypt from the eighth century. The unique Lamu version is believed to have been developed by Habib Swaleh Jamal Lely, an Arab from the Comoros Islands who came to Lamu in 1866 and established the Riyadha mosque. It attracts pilgrims from Zanzibar, Somalia, Uganda, and the Comoros Islands, when the population of Lamu doubles. Maulidi celebrations take different forms and are normally held in early June. The main religious celebrations take place in and around the Riyadha Mosque, when the central square outside the mosque is partitioned into areas for men and women for traditional dancing accompanied by drumming groups. The best known of these dances is the Goma, which involves lines of men standing together holding long walking sticks known as Bakora. Swaying to the rhythm of the drums, the men extend the sticks forward or interlink them among their drums. More solemn are the all-night prayer vigils, when the townspeople gather around the mosque for group prayer. On the last day of Maulidi, the men gather at the town cemetery and, following prayers, begin a procession into town. The colourful, energetic procession winds along the seafront towards the centre of town, with the crowds singing and dancing.

During the festival there are also a number of sporting events. These include a donkey race along the waterfront, running the length of the town. For the donkey jockeys, victory in this annual race is a much-coveted title. The race attracts most of the townspeople, who gather along the waterfront or anchor offshore in *dhows* to watch the action. Other events include a swimming race, a cross-country race and football matches. There's also a *bao* competition in the large open square in front of Lamu's fort. *Bao* is probably the oldest-known board game in human history, with archaeological evidence suggesting that the game has been played throughout Africa and the Middle East for thousands of years. The game is based around a basic board of four lines of holes, and involves beads, seeds or stones being placed in the holes, and each player then moving these objects around the board by following a simple set order. The winner is the one who places theirs in a set pattern before the other can.

The annual three-day Lamu Cultural Festival usually held at the end of November is a similar (though not religious) event and has gained in popularity since it was established in 2001. Like Maulidi, there are *dhow*, donkey and swimming races plus performances by Taarab musicians, Kiswahili poetry competitions, traditional handicrafts and henna painting are demonstrated and there is a mock Swahili bridal ceremony and a Swahili food bazaar.

Although they have not yet been excavated you should be able to make out the town walls, houses, mosques and tombs.

The age of the town is disputed – the earliest remains that have been found are from the 13th century – although according to some accounts the town dates back to the eighth century. The town was reasonably prosperous up to 1600, although by the time the Portuguese first arrived it had begun to decline. The Portuguese did not have much success and by the 17th century had withdrawn to Mombasa. The final decline of Pate was the war with Lamu. There had been an ongoing dispute between the two islands. Over the years the port at Pate silted up, so Lamu was used instead by the bigger *dhows*, and the tensions increased. The situation reached a climax in 1813 when the army from Pate was defeated at Shela and the town went into a decline from which it has never recovered.

Siyu

The channel that Siyu is sited on is so silted up that only the smallest boats can reach Siyu. It is therefore necessary to approach the town by foot – either from Pate (about 8 km) or from Faza (about 10 km). Unless you are happy to get lost and therefore walk for hours, you would be advised to take a guide, as the route (particularly from Pate) is complicated. Siyu is a stone-built town dating from about the 15th century. It became most well known as a centre for Islamic scholarship and is believed to have been an important cultural centre during the 17th and 18th centuries. At one time is said to have had 30,000 inhabitants. Today there are probably fewer than 4000 people living in the town and the inhabited part of the town is slightly apart from the ancient ruined area. A creek separates the residential area from the **fort**, built by Seyyed Said, believed to date from the mid-19th century when the town was occupied by forces of the Sultan of Zanzibar. The fort has some impressive canons and has been partly renovated. The town is fairly dilapidated and outside the town are coconut plantations. It is a small fishing village that has a thriving crafts industry – you will be able to see leather goods being made, and doors, furniture and jewellery.

About one hour's walk from Siyu there are the **Shanga Ruins**, but they are almost impossible to find without the help of a local guide. Ask around in Siyu for someone to show you the way. There have been excavations in recent years and they show signs of unearthing impressive remains. There are buildings from the 13th and 14th century and many artefacts have been found dating back to the eighth and ninth centuries. There is a pillar tomb, a large mosque, a smaller second mosque, about 130 houses and a palace. The whole town was walled with five access gates and outside the wall is a cemetery containing well over 300 tombs. If you are visiting the islands by *dhow* and would rather not walk you can ask your boatman to take you to Shanga direct.

Faza

Faza is about 18 km from Pate Town, and 10 km northeast of Siyu. Although the town of Faza is believed to date from the 13th century and possibly as early as the eighth century, there is little in the way of ruins left here. Today it's a ramshackle place of mud thatched huts crammed together and piles of rubbish everywhere. In 1990, there was a huge fire that destroyed most of the houses in the town so the huts are the replacement. However, the town is important in that it is the district headquarters of Pate Island and some of the mainland. It therefore has a number of modern facilities that are not found elsewhere on the island – such as post office, school, telephone exchange, a police station (where the police force has nothing to do) and some simple shops and restaurants.

The original town is believed to have been completely destroyed in the 13th century by the nearby town of Pate, rebuilt, and destroyed again in the late 16th century this time by the Portuguese. It was again rebuilt and joined forces with the Portuguese against Pate. However, its significance declined until recently when, being the district headquarters, it resumed its position of importance.

Shela stash

In 1915 a man called Albert Deeming was convicted of the murder of a woman and two children in Melbourne, Australia. He was sentenced to death but before his execution he prepared a document detailing the whereabouts of 50 kilos of gold bars buried on Lamu Island.

In 1901, Deeming had boarded the bullion train from Pretoria to Laurenco-Marques, shot two guards and forced a third to open the bullion compartments. Grabbing as many bars as he could carry he jumped the train and made his way to the coast. At Delgoa Bay, he sailed by *dhow* to Lamu, but locals were suspicious, and he hid the gold at a small European graveyard at Shela, in the grave of William Searle, a British sailor.

Deeming's belongings were eventually returned to his relatives in South Africa, and one of them made a visit to Lamu in 1919, but was unable to locate the grave.

In 1947 the documents passed to a Kenyan farmer, who with a couple of companions travelled to Lamu and found the Shela graveyard. Four graves were marked, but none of them had the name of William Searle. Convinced that this must be the graveyard described by Deeming they began probing the sands. They located a solid object and removed the covering of sand. It was a gravestone with a well-weathered crack. Deeming's instructions were that the gold was in a small wooden box at the head of the grave, at a depth of two feet. Despite extensive excavations they found nothing. They were curious over the fact that an area of sand appeared less compacted than that of its surroundings. Also, when they examined the gravestone, it had some cracks that looked quite recent. They made discreet enquiries in Lamu Town. Four weeks earlier a party of three Australians from Melbourne had visited Lamu and had spent two days at the Shela sand dunes.

Close to where the ferries anchor are the ruins of the **Kunjanja Mosque**. Although no more than a pile of rubble, you can still see some the Mihrab, which points to Mecca and which is a beautiful example with fine carvings. There are some splendid Arabic inscriptions above the entrance. Outside the town there is the tomb of Amir Hamad, the commander of the Sultan of Zanzibar's army who was killed here, in action, in 1844. Faza makes an interesting place to walk around. From Faza you could, if you wanted, walk on to the other villages on the island, all within 40 minutes of Faza: Kisingitini, Bajumwali, Tundwa, and the closest, Nyambogi.

Kiunga Marine National Reserve

In the far northern part of the Kenyan coast, stretching from Boteler Islands to 20 km north of Kiunga, this marine national reserve, opened in 1979, has a reputation for having some of the best coral reefs interspersed with limestone islands in Kenya, but it suffers from being impossibly remote. Sadly, this area has suffered from the problems to the north in Somalia, and so there have been virtually no visitors in recent years. It is 250 sq km from the northeast coastal border of mainland Kenya to the Pate Island. The park has a chain of about 50 calcareous offshore islands and coral reefs running for some 60 km parallel to

New Year's Day dhow race

The people of Lamu are fiercely proud of their maritime tradition and there is an annual *dhow* race on New Year's Day at Shela Beach. This event is an important event on the island, and winning the race is a great honour among *dhow* captains. Like the annual donkey race, it brings the island to life and the shorelines throng with supporters. Individual *dhows* are brightly decorated, and festivities on race day last well into the night. Local captains and their crews compete on a course that tests their skills and prowess, and race day is one of showmanship and celebration. Until recently *dhows* were built entirely without nails – sewn with coconut cord and pegged by wooden dowels. All *dhows* have eyes painted on the bows for protection and to see dangerous rocks. A poignant, well-used Kiswahili proverb, 'You cannot turn the wind, so turn the sail', originates from the sailors of Lamu.

the coastline off the northern most coast of Kenya and adjacent to Dodori and Boni National Reserves on the mainland. Composed of old, eroded coral, the islands mainly lie inland around 2 km offshore and inshore of the fringing reef. They vary in size from a few hundred square metres to 100 ha or more. Leatherback turtles, dugongs and nesting migratory sea birds are to be found here. Dugongs resemble large sea lions and have been almost hunted to extinction, making them one of the rarest sea mammals. They give birth to live pups that suckle on teats situated high on the female's chest wall. They are believed to be the origin of sailor's mermaid sightings as it was thought that they had 'breasts'. The coastal area is made up of scrubland and mangroves surrounded by microscopic marine plants and dugong grass. The coral here is extensive. As you would expect, there is a good variety of marine birds with colonies of various gulls and terns.

Kiwayu Island is located on the far northeast of the Lamu Archipelago and is part of the reserve. The Island itself is 19 km long and roughly 1.5 km wide. There are lots of caves and coves to explore, and there are two villages on the island, **Kiwayu** and **Chandani**. The highlight here is the 10-km-long virgin beach and the spectacular snorkelling on the unspoilt coral reefs. There is an airstrip that serves the two luxury lodges, see page 136, which can also organize *dhow* and speed-boat launches from Lamu.

Dodori and Boni national reserves

Dodori and Boni national reserves are in the far north of the Kenyan coast close to the Somali border. Gazetted in 1976 they cover an area of 2590 sq km. Dodori National Reserve is in Coastal Province and is 877 sq km extending from northeast Lamu District up to Kiunga. It is named after the river ending in the Indian Ocean at Dodori Creek, a breeding place for dugongs. The vegetation consists of mangrove swamp, lowland dry forest, marshy glades and groundwater forest and is bisected by the Dodori River. Dodori Reserve was established to protect an antelope called the Lamu topi, as this area is a major breeding ground. There are also a few elephant, buffalo, giraffe, duikers and lesser kudu in the reserve. In addition the area is rich in birdlife. Pelicans are particularly common here. Boni National Reserve is one of the large, remote parks in the northeast of the country, contiguous with the Somali border down to the coast in Northeastern Province. It is 1340 sq km, and contains the only coastal lowland groundwater forest in Kenya. The diversity of the vegetation consist of coastal and riverine forests, mangroves, swampy grasslands and savannah. Away from the rivers and channels, impenetrable thornbush is scattered with gigantic baobabs. Unfortunately there is little information about what wildlife is in the reserve, and given that it borders Somali, the antelope here may well have been targeted by poachers for meat.

To reach the reserves, from Mokowe opposite Lamu take the road D568 inland and turn right at Bodhei. This track leads to Kiunga, on the northern limit of the Kenyan coast, passing between both reserves. Along the road, at the town of Mangai, a track allows for wildlife observation at both banks of Dodori River. Once in Kiunga, the road to Mkoconi borders the coast and provides access to some waterholes amongst the bush. However, the area is only passable in the dry season. The easiest access is by sea, especially if you wish to watch the sea wildlife at Dodori. You can travel by boat or *dhow* to Dodori Creek and from there sail the channels and mangroves. However, there are no camp sites or facilities at these reserves and given its proximity to the Somali border, most parts of this national reserve have been out of bounds to tourists for a while. If you want to go up here be sure to check with the local authorities and tour agencies before departure.

Lamu archipelago listings

For Sleeping and Eating price codes and other relevant information, see pages 11-16.

🛌 Sleeping

Price varies with the season. Peak periods are Dec and Jan for upmarket travellers, and Jul-Sep for families and budget travellers. At other times, there's plenty of scope for negotiation, especially if you plan to stay for more than 1 or 2 days. If you are planning to stay here for a longer holiday and are in a family or group then it is worth renting a house (with staff). Many are holiday homes of Kenya residents and offer high-quality accommodation at a very modest price. People post details of houses to rent on notice board at the museum or visit www.lamuretreats.com or www.kenya safarihomes.com. At the lower end of the price range, the hotels in Lamu tend to be hot and suffer from frequent problems with the water supply (expect cold buckets), but nevertheless are still mostly housed in traditional and atmospheric old houses.

Lamu Island *p116*
Lamu Town
$$$ Baytil Ajaib, to the west of the Donkey Sanctuary, T042-632 033, www.baytil ajaib.com. A recently and immaculately restored house with 4 spacious en suite rooms, or a group can rent it singularly. With verandas and an open courtyard on each floor supported by gracious columns and arches, where there are comfortable sitting areas with day beds piled with cushions and Swahili and other African artefacts on display. The name means 'House of Wonder' and there are great views over the town and the Lamu Channel. Rates are bed and breakfast or ½ board and you can discuss menus with the chef.

$$$ Lamu House, near the Lamu Social Hall, T042-633 491, www.lamuhouse.com. 2 upmarket houses near the waterfront and the most luxurious place to stay in Lamu Town with 5 beautiful and stylish rooms, each decorated with lattice windows, dressing rooms and private terraces, and a lovely whitewashed courtyard with a refreshing plunge pool and day beds. Rates include breakfast and a free *kikoy*, lunch and dinner are US$25 each and the service is excellent. Can organize day trips or dinner on their *dhow*.

$$$ Lamu Palace Hotel, T042-633 104, islands@africaonline.co.ke. Located on the harbour front at the south end of town, now managed with **Petley's Inn**. Set in an imposing 3-storey block, this has 22 a/c rooms and is very attractively decorated. The pleasant patio restaurant has average and bland buffet set meals, but the à la carte seafood is very good. It's possible to negotiate a better rate off season, Oct-May, and it's one of few places that sells alcohol in Lamu. Friendly and helpful set up and can organize *dhow* excursions.

$$$ Petley's Inn, Kenyatta Rd, reservations through Lamu Palace, above. A historic hotel founded by an Englishman called Percy Petley in 1962 who fell in love with Lamu whilst recovering from a safari accident. The hotel has 11 rooms and a swimming pool on the 1st floor. The rooms are very pleasant, in traditional Swahili style, the 2 front rooms have a private terrace. The restaurant no longer exists, but the 2 bars survive and remain popular, and it's one of the few places that serves chilled beers.

$$$ Stone House Hotel, near the Swahili House Museum, T042-633 544, www.stone househotellamu.com. This is a quiet friendly and good-value option where the small interior coral-walled garden at the entrance provides a nice welcome, and it's one of the best preserved of Lamu's 18th-century houses. It has 10 simple en suite rooms and 4 sharing a bathroom, with Swahili furniture and 4-poster beds, mosquito nets and fans and a reliable source of (cold) water. The small rooftop restaurant has good views and serves seafood and Swahili dishes, as well as cold drinks and fresh juices.

$$$ Wildebeest, T042-632261, www.wilde beeste.com. Several lovely traditional apartments in 2 houses, sleeping between 2-7 people (the floor-level beds are draped with mosquito nets), each has a small kitchen. There are fantastic stone terraces dotted at various levels with comfortable day beds for lounging, steep stone steps around courtyard gardens and, *makuti* roofs. Downstairs is an art shop and gallery. Larger apartments are around US$130, so for groups the cost per person is very reasonable, rates include a house boy.

$$ Amu House, T042-633 420, a few streets behind the **Standard Chartered Bank**. This very central and a charming place, owned by an American woman, is a reworked 18th-century Swahili house with plaster carvings and niches, pretty Swahili furniture and canopy beds, some rooms have a veranda. Breakfast included but other meals are only available on request.

$$ Jannat House, north end of town, near Mwana Mshamu mosque, T042-633 414, www.jannathouse.com. This dates from the 18th century and was built as a merchant's house. The 16 rooms have Swahili furniture, warm (not hot) water and mosquito nets, and it offers Kiswahili language courses. Good food in pleasant garden atmosphere and is one of the few hotels with a swimming pool. Rates are bed and breakfast or ½ board, expect pay in the region of US$80 for a double but this drops considerably in low season.

$$ Kipepeo Guest House, on the waterfront to the north of Lamu House, T042-633 569, www.kipepeo-lamu.com. Opened in 2005, this imposing white 4-storey block run by a German woman has 7 simple but comfortable doubles, with or without tiled bathrooms, and offers some of the best views of the Lamu Channel from the rooftop terrace. You can self-cater in the kitchen or breakfast is available for US$3. Groups can hire a whole floor (with the kitchen) and fit in as many as they like to a maximum of 13 from about US$120.

$$ Sunsail Hotel, on the waterfront near the District Commissioner's Office, T042-632 065, sunsailhotel2004@hotmail.com. 18 double rooms in a fully restored 100-year-old building that was once the sugar depot, with whitewashed walls and an impressive large carved front door. Smart rooms with fans and Lamu beds, tiled bathrooms, restaurant under thatch on the roof with new windows and views of the busy jetty, big discounts during low season, very friendly management.

$ Casuarina Rest House, above the Kenya Airways office near the Lamu Museum, T042-633 123. Another popular budget option in a great location on the waterfront, with 10 clean and spacious rooms, 6 have their own bathroom while 4 have shared bathrooms, mosquito nets and fans in a building that used to be the Police Station and it's well run and friendly. There is a large rooftop area and breakfast is included, and they claim that they do not give commission to touts, so go alone.

$ Hapa Hapa, to the rear of the **Hapa Hapa** restaurant on Main St. Fairly simple but spacious, with clean shared bathroom, some rooms look out over the Lamu Channel, no fans though so ask for one of the top rooms, which catch the sea breezes.

$ Lamu Archipelago Villas, on waterfront at southern end, T042-633 247. Good location, 12 rooms in an imposing white building, some with their own bathrooms, includes breakfast, fans, nets, efficiently run, though rooms are a little grubbier than others in town.

$ Pole Pole, just inland, north end of town, T042-633 344. This is one of the highest buildings in Lamu, with good views from the roof, but is quite run down now. It offers very basic board and lodgings with beds that are falling apart, mosquito nets and fans, some of the 15 rooms have bathrooms with cold water although water cannot be relied upon. Nevertheless cheap from about a negotiable US$8.

$ Yumbe House, near the Swahili House Museum, T/F042-633 101. This is a basic but wonderful hotel full of atmosphere and excellent value and is consistently popular

with backpackers. It's a traditional house of 4 storeys and is airy and spacious, clean, friendly, has a good water supply and the price includes breakfast. The garden courtyard is especially pretty.

$ Yumbe Villa, located near the fort, see Yumbe House, above, for contact details. This is the annex of Yumbe House where you'll stay if that's full and is another traditional house with Zidaka niches in the ground floor walls, and clean and tidy rooms with traditional Lamu beds, mosquito nets, en suite shower and toilet, some have fans and fridges.

Shela p121

In recent years there has been much restoration work going on in Shela (left to its own devices Shela would probably be far more dilapidated than it is today), and there are now some wonderful places to stay. By comparison, Lamu town is definitely the poorer cousin. Some of the houses are now very luxurious and are popular with wealthy Europeans: Princess Caroline of Monaco for example owns a house in Shela.

$$$$ Johori House, reservations through **Kenya Safari Homes**, Nairobi, T020-890 699, www.kenyasafarihomes.com. Another well-restored 18th-century house, sleeping up to 6 on 3 floors, with excellent views. The top floor features a covered rooftop with hammocks and day beds. There is a lovely outside area for al fresco dining, fully equipped kitchen, and staff includes houseboy and cook. Other similar houses for rent in the village are **Kisimani House** and **Mnarani House**, which both sleep 8, and **Jasmine House** which sleeps 7. Rates start from around US$300 per night depending on season but shared among a group they represent good value.

$$$$ Kijani House Hotel, on water's edge between **Peponi's** and Shela Beach, T042-633 235, www.kijani-lamu.com. Here are 10 en suite rooms in a collection of restored old Swahili houses, with fine gardens, traditional furniture, white archways, verandas, 2 small swimming pools, seafood, Swahili dishes, and a touch of Italian cuisine in the Kijani restaurant, excellent standards. Room rates are bed and breakfast, half or full board and include boat transfers from the airport. Offers fishing, snorkelling and guided tours of Lamu town. Closed May-June.

$$$$ Kizingo, T0733-954 770, www.kizingo.com. This is a small peaceful eco lodge situated at the end of Shela Beach with 8 thatched cottages set well apart from each other, with verandas with hammocks and unrivalled sea views. Room rates include all meals as well as afternoon tea with homemade cake and boat transfers from Manda Island. Fine wines from South Africa, Chile and Italy and cocktails are extra. Supports a local turtle conservation project, and activities include visiting the turtles laying their eggs on the beach, fishing, snorkelling, and bird and bush walks or guests can hire bikes to explore the local villages. Closed May-Jun.

$$$$ Shela House, T042-633 419, www.shela house.com. This is a collection of 4 luxury houses in the village: **Shela House**, **Beach House**, **Garden House** and **Palm House**. The decor is very luxurious with lots of dark wood and cream walls, floors and furniture, and each house has 3 staff including a cook and must be booked for a minimum of 3 nights (7 nights in high season). You can self-cater or full-board meals are an additional US$70 per person per day, US$35 for children under 12. **Shela House** (from US$650 per night) is built on 3 floors around an open courtyard, the house well and an ancient gardenia. The entrance hall leads into the courtyard, edged by a *baraza* sitting and eating area, the upper rooms comprise 5 en suite bedrooms, nursery room and a day room and terrace; there are also hammocks on the rooftop. **Beach House** (from US$1300 per night) is a large house with 4 double and 1 triple en suite bedrooms, an infinity, fresh-water swimming pool, bar area and low

comfortable *baraza* seats. Up the 1st flight of stairs is a large dining and living room, leading on to a terrace. **Garden House** (from US$300 per night) has a ground-floor dining and seating area, a double bedroom and a children's twin on the 1st floor and a top-floor master bedroom with a shaded rooftop *baraza* and open terrace with sun beds. **Palm House** (from US$650 per night) is designed around an open courtyard, with 2 doubles and 1 twin bedroom, all en suite with private balconies. There is a panoramic view from the covered rooftop, with a bar, sun beds and *baraza* lounging area.

$$$ Baitil Aman Guesthouse, in the middle of the village, T042-633 022, www.baitil aman.com. Newly opened in 2006, this 18th-century house took over 7 years to restore and now features some particularly fine examples of Zidaka niches in the walls and some splendid carved wooden doors. There are just 8 en suite rooms with mosquito nets, fans and outdoor seating areas. Rates are bed and breakfast, dinner is US$20 extra per person, which is served in the dining room or on Swahili mats on the rooftop terrace. The name means 'House of Peace'.

$$$ Banana House, in the village, 50 m back from the beach, T042-632 044, www.banana house-lamu.com. This is run by a friendly Dutch woman as a holistic place to stay, it offers daily yoga sessions and guests are required to wash their feet in a small pool before entering the house barefooted. There are 6 en suite rooms, plus 1 more for children that shares a bathroom with parents, a 2nd-floor restaurant, attractive sitting areas with hammocks and day beds and 1 lounge area has an interesting wall embedded with hundreds of coloured bottles.

$$$ Fatumu's Tower, in the village, T042-632 213, www.fatumastower.com. Another nicely restored house, this has 5 en suite doubles plus a ground floor 3 bedroom family apartment, furnished in local antiques and fabrics, with several balconies and terraces for relaxing and a small plunge pool with a waterfall in the garden. On the 1st floor is a bright white yoga hall, which lets light in through slit windows, where yoga classes are held in the early evening and massages are available. You can either self-cater, a cook is provided, or lunch and dinner are US$20/25 respectively.

$$$ Peponi's, Shela Beach, T042-633 4213, www.peponi-lamu.com. Facing the channel that runs between Lamu and Manda, this is a really wonderful setting with about 500 m of private beach. The hotel is made up of a series of cottages each with a veranda and full facilities. There is an excellent restaurant (see under Eating, below) as well as a bar. The hotel provides full watersports facilities, probably the best and most extensive on the island and organizes excursions. Very efficiently run and booking well ahead is advised. Closed mid-Apr to end of Jun.

$$$ Shella Royal House, in the village, T0722-698 059, www.shellaroyalhouse.com. Here there are 2 houses, 1 with 3 storeys and 1 with 4 storeys, with 13 spacious and airy rooms, all but 1 are en suite, with traditional furnishings and whitewashed walls, and a lovely roof terrace with day beds for relaxing. Rates are half board and Swahili dinners feature plenty of fish and seafood. They also have a *dhow* for excursions, some tents and can arrange overnight camping trips to the other islands.

$$ Stop Over Guest House, on the beach, reservations through **Lamu Homes**, Nairobi T020-444 7397, www.lamuhomes.com. Newly renovated and locally owned, 5 clean rooms, simply furnished with fans and mosquito nets and have good views of the sea and plenty of sea breezes. The 3 rooms on the 1st floor can be rented as an apartment with access to kitchen facilities on the same floor. On the ground floor is a restaurant serving Swahili dishes, fresh juices, soft drinks and seafood.

$ Shela Bahari Guest House, on the beach, close to Peponi's, T042-632 046. A similar set

up to the nearby **Stop Over** with spacious rooms, big beds, nets, fans, Swahili furniture, the rooms open out on to a broad balcony that is right above the water at high tide, and the ones at the back without a view are cheaper. The top room here is the best and very private with its own balcony and hammock and there's a small restaurant where you can discuss what you want for dinner beforehand.

$ Shela Pwani Guest House, very close to **Peponi's** and the jetty, above the shop selling *kikoys*, T042-633 540. Has 4 double rooms and 1 triple, the top double room is the best, though all have bathrooms (cold water), fans and mosquito nets, set in an old house with some nice traditional plasterwork and well managed. There is a small dining room downstairs, where it is possible to organize meals that include seafood and Swahili dishes and the rooftop terrace has fine views.

Southern shores *p121*

$$$$ Kipungani Explorer, reservations **Heritage Hotels**, Nairobi, T020-444 6651, www.heritage-eastafrica.com. The 1st of Heritage Group's highest standard 'Explorer' resorts, this lodge, with just 14 *makuti* thatched cottages made from local palm leaf mats, is located at the southern tip of Lamu Island. All are extremely spacious and comfortable and each has a veranda. It organizes various excursions and snorkelling trips, and there is a sea-water swimming pool, good restaurant and bar where non-guests can visit for lunch. Boats to get there depart from **Peponi's**. The property has an extremely close bond with the people of neighbouring Kipungani Village, who will show you their ancient boat-building and mat-weaving techniques, or take you fishing or prawn-netting in the remote Dadori Nature Reserve. Rates are full board and include boat transfers from Manda Island. Closed mid-Mar to 1st July.

Other islands
Manda Island p121

There is no fresh water on Manda Island; it is brought over from Lamu daily. Consequently water is used carefully at the lodges and water conservation is encouraged.

$$$$ Manda Bay, T042-633 475, www.manda bay.com. An exclusive resort offering water sports and *dhow* safaris, all the buildings are constructed with local materials in traditional coastal style, with palm-thatch roofs and woven matting covering the floors. 16 spacious and comfortable cottages with their own bathrooms and verandas. Meals, seafood and Italian, are relaxed and casual, served in the dining room, on the beach, or on a *dhow*. Rates are full board and include soft drinks, beer and wine. Closed mid-May to mid-July.

$$$ Diamond Village, T0720-015001, www.diamondbeachvillage.com. Very comfortable and affordable *bandas* on the beach with thatched roofs, 1 for families that sleeps 4-8 people, and the others with a double bed downstairs and a single bed mounted in the roof, each has a front porch and en suite shower and sink. Because of the lack of water, toilets are pit latrines. There is also a rather unique treehouse in the arms of a baobab tree, which has a wooden deck all the way around the trunk. Very good food in the open-air restaurant. A rather special feature of the lodge are the giant clam shells that act as bird baths and attract a colourful array of birds at both dawn and dusk.

$ Camping, is available at a pretty site close to the Takwa Ruins, though there are no facilities and you will need to be completely self sufficient. Bring plenty of water as none is available on the island.

Pate Island p122

Every few years a lodging house opens in Faza, but the lack of visitors forces them to close sooner or later. Private accommodation, though, is easy to find and you can ask around to stay at a family house and people may also approach

you. Again in Siyu it is possible to rent rooms in local houses – there are no formal guesthouses. It's possible you may get offered food by your hosts and other than that there are only basic provisions available from small shops and stalls.

Kiunga Marine National Reserve p125

$$$$ Kiwayu Safari Village, to the north of Lamu on the Kiwayu Peninsula, in a beautiful bay on the mainland opposite Kiwayu Island, reservations, Nairobi, T020-600 107, www.kiw ayu.com. Nestled among the dunes overlooking a sheltered lagoon, here there are 18 luxurious, traditional-style thatched *bandas*, a restaurant, bar and shop. The hotel has a fleet of deep-sea fishing vessels and game fishing, boat trips into the mangrove swamps and waterskiing are on offer, and the beach is wonderful. The food is excellent and non-seafood dishes are available on request. The honeymoon suite is so intimate and secluded it's a boat ride away on the opposite beach nestled amongst some baobab trees. Closes for 2 months from mid-Apr during low season.

$$$$ Mike's Camp Kiwayu, on Kiwayu Island, reservations Nairobi, T020-512 213, www.mikescampkiwayu.com. Formerly known as Munira Island Camp, this camp is totally eco-friendly running on solar and wind power, the water is brought in by a team of donkeys from a nearby well. 7 comfortable and spacious *bandas*, built of *makuti* and *jambies* (local matting made from palm fronds), each with panoramic ocean views. Rates are US$250 per person full board, food is predominantly seafood and is served in a communal mess tent. Game fishing on a deep-sea fishing boat, diving, waterskiing and windsurfing are available and you can walk to the 2 simple villages on the island or explore the nearby mangrove creek.

🍴 Eating

Lamu Island p116

You will find lots of yoghurt, pancakes, fruit salads, and milk shakes as well as good-value seafood. If you are looking for the traditional food that you find in upcountry Kenya, such as *ugali*, beans, curries, chicken and chips, there are a number of places that do these, mainly on Harambee Av – particularly in the southern end of town. One of the highlights of eating in Lamu is the availability of fresh and cheap fruit juices and a pint of juice goes for little more than KSh50. They are made to order as attested to by the constant rumblings of electric blenders in the restaurants. There's a wide variety of fruit including orange, mango, lime, pineapple, pawpaw, avocado, banana, tamarind and coconut. They do tend to add sugar so you must tell them beforehand if you want your juices natural. Restaurants close fairly early, usually about 2100, so if you want a beer after dinner the only choices are the terrace bar at the **Lamu Palace Hotel** and the downstairs and rooftop bar at **Petley's**. In Shela, you can get a single malt on the terrace at Peponi's, and elsewhere on the island the **Kipungani Explorer**, and the **Kizingo** resorts have bars. Bear in mind that Lamu is a predominantly Muslim society, so during Ramadan – the month of fasting – many of the restaurants and cafés will remain closed all day until after sunset and it is considered highly impolite to eat and drink (and smoke) in public until after dark. Stomach upsets are fairly common so stick to bottled water and avoid ice. If you are self-catering, the fresh produce market near the fort has everything you may need including fresh seafood, though the catch comes in early in the morning so get there before 0900.

Lamu Town *p116*

$$$ Lamu Palace Hotel, southern end of waterfront, T042-633 104. Daily 0800-2300. This is a pleasant restaurant looking out over the waterfront with some tables on a very attractive terrace surrounded by plants, serving seafood, grills, Indian food, and alcohol including wine. Set meals at dinner are rather bland but presented nicely; the à la carte dishes although more expensive are far superior. Towards the back of the restaurant is an extremely comfortable bar and lounge area.

$$ Bush Gardens, on the waterfront near the fort. Daily 0700-2100. This is a very good seafood restaurant and specialities include lobster cooked in coconut sauce, poached monster crab, jumbo prawns and oysters, good fresh juices, cheaper briyanis and stews, it is friendly but service can be extremely slow, especially when full. Tables are set outside under *makuti* thatched roofs.

$$ Hapa Hapa Restaurant, on the waterfront close to Bush Gardens (above). Daily 0800- 2100. One of the most popular restaurants with tourists, this has a long menu of pasta and pizza, good fruit juices and snacks, lots of fish including an overloaded seafood platter and jumbo prawns, occasionally barracuda, shark and tuna on the menu. Very simple decor under thatch but a lively place with excellent food. Breakfasts are good here too; try the banana or mango pancakes with honey.

$$ Stone House Hotel, near the Swahili House Museum, T042-633 544, www.stone househotellamu.com. This small but lovely rooftop restaurant is open to non-hotel guests and has enchanting views of the narrow alleyways and Lamu's *makuti* rooftops. Tables are set in open Arabian archways. With low lighting and sea breezes it's quite romantic. There's a short but neat menu of pasta, seafood and Swahili dishes and vegetarians are catered for.

$$ Whispers, Harambee Av, T042-633 355. Daily 0900-2100, may close in the afternoon if it's quiet, though it stays open during Ramadan. Set in a lovely coral rag-built house with tables outside in the beautiful tropical garden courtyard, this is a high-quality café with juices, cappuccino, ice cream, spaghetti, pizzas, sandwiches, homemade cakes and serves wine.

$ Coconut Juice Café, Harambee Av, southern end. Daily 0800-2000. This is a 2-storey cafeteria and as the name suggests, serves specialist juices that are freshly made, with combinations of lime, peanut, avocado, papaya, mango, coconut and banana, and you can also ask them to blend them with their homemade yoghurt. Also serves basic local and fairly greasy meat and fish dishes.

$ New Minnaa, just off Harambee Av, to the southern end. Upstairs daytime cafeteria, very popular with local people and cheap with clean plastic tables that are continuously cleared, and serves local stews, biryanis, fried fish, chapattis and local specialities like *mkata wa nyama* (a kind of pizza) or *maharagwe* (beans in coconut sauce). If you are hankering after Nairobi-style chicken and chips, this is the place to come.

$ New Star Restaurant, Harambee Av, southern end, near the German Post Office Museum. Another cheap local canteen serving dishes like rice and beans, *ugali* and beef stews but under a tatty *makuti* roof and in a fairly grubby environment. It does open very early for breakfast though, from 0530.

$ Olympic Restaurant, south of the town also on the waterfront. Daily from 0800. A *makuti*- roofed eating area with only a handful of tables, to find it look out for the blackboard of specials outside but worthwhile for the excellent cheap food. If you're lucky and prepared to wait for about an hour you might get grilled red snapper with tamarind sauce and coconut rice, prawn biryani or crab served with fresh limes and salad. Also good juices and fruit pancakes for breakfast. Very friendly.

$ Seafront Cafe, on the waterfront east of the German Post Office Museum. Daily 0800-2200. Another *makuti*-thatched tourist restaurant that stays open later than most, and with shorter waiting times for food, this sells the usual fare including good fish curries with coconut rice, an excellent crab soup and seafood salads served with a chapatti plus juices and milkshakes. Ask about the catch of the day.

Shela *p121*

$$$ Barbecue Grill, at Peponi's, T042-633 421-3, www.peponi-lamu.com. Daily 1200-1600, 1900-late. Excellent and open to non-residents, the food is of a very high standard, is probably the best on the island. The beautiful dining room has cool white arches and Swahili copper pots and furniture or there are tables on the terrace shrouded with bougainvillea. Service is excellent and discreet. Superb seafood, including oysters, lobster and crab and the giant prawns cooked in chilli and lime are to die for. Alternatively choose the Swahili menu, which is a variety of dishes served on a copper platter to share. The friendly bar serves a full range of alcohol including cocktails and international spirits and is popular with Shela's expat community.

$ Stop Over Restaurant, at the hotel of the same name. Serves simple, basic but good-value food, including pancakes for breakfast, grills and some seafood such as fantastic grilled prawns with coconut rice, fresh fruit juices, and it also has a great location right on the beach, which is just as well as food takes a long time to appear.

▲▲ Activities and tours

Lamu Island *p116*

Watersports can be organized from **Peponi's** in Shela (see Sleeping) and include wind-surfing (with instruction), waterskiing, snorkelling, sailing, and scuba diving (Nov-Mar). They also have their own fully equipped boat for deep-sea fishing and offer day trips with a picnic lunch and drinks from US$200 for 4 people.

Taking a *dhow* trip is almost obligatory and drifting though the mangroves is a wonderful way to experience the islands. Take your time to shop around and find a *dhow* captain you like. Prices vary, and expect to haggle hard, but generally it's around US$8 per person for half a day and US$12 for a full day per person for groups of

4-5 people. The boats aren't big enough for more than 5. If you are a solo traveller, ask around the budget hotels to see if you can tag along with another group. There are a number of options, but whatever you arrange, make sure you know exactly how much you'll be paying and what that will include, and don't hand over any money until the day of departure except perhaps a small advance for food or a deposit to hire snorkelling equipment. The most popular trips are the slow sail across to Manda Island with a barbeque lunch on the beach there, and perhaps a visit to the Takwa Ruins or a sail down the Lamu Channel to the southwest corner of Manda Island around Kinyika Rock to snorkel on the reefs. *Dhows* can be hired for trips to Pate, and full-moon trips can also be arranged. During the day, take a hat and sunscreen, as there is rarely any shade on the *dhows*. Also remember, *dhows* without motors are dependent on the tides, so departure and return times are obviously arranged around the tide times.

Around both Lamu and Shela you may be approached by ladies, usually in the restaurants, who offer to do henna tattoos on your hands and feet.

Shopping

Lamu Town *p116*
Books
The museum has a very good collection of books on Lamu, its history and culture. **Lamu Book Centre** has a reasonable selection as well as the local newspapers, and there are a couple of second-hand book stalls along the waterfront.

Souvenirs
Boys walk around selling hand-built model *dhows*, which are not too easy to carry around so get them at the end of the trip. Other items to buy include carved chests, cloth, especially *kikoys*, jewellery (silver in particular), plus all manner of carved wooden

curios. There are a few stalls on the waterfront and some shops, silversmiths and tailors along Harambee Av, and to the north of town are some wood-carving workshops where you'll see mostly chests and furniture being made, including the distinctive 4-poster beds. You can get things made for you but be prepared to bargain, and there is the question of getting it home.

Baraka, Harambee Av, T042-633 264. This is Lamu's best and most beautiful gallery adjoining the **Whispers Restaurant** that sells high-quality but expensive carvings, Lamu chests, jewellery, and clothing, and there are pieces on display from across Africa.

Wildebeest, see page 128, sells contemporary paintings as well as wall hangings made from goat hair and other fabrics. The gallery is on the ground floor and the workshop on the 2nd floor.

Transport

Lamu Island *p116*
Air
Air Kenya, has a daily flight between Lamu and **Nairobi**, which departs Nairobi at 1530, arrives in Lamu at 1640, departs again at 1710, and arrives back in Nairobi at 1855, 1 way from US$142. For the Lamu flight, Air Kenya baggage allowance is just 15 kg. **Fly 540**, has 1 daily flight between **Nairobi** and Lamu, which departs Nairobi at 1040, arrives in Lamu at 1240, departs again at 1255 and arrives back in Nairobi at 1440. 1 way from US$139. **Kenya Airways**, flies between **Nairobi**, and Lamu daily with a stop in **Malindi**. Flights depart Nairobi at 1100, arrive in Lamu at 1310, depart Lamu 1410, arrive Malindi 1340, depart Malindi at 1440, and arrive back in Nairobi at 1550.

Mombasa Air Safari, has daily flights between **Mombasa**, **Malindi** and Lamu. The flight departs Mombasa at 0800, arrives at Malindi at 0840, departs again at 0845 and arrives in Lamu at 0915. On the return leg it departs Lamu at 1700, arrives in Malindi at

1730, departs Malindi at 1750, and arrives in Mombasa at 1810. Check-in time is 30 mins before take off from the Manda airstrip. Allow plenty of extra time to arrange a boat transfer or *dhow* taxi to get to Manda, the crossing itself takes about 15 mins from Lamu town and about 30 mins from Shela.

Airline offices **Air Kenya**, Baraka House, T042-633 445, near the Whispers Restaurant, or reservations at Wilson Airport, Nairobi, T020-605 745, www.airkenya.com. **Fly 540**, ABC Place, Westlands, Nairobi, T020-445 3252, www.fly540.com. **Kenya Airways**, on the waterfront, on the ground floor of Casuarina Rest House, T042-632 040, www.kenya-airways.com. **Mombasa Air Safari**, Moi International Airport, Mombasa, T041-343 3061, www.mombasaairsafari.com.

Bus

The **Pwani Tawakal Bus Company**, on Main St near the fort in Lamu, T0722-550 111, T042-633 380, http://pwanitawakal.com, has 3 services a day in each direction between Lamu and **Malindi/Mombasa**. The buses stay overnight at **Mokowe** and return to Malindi and Mombasa from 0700. Allow plenty of extra time for the ferry from the main jetty to Mokowe and you need to be at the jetty before sunrise, but there are boats waiting to connect with the buses from 0600 and plenty of people waiting for them.

Pate Island *p122*

For details about getting to Pate from Lamu by ferry and *dhow*, see page 135.

Kiunga Marine National Reserve *p125*

The 2 luxury camps here are usually accessed by private air charter from Nairobi's Wilson Airport to the Kiwayu airstrip. Alternatively the lodges can arrange slow *dhow* transfers

or much quicker speedboat transfers (about 2 hrs) from Lamu. A cheaper option to get here is to get a group of 5 or 6 together and charter a *dhow*. This should include food and water as well as snorkelling gear and should work out at around US$70-80 per day. The journey is dependent on the winds and the tides and so be prepared for the journey in each direction to be anything between 8 and 36 hrs. For sleeping the only option is to sleep on the *dhow* or camp on the beach.

❻ Directory

Lamu Island *p116*

Banks There are 2 banks on the island, **Standard Chartered** and **Kenya Commercial Bank (KCB)**, both on the waterfront, south of the Lamu Museum, which have ATMs and can change foreign currency and TCs, and accept Visa cards for cash withdrawals (but not Mastercard), although service can be very slow, open 0900-1500 on weekdays, and 0900-1100 on Sat. Internet It is possible to email from the post office and in the past there have been internet cafés, but they have never lasted long as internet connection is sporadic on Lamu and is often down. Nevertheless, keep your eyes peeled for new spots. Medical services **Lamu District Hospital**, T042-633 425, located in the southern end of the town to the south and inland from the fort, which does malaria tests but other than that is poorly equipped and busy so anyone with serious medical conditions should try to get to Mombasa. Immigration At the District Commissioner's Office near the jetty. Post office Just to the south of the jetty, Mon-Fri 0800-1230 and 1400-1700; Sat 0900-1200. There are some card phones outside and phone cards can be bought inside, though they sometimes run out.

Contents

Footnotes

Useful words and phrases

Attempting a few words in Kiswahili will be much appreciated by Kenyans.

Good morning	*Habari ya asubuhi*
Good afternoon	*Habari ya mchana*
Good evening	*Habari ya jioni*
Good night	*Habari ya usiku*
Hello!	*Jambo!*
A respectful greeting to elders, actually meaning: "I hold your feet"	*Shikamoo*
Their reply: "I am delighted"	*Marahaba*
How are you?	*Habari yako?*
I am fine	*Nzuri / Sijambo*
I am not feeling good today	*Sijiziki vizuri leo*
How are things?	*Mambo?*
Good/cool/cool and crazy	*Safi / poa / poa kichizi*
See you later	*Tutaonana baadaye*
Welcome!	*Karibu! (Karibu tena!)*
Goodbye	*Kwaheri*
Please	*Tafadhali*
Thank you	*Asante*
Sorry	*Pole*
Where can I get a taxi?	*Teksi iko wapi?*
Where is the bus station?	*Stendi ya basi iko wapi?*
When will we arrive?	*Tutafika lini?*
Can you show me the bus?	*Unaweza ukanioyesha basi?*
How much is the ticket?	*Tiketi ni bei gani?*
Is it safe walking here at night?	*Ni salama kutembea hapa usiku?*
I don't want to buy anything	*Sitaki kununua chochote*
I have already booked a safari	*Tayari nimeisha lipia safari*
I don't have money	*Sina hela*
I'm not single	*Nina mchumba / siko peke yangu*
Could you please leave me alone?	*Tafadhali, achana na mimi*
It is none of your business!	*Hayakuhusu!*
One	*moja*
Two	*mbili*
Three	*tatu*
Four	*nne*
Five	*tano*
Six	*sita*
Seven	*saba*
Eight	*nane*
Nine	*tisa*
Ten	*kumi*

Index

Titles available in the Footprint *Focus* range

Latin America	UK RRP	US RRP
Bahia & Salvador	£7.99	$11.95
Buenos Aires & Pampas	£7.99	$11.95
Costa Rica	£8.99	$12.95
Cuzco, La Paz & Lake Titicaca	£8.99	$12.95
El Salvador	£5.99	$8.95
Guadalajara & Pacific Coast	£6.99	$9.95
Guatemala	£8.99	$12.95
Guyana, Guyane & Suriname	£5.99	$8.95
Havana	£6.99	$9.95
Honduras	£7.99	$11.95
Nicaragua	£7.99	$11.95
Paraguay	£5.99	$8.95
Quito & Galápagos Islands	£7.99	$11.95
Recife & Northeast Brazil	£7.99	$11.95
Rio de Janeiro	£8.99	$12.95
São Paulo	£5.99	$8.95
Uruguay	£6.99	$9.95
Venezuela	£8.99	$12.95
Yucatán Peninsula	£6.99	$9.95

Asia	UK RRP	US RRP
Angkor Wat	£5.99	$8.95
Bali & Lombok	£8.99	$12.95
Chennai & Tamil Nadu	£8.99	$12.95
Chiang Mai & Northern Thailand	£7.99	$11.95
Goa	£6.99	$9.95
Hanoi & Northern Vietnam	£8.99	$12.95
Ho Chi Minh City & Mekong Delta	£7.99	$11.95
Java	£7.99	$11.95
Kerala	£7.99	$11.95
Kolkata & West Bengal	£5.99	$8.95
Mumbai & Gujarat	£8.99	$12.95

Africa	UK RRP	US RRP
Beirut	£6.99	$9.95
Damascus	£5.99	$8.95
Durban & KwaZulu Natal	£8.99	$12.95
Fès & Northern Morocco	£8.99	$12.95
Jerusalem	£8.99	$12.95
Johannesburg & Kruger National Park	£7.99	$11.95
Kenya's beaches	£8.99	$12.95
Kilimanjaro & Northern Tanzania	£8.99	$12.95
Zanzibar & Pemba	£7.99	$11.95

Europe	UK RRP	US RRP
Bilbao & Basque Region	£6.99	$9.95
Granada & Sierra Nevada	£6.99	$9.95
Málaga	£5.99	$8.95
Orkney & Shetland Islands	£5.99	$8.95
Skye & Outer Hebrides	£6.99	$9.95

North America	UK RRP	US RRP
Vancouver & Rockies	£8.99	$12.95

Australasia	UK RRP	US RRP
Brisbane & Queensland	£8.99	$12.95
Perth	£7.99	$11.95

For the latest books, e-books and smart phone app releases, and a wealth of travel information, visit us at: www.footprinttravelguides.com.

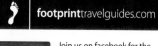

footprinttravelguides.com

Join us on facebook for the latest travel news, product releases, offers and amazing competitions: www.facebook.com/footprintbooks.com.